Monsters in the Classroom

Noam Chomsky, Human Nature, and Education

Philip G. Hill

Series in Education

VERNON PRESS

www.vernonpress.com

In the Americas:
Vernon Press
1000 N West Street, Suite 1200
Wilmington, Delaware, 19801
United States

In the rest of the world:
Vernon Press
C/Sancti Espiritu 17,
Malaga, 29006
Spain

Series in Education

Library of Congress Control Number: 2023946582

ISBN: 978-1-64889-938-6

Also available: 978-1-64889-789-4 [Hardback]; 978-1-64889-810-5 [PDF, E-Book]

Cover design from Vernon Press with resources from Freepik.

I dedicate this book to my two children, Christopher and Bianca. Please accept the words in this manuscript as an expression of the honour and privilege it is for me to be part of your lives.

> *Yet I do not know what gifts of mine could more aptly repay yours - though my greatest gifts could never repay yours, for they cannot be equalled by any barren gratitude of futile words.*

John Milton

I also dedicate this book to my wife, Rosa Maria Cepeda, for her endless encouragement and constant support.

And finally, I dedicate this book to the memory of Plata and Darwin, my two truly loyal companions.

Table of Contents

List of Acronyms

EST	Extended Standard Theory
FLB	Faculty of Language - Broad Sense
FLN	Faculty of Language - Narrow Sense
FLS	Functional Language System
GB	Government Binding
HCF	Hauser, Chomsky, Fitch paper
LP	Locality Principle
LSLT	The Logical Structure of Linguistic Theory
MIT	Massachusetts Institute of Technology
MP	Minimalist Program
P&P	Principles and Parameters
SLORC	State and Order Restoration Council
SPDC	State Peace and Development Council
TGG	Transformational Generative Grammar
UG	Universal Grammar

Foreword

It is a great honor to be asked to write this foreword for *Monsters in the Classroom: Noam Chomsky, Human Nature, and Education.* I thoroughly enjoyed reading Phillip Hill's book and hope you will gain insight from his analysis as I have. As a lifelong educator and Noam Chomsky follower, I am grateful to have read such a thoughtful overview of his life, linguistic work, and political views. But Phillip Hill's analysis of how Noam Chomsky's work relates to education is what makes this book a notable contribution to the educational field.

I originally learned of Noam Chomsky in the early 1980s when I took a language development class as part of my special education teacher preparation program. Though I was well-versed in behavioral learning theories, I believed there was something more magical about how naturally children learn language. So, it was validating to learn of Chomsky's view that language development draws from more than imitation and reinforcement. As Phillip Hill describes, Noam Chomsky believes linguistics are tied to human nature and evidence of our innate creativity.

Noam Chomsky is considered one of the greatest intellectuals of our time, yet a controversial figure for his linguistic and political views. It is this controversy that kept my interest in Chomsky's work while I pursued my own career in education, first as a teacher, then a professor of education, for over forty years. In 2013, I was asked to write a chapter about a critical pedagogue in James Kirylo, "A Critical Pedagogy of Resistance: 34 Pedagogues We Need to Know." Even though Noam Chomsky was my first and only choice, it was incredibly difficult to condense so much information into only five pages. Though I tried my best to do the man justice, I always regretted that I was so limited in exploring Noam Chomsky's impact on education.

So, this book is close to the one I would have liked to have written. I am especially jealous that Hill got the opportunity to interview Noam Chomsky, which is included at the end of the book. Phillip Hill did an excellent job describing Chomsky as a person, his linguistic theories, his political views, and how his works can be applied to education. In fact, the pedagogy Hill developed based on Chomsky's views shares similarities with the evidence-based CREDE Pedagogy and project-based and service learning I have utilized in my own classrooms for decades. Like Hill, I recognize that students who are free to construct their own learning, when given opportunities and support, can have transformational experiences even in our currently flawed, over-encumbered schools.

Despite the development of standardized teaching and learning systems, we are fortunate for the creative teachers who subvert these systems to encourage more authentic learning. I believe our focus within schools should be to support creativity, teach critical thinking, and actively model problem solving with our students. From the examples provided, it is apparent that Phillip Hill is a wonderful teacher who creates learning experiences that can empower students to reach human potential beyond the standard curriculum. These transformational experiences should be what all educators strive to accomplish. I hope you enjoy reading Phillip Hill's pedagogical journey and can apply it to your own understanding of educational practice.

Sincerely,

Janna Siegel Robertson, Ph.D.
Professor Emerita, University of North Carolina, Wilmington

Acknowledgements

I would like to thank Professor Noam Chomsky for finding the time, many years ago, to meet with me, and, more recently, to review parts of my manuscript and provide constructive criticism. I would also like to thank Professor Janna Siegel Robertson for her insightful and extremely generous foreword to the manuscript. In addition, I would like to express my gratitude to the two anonymous reviewers of my manuscript for offering me valuable commentary. Similarly, I would like to acknowledge the generosity of the Canadian Centre for Policy Alternatives for granting me permission to include in the manuscript my published conversation with Noam Chomsky. Likewise, I would like to thank my editors at Vernon Press - Blanca Caro, Javier Rodriguez, and Argiris Legatos - for their generosity and constant support. And finally, I would like to thank all the students I had the privilege to teach over the past 30 years. Their creative minds and compassionate hearts constantly provided me with an authentic love of teaching, a love that never died. For that alone, I am truly grateful.

Introduction

A word in earnest is as good as a speech.

Charles Dickens, *Bleak House*

Surprisingly, the ideas of Noam Chomsky, one of the greatest intellectuals in history, who, according to numerous citation indexes, is in the distinguished company of Sigmund Freud, Karl Marx, and Charles Darwin, and has single-handedly redefined the scope and parameters of discourse in modern linguistics, cognitive science, psychology, political criticism, media studies, and a vast array of other disciplines, are suspiciously absent from consideration and debate in faculties of education and standard school curriculum. The influence of Chomsky's thought is so profound and far-reaching that it will most likely take centuries before the dust settles and a consensus is reached regarding his overall impact on human thought. Yet, he is not a household name among educators. In fact, Chomsky's ideas are still relatively unknown in the educational community despite the wide appeal and general applicability of his ideas. Teachers tend to cherish old, outdated relics and profess ideas in the classroom that were often discarded by academics decades ago. For instance, as will be noted later, a Skinnerian approach to learning was dismissed by the academic community six decades ago, but radical behaviourism is commonly preached in faculties of education and applied regularly in classroom settings. It is rather difficult to grasp the seriousness of this matter, but it definitely reflects poorly on the teaching profession. For some inexplicable reason, the absence of Chomsky's ideas in educational discourse does not seem to be problematic for either education theorists or classroom teachers.

The primary purpose of this manuscript is to critically examine the relationship between Chomsky's understanding of human nature and education, and explore how it can be used to develop a new approach to teaching and learning. To my knowledge, this is a relatively unexplored area of study. There are only two works that address Chomsky's views on education, but they are edited collections of his essays and speeches which only address education in a general manner. For instance, in *Chomsky on Democracy and Education* (2003), C. P. Otero offers a broad collection of readings on various topics related to education, directly or indirectly, but these readings lack a thorough and systematic presentation of Chomsky's ideas on the teaching and learning process. Likewise, a second work, Donaldo Macedo's *Chomsky on MisEducation* (2000), contains four essays by Chomsky, in addition to a conversation between Chomsky and Macedo, but, once again, lacks a thorough exploration of Chomsky's understanding of education.

In this manuscript, I approach Chomsky's views on education in a systematic fashion. I claim that his understanding of human nature, with its reliance both on his studies in linguistics and his political discourse, combined with his views on education, can be used as key elements of an effective and highly innovative approach to contemporary schooling. Even though the expression 'human nature' is often misinterpreted, in this manuscript, I understand it to mean a set of traits unique to human beings that clearly define what it means to be human. Later on, I expand on this definition, but for the moment, this should suffice. Similarly, the verb 'to educate' is often misunderstood in educational discourse. Its Latin roots, *educare*, to train or to mould, and *educere*, to lead out, play a key role in Chomsky's understanding of education. Normally, the noun 'education' includes formal educational settings, such as elementary, secondary, and post-secondary institutions, but it can also include adult education centres, community-based literacy programmes, and other non-formal teaching and learning environments. In this manuscript, I focus primarily on the implications of Chomsky's thought for secondary education, but the findings can be easily modified to meet the goals and expectations of other institutions of learning or informal centres of education. The overall thrust of the manuscript is praxis-oriented. It focuses on two key elements found commonly in educational discourse, that is, theory and practice. Chomsky's ideas, especially in linguistics and cognitive science, can often appear to be abstract and highly theoretical. Even so, it is often the case that these ideas can be applied relatively easily in a concrete classroom setting. Therefore, immediately following a consideration of Chomsky's thoughts on human nature and education, I use his ideas to develop a pedagogy that, when put into practice, offers a rather unique and dynamic approach to teaching and learning. Even though the theoretical part of the argument comes primarily from Chomsky; nevertheless, the particularly dynamic and highly efficacious approach to pedagogy that I explore is based on 30 years of teaching experience as a high school educator. My endeavour to use Chomsky's thought as the foundation of a pedagogy is a worthwhile one, because, as will become apparent, Chomsky has a lot to offer educators. My initial intuition is supported by Otero, who states,

Chomsky's theory of knowledge, and above all the epic-making scientific discoveries that underlie it, furnishes a much needed basis for a truly principled conception of democracy and education. In fact, the science of human language that he initiated in the mid-1950s, which is the first and still the most advanced of the cognitive natural sciences, is at the very core of the study of everything human.[1]

I had the good fortune to meet personally with Chomsky in his office at the Massachusetts Institute of Technology (MIT), and discuss with him many of the ideas that are developed in this manuscript. The entire conversation is included in the final chapter of this work, along with some additional commentary (in square brackets), and acts as a synthesis of some of the ideas on education expressed in the manuscript.

It is important to highlight a fundamental assumption that acts as the basis of the entire structure of the manuscript, an assumption that is commonly shared by Chomsky and other critical educators. It is assumed throughout the work that approaches to teaching and learning are based on a particular understanding of human nature. Educators may regard pedagogy from entirely different socio-political and economic points of view, but their approaches to teaching are grounded upon a specific understanding of what it means to be human. Unfortunately, this understanding may not be well articulated, even though it is the basis of and a motivational factor for the entire educational process. For instance, a pedagogy rooted in Latin American soil, with an emphasis on the emancipatory capacities of individuals and communities, highlights an understanding of human nature that is in complete contrast to a pedagogy which emphasises the social importance of hierarchy and authority. Even so, both forms of pedagogy perpetuate a particular understanding of human nature. Therefore, prior to any valuable discussion about the various facets of teaching and learning, educators need to address the issue of what it means to be human. What is it teachers are trying to do in the classroom? Are they training students to be passive and obedient, or are they encouraging students to think independently? Are teachers moulding students into prefabricated products or encouraging them to explore the world in a creative fashion? Are teachers merely producing workers for the workforce, or are they instilling in students an authentic love of learning? These are important questions for educators to ponder, and their responses will be determined, to a significant degree, by their understanding of human nature.

In Chapter One, I provide a brief biographical sketch of Noam Chomsky. His publication output alone, regardless of the complexity of many of the issues he addresses, is a breathtakingly incomprehensible feat for any human being, to say the least. Thus, it would be far beyond the scope of this manuscript to

---

[1] C.P. Otero, *Chomsky on Democracy and Education* (New York: Routledge Falmer, 2003), p.xiv.

highlight each and every key event in Chomsky's life, and discuss in a critical fashion his particular position on a vast array of academic subjects. In this chapter, I consider a few key topics of biographical interest that relate, either directly or indirectly, to Chomsky's understanding of the nature and dynamics of education. In addition, I highlight the way freedom and creativity were promoted in his home environment and also in the Deweyite elementary school he attended as a young child. I contrast this creative approach to learning with a typically rigid and authoritarian approach to pedagogy, as experienced by Chomsky in his high school and early university years and also practised commonly in schools today. I discuss some of Chomsky's achievements as the founder of modern linguistics and also his involvement in American domestic and foreign policy. Then, I reflect on the "tenuous thread" between Chomsky's career as a linguist and his political discourse.

In Chapter Two, I offer for critical consideration the relationship between Chomsky's linguistics and his understanding of human nature. The age-old debate between nature and nurture is revisited, and I argue, especially in light of Chomsky's findings in linguistics and contrary to the assumptions upheld in contemporary education, that the nature side of the debate provides valuable insights into our understanding of human nature, and also into the way we approach classroom teaching and learning. This is followed by a fairly detailed analysis of the relationship between Chomsky's findings in linguistics and human creativity, and compared to an outdated radical behaviourist approach promoted commonly in schools.

In Chapter Three, I consider the views of Chomsky and others on the evolution of language. Then, I discuss what seems to be two problems associated with Chomsky's understanding of human nature, especially in light of his fundamental position in linguistics. The two problems, or what I refer to as bones of contention, are highlighted, and speculative solutions are offered in an attempt to resolve what appears to be a valid challenge from Darwinian thought. This is a particularly important matter because the entire manuscript is based upon Chomsky's understanding of human nature, and if this matter is not addressed adequately, then the edifice of the manuscript can be easily dismantled.

In Chapter Four, I consider Chomsky's political discourse and show how it has something significant to contribute to his understanding of human nature. Various themes are highlighted that are prevalent in Chomsky's works, including his role as a critic of American foreign policy, analysis of the mass media and its role in perpetuating a corporate-defined worldview, the responsibility of intellectuals (especially teachers), and intellectual self-defence, and show how freedom plays a key role in his political analysis.

In Chapter Five, I explore Chomsky's understanding of libertarian education, with an emphasis on the roles played by freedom and creativity in the teaching and learning process. This is compared to ideas promoted by other progressive and libertarian educators. The chapter begins by exploring key figures who have influenced Chomsky's view of education. Then, I focus on liberatory educators who actually founded and operated schools, in order to highlight the practical nature of many of their fundamental ideas, especially those ideas embraced by Chomsky. I consider in detail the alternative schools founded by Henry Thoreau, Leo Tolstoy, Francisco Ferrer, Bertrand Russell, and John Dewey. Also, I offer for consideration a brief comment on the relationship between Chomsky's views on education and critical pedagogy.

In Chapter Six, I present a dynamic and practical pedagogy based on Chomsky's understanding of human nature and education. A few implicit factors associated with a Chomskyan approach to pedagogy are considered, followed by a detailed presentation of the pedagogy's four moments - thematic dialogue, tradition, synthesis, and transformation. It is shown through the use of a detailed case-study, based on personal teaching experiences, how a Chomskyan approach to pedagogy developed earlier can be used in a classroom setting. The pedagogy is applied to a unit in a Grade 12 social science course, and I explore how each moment of the pedagogy unfolds in a dynamic fashion and leads to a highly effective form of transformative action.

In Chapter Seven, I revisit a conversation I had with Chomsky on education. I include some additional commentary to parts of the discussion, and the conversation is used, in a certain fashion, as a synthesis of some of the material considered earlier in the manuscript.

It is worth noting at the outset that the approach taken here to Chomsky's work in linguistics and politics is that of a classroom-based educator. The pedagogy to follow is not the product of research in the dusty halls of academia. Rather, it comes from 30 years of experience as a high school teacher, and also involvement in various non-formal educational settings. I taught in high schools in the Toronto area and also in Mexico. In addition, I participated in non-formal, community-based educational activities in rural Mexico, and in a research centre in the maquiladora region of the U.S.-Mexico border. Also, my non-formal educational activities include grassroots work in a cultural centre in Cuernavaca, Mexico, and participation in an annual international conference of educators from Canada, the U.S., and Mexico. I first heard Chomsky speak while I was a doctoral candidate at the University of Toronto, and that speech was an initial motivating factor behind this manuscript. Throughout my teaching career, I kept Chomsky's ideas nearby and, over the years, developed an approach to teaching rooted in his understanding of the relationship between human nature and education. It is a practical, hands-on pedagogy that has been implemented, modified, and refined many times in a classroom setting. The pedagogy to follow should not be treated as an end in itself; rather, it should be regarded as a tool for classroom teachers and students in faculties of education to use and modify in their attempts to provide students with a dynamic and highly creative learning environment. As Alfred North Whitehead suggests, "[t]here is no royal road to learning through an airy path of brilliant generalisations."[2]

The ideas to follow are rooted in various disciplines of study, including linguistics, evolutionary biology, cognitive science, psychology, politics, and educational theory. Inevitably, the overall scope of the manuscript suggests that many of the ideas raised for consideration will be presented in a summary fashion, and this might leave me vulnerable to criticism. Regardless, I will leave the fine details for scholars in each discipline to debate. Derek Bickerton, in his *Language and Species* (1990), expresses similar concerns regarding the overall nature of his work. He states,

> The alternative course, pursued here, is by its nature a risky one. It entails crossing disciplinary boundaries and trespassing on fields so various that no single scholar could hope to encompass them all. It is, therefore, inevitable that anyone who attempts such a course may, here and there, quite unintentionally oversimplify or distort the findings of others. The most one can do is to try to keep such errors to a minimum. In any case, the risks seem well worth taking."[3]

But, who is Noam Chomsky? Who is this person who is ranked in the same category as Freud, Marx, and Darwin? In the following chapter, I briefly consider some key events in the life of Chomsky that significantly influenced his views on education.

---

[2] Alfred North Whitehead, *The Aims of Education and Other Essays* (New York: The Free Press, 1967), p.6. Originally published in 1929.

[3] Derek Bickerton, *Language and Species* (Chicago: University of Chicago Press, 1990), p.5.

Chapter 1

A Biographical Sketch

Great geniuses have the shortest biographies.

Ralph Waldo Emerson, Plato, or the Philosopher

Noam Chomsky is a giant by any standards. He is a world-renowned scholar and social activist. At present, he is a Laureate Professor of Linguistics at the University of Arizona and an Institute Professor Emeritus at the Massachusetts Institute of Technology (MIT). He is the founder of modern linguistics, and has published more than 150 books in a vast array of subject areas. In addition to his scientific work, Chomsky is a recognized thorn in the side of defenders of American domestic and foreign policy. He classifies himself as a libertarian socialist, or anarcho-syndicalist, and borrows ideas from Enlightenment thinkers, classical liberalism, Marxism, socialism, and anarchism. In a saner world, Chomsky would have been awarded the Nobel Peace Prize for his enduring efforts in the political realm, but powerful social forces on the right end of the political spectrum make sure he is kept a safe distance from Stockholm. In the brief biographical sketch to follow, I focus primarily on events in Chomsky's life that relate to his understanding of education. I hope these events may inspire educators, both young and old.

Times were extremely tough for people living in Philadelphia during the Depression, especially if one was a Jew living in a predominantly Irish Roman Catholic district. Massive levels of unemployment and poverty led naturally to starvation, desperation, discrimination, and violence. In the early 1930s, more than a quarter of the workforce were unemployed, and the majority of the employed workers worked part-time jobs. Anti-Semitism was on the rise. For some reason, the ignorant side of history tends to repeat itself, and Catholics, once again, blamed the Jews for the current state of affairs. This is the milieu into which Noam Chomsky was born.

Noam Chomsky was born on December 7, 1928, in Philadelphia, Pennsylvania. His parents, William Chomsky and Elsie Simonofsky, taught at the religious school of the Mikveh Israel congregation, and William Chomsky eventually became the school's principal and one of the world's foremost Hebrew grammarians. He authored *Hebrew, the Eternal Language* (1957) and numerous works related to teaching and learning. William Chomsky was appointed to the faculty of Gratz College, a reputable teacher's training college, and eventually became faculty president, a position that he held for 45 years.

The apple doesn't fall far from the tree. This is especially so in the case of Noam Chomsky and his parents. Both parents had towering intellects, and each side of the nature-nurture debate played a key role in Chomsky's development as a scholar and social activist. It is obvious that Chomsky inherited an enriched genetic structure from his parents, but he also lived in a family environment that promoted critical thought and a passion for social justice. According to Otero, William Chomsky regarded his career as an educator as "the education of individuals who are well integrated, free and independent in their thinking, concerned about improving and enhancing the world, and eager to participate in making life more meaningful and worthwhile for all."[1] These words envelop a classical liberal, Deweyite sentiment found commonly in the works of left-wing libertarian thinkers. Otero also highlights the important role played in Chomsky's life by his mother. Apparently, she was further to the left end of the political spectrum than her husband, and influenced her son "in the area of general concern about social issues."[2] Obviously, both parents guided the overall development of their son. "During childhood," according to Chomsky, "there was always plenty of discussion in (our) home about really interesting and important issues."[3] As a young child, Chomsky often read nineteenth- and twentieth-century Hebrew literature with his father. He spent much of his childhood in Hebrew school and later became a Hebrew teacher. Even at a young age, Chomsky showed signs of excellence as a student. In Hebrew school, he often appeared to be somewhat inattentive in class, but this was because he had covered the material beforehand under his father's guidance. Itzhak Sankowsky, a Hebrew teacher at that time, states, "it was expected from his family background that he should know more Hebrew than anybody else. Superficially, you couldn't tell there was something unusual there. You had to bring it out with a debate or a bit of knowledge. Then you knew."[4]

Chomsky's early education was formed in numerous ways by his parents. Nevertheless, Chomsky also recognised the importance of informal education in his overall personal development. He often claims that his political education may have started with his mother's passion for social justice, but was solidified through interaction with members of his working-class extended

---

[1] Robert Barsky, *Noam Chomsky: A Life of Dissent* (Toronto: ECW Press, 1997), p.11. Many of the biographical details to follow are influenced significantly by Barsky's biography of Chomsky.

[2] Ibid.

[3] Ibid.

[4] Ibid., p.14.

family, including members of radical political movements. According to Chomsky, his cousins, aunts, and uncles "were in the Communist Party, some militantly anti-Communist Party (from the left), some Roosevelt Democrats, and everything else from left-liberal to anti-Bolshevik left (whether the Communist Party fits in that spectrum is not obvious, in my opinion)."[5] In part, his extended working-class family and his mother's left-wing tendencies influenced Chomsky's overall commitment to social justice, but it was also ignited by his personal experiences in elementary school. He states,

> I remember when I was about six, first grade. There was the standard fat kid everybody made fun of. I remember in this schoolyard he was standing outside the school classroom and a bunch of kids outside were taunting him. One of them brought over his older brother from third grade, a big kid, and we thought he was going to beat him up. I remember going up to stand next to him feeling somebody ought to help him, and I did for a while, then I got scared and ran away. I was very much ashamed of it. I felt, I'll never do that again. That's a feeling that's stuck with me: You should stick with the underdog ... I think everybody must have personal experiences of this kind that sort of stick with you and colour your choices later on.[6]

Chomsky has spent practically his entire life in academic institutions, and his views on education that I will explore later incorporate an incredible amount of personal experience, both as a student and a teacher. His initial exposure to formal education began shortly before his second birthday and extended until he was 12 years old. He attended Oak Lane Country Day School, a Deweyite experimental school in Philadelphia operated by Temple University. It promoted John Dewey's progressive ideas about the teaching and learning process, and encouraged a high level of critical thought in a creative, non-hierarchical, non-competitive milieu. An authentic love of learning supplanted the traditional view of schools as grounds of competition between students. As Chomsky states,

> at least as a child, that was the sense one had - that, if competing at all, you were competing with yourself. What can *I* do? But no sense of strain about it and certainly no sense of relative ranking. Very different from what I notice with my own children, who as far back as the

---

[5] Ibid.
[6] Quoted in Milan Rai, *Chomsky's Politics* (London: Verso, 1995), p.6.

second grade knew who was 'smart' and who was 'dumb,' and who was high-tracked and who was low-tracked.[7]

In fact, Chomsky had no idea he was a so-called 'gifted' student until he entered Central High School in Philadelphia. His high school experiences were a particularly dark moment in his life. Unlike his Deweyite experiences in Oak Lane Country Day School, his high school promoted competition between students, a rigid social hierarchy, and an overall lack of creative thinking. Grades were the defining line between success and failure. The pursuit of freedom, creative thought, and an authentic love of learning were replaced by a strict, overly competitive pursuit of high grades. For Chomsky, his years in high school were fundamentally a "period of regimentation and control, part of which involves direct indoctrination, providing a system of false beliefs."[8] A high school environment of this sort could not provide Chomsky with a suitable climate to develop and express his political thought, so he often visited radical members of his extended family in New York City. Here, he was exposed to Marxist and libertarian socialist ideas. He states,

> The Jewish working-class culture in New York was very unusual. It was highly intellectual, very poor; a lot of people had no jobs at all and others lived in slums and so on. But it was a rich and lively intellectual culture: Freud, Marx, the Budapest String Quartet, literature, and so forth. That was, I think, the most influential culture during my early teens."[9]

In his later teen years, Chomsky broadened his political vision, made contact with key figures in left-wing circles, and expanded his reading to include the works of the British writer George Orwell, German Marxist philosopher Karl Korsch, Dutch revolutionary Anton Pannekoek, Russian revolutionary anarchist Mikhail Bakunin, and British philosopher Bertrand Russell. By the end of his high school years, Chomsky had become an anarchist, or what he often calls a 'libertarian socialist'. Interestingly, Chomsky's initial exposure to anarchist thought was not merely an adolescent fad. His political stance has remained consistent throughout his lifetime, and he remains a committed libertarian socialist thinker.

In 1945, Chomsky entered an undergraduate program at the University of Pennsylvania. He enrolled in a general program of study, in order to further enrich his recently self-acquired knowledge in politics, philosophy, logic, and

---

[7] James Peck (ed.), *The Chomsky Reader* (New York: Pantheon Books, 1987), p.5.
[8] Ibid., p.21.
[9] Peck (ed.), *The Chomsky Reader*, p.11.

languages. Unfortunately, Chomsky felt that his undergraduate university studies were quite similar, in many respects, to his experiences in high school. Competition, once again, was the measuring stick for success, and any creative thought was quickly extinguished. In fact, the situation became so dark for Chomsky, that he seriously considered withdrawing from university and moving to a kibbutz in Palestine. In 1947, Chomsky met Zellig Harris, a professor of linguistics at the University of Pennsylvania, and Harris convinced Chomsky to continue his studies. It was Harris who, in fact, introduced Chomsky to the field of linguistics. Chomsky states,

> My formal introduction to the field of linguistics was in 1947, when Zellig Harris gave me the proofs of his *Methods in Structural Linguistics* to read. I found it very intriguing and, after some stimulating discussions with Harris, decided to major in linguistics as an undergraduate at the University of Pennsylvania. I had some informal acquaintance with historical linguistics and medieval Hebrew grammar, based on my father's work in these fields, and at the same time was studying Arabic with Giorgio Levi Vida. Apart from some introductory work in logic and philosophy, I had studied nothing else related to the material under consideration here.[10]

This quotation highlights a couple of important points associated with Chomsky's understanding of education. First, his inspiration for the study of linguistics did not originate in stale undergraduate lecture halls; rather, it found the light of day through his informal meetings with an inspiring figure. Second, Chomsky, once again, recognises the influence of his father on his intellectual development. This emphasis on informal education, the same kind of education that he experienced in New York City's bookstores and at his uncle's newspaper stand, plays a key role in Chomsky's overall view of teaching and learning.

In 1949, Chomsky entered a graduate program at the University of Pennsylvania, worked on a revised version of his undergraduate thesis, and within two years, graduated with a master's degree. His graduate thesis was eventually published under the title of *Morphophonemics of Modern Hebrew* (1979). By 1951, Chomsky was nominated to the Society of Fellows at Harvard University. His years as a Junior Fellow granted him the freedom to pursue ideas which interested him. He states,

---

[10] Noam Chomsky, *The Logical Structure of Linguistic Theory* (Chicago: The University of Chicago Press, 1975), p.25.

These years were an extraordinary opportunity for me. I was able to pursue a line of inquiry that seemed to many professional linguists unpromising if not exotic, free from external pressures, and with the resources of Harvard University available to me. It would be difficult to imagine more ideal circumstances for graduate study and research.[11]

Nevertheless, Harvard University's particular culture would, at times, conflict with the values that played a key role in Chomsky's upbringing. He states,

I grew up in a lower-middle class urban environment without any particular social graces, and when I went to Harvard as a graduate student in the early 1950s, in a special high-class research outfit that had all sorts of prestigious elite people, I discovered that a large part of the education was simply refinement, social graces, what kinds of clothes to wear, how to have polite conversation that isn't too serious, all the other things that an intellectual is supposed to do. I remember a couple of years later asking a distinguished English professor from Oxford, which was the model that this organization was attempting to imitate, how he thought that Harvard's imitation compared with Oxford's original. He thought for a while and he said that he thought it was the difference between genuine superficiality and phoney superficiality. This is a large part of what is called education. And it is teaching conformity to certain norms that keeps you from interfering with people in power and all sorts of other things.[12]

In 1955, Chomsky received his Ph.D. from the University of Pennsylvania. Shortly after Chomsky completed his doctoral studies, he acquired a teaching position at the Massachusetts Institute of Technology (MIT) in the Modern Languages Department and a joint appointment in the Research Laboratory of Electronics. On the surface, the joint position appeared to be a far cry from his interests in linguistics, but in reality, the position had nothing to do with electronics or U.S. military research. He prepared various graduate students for their doctoral exams, taught undergraduate courses on language and philosophy, and eventually established a distinguished philosophy department. For Chomsky, MIT "has always been a pretty free and open place, open to experimentation and without rigid requirements. It was just the place for someone of my idiosyncratic interests and work."[13]

---

[11] Chomsky, Ibid., p.2.

[12] Barsky, *Noam Chomsky*, p.79.

[13] Ibid., p.87.

At this time, a version of his monumental classic of modern linguistics, entitled *The Logical Structure of Linguistic Theory* (LSLT), circulated among his peers. It represented Chomsky's initial exposition of ideas regarding transformational-generative grammar. The work was concerned with three concepts: language, grammar, and structure. A language L, according to Chomsky, is "a set (in general infinite) of finite strings of symbols drawn from a finite 'alphabet.'"[14] A grammar of L "is a system of rules that specifies the set of sentences of L and assigns to each sentence a structural description."[15] A structural description of a sentence S "constitutes, in principle, a full account of the elements of S and their organization."[16] Therefore, the structure of L would be "the set of structural descriptions of sentences in L."[17] According to Robert Lees, who reviewed LSLT prior to its publication, the work "is one of the first serious attempts on the part of a linguist to construct ... a comprehensive theory of language which may be understood in the same sense that a chemical, biological theory is ordinarily understood in the fields."[18] A chapter of the manuscript was used as his doctoral dissertation, and entitled *Transformational Analysis* (1955). In 1956, LSLT was completed and submitted for publication, but was rejected "with the not unreasonable observation that an unknown author [is] taking a rather unconventional approach."[19] A year later, Chomsky revised some lecture notes for an MIT undergraduate course and published them under the title *Syntactic Structures* (1957).

During the 1958-9 academic year, Chomsky conducted research at the Institute for Advanced Study in Princeton and completed a full-scale revision of LSLT. In part, his revisions were a product of his discussions, at that time, with Zellig Harris, Nelson Goodman, and other leading scholars, and, in prior years, with other leading linguists and philosophers, including Peter Elias, Morris Halle, Israel Scheffler, and W.V.O. Quine.

In 1961, at the extremely young age of thirty-two, Chomsky was granted tenure, and became a full professor in the Department of Modern Languages and Linguistics at MIT. In the early sixties, Chomsky became recognised as a public intellectual. Until that time, he developed a reputation in academic circles as being an original and highly gifted thinker, but he was a completely unknown figure to the general public. In the 1960s, Chomsky's progress in linguistics was astronomical. In fact, he quickly became the "*de facto*

---

[14] Chomsky, *The Logical Structure of Linguistic Theory*, p.5.
[15] Ibid.
[16] Ibid.
[17] Ibid.
[18] Barsky, *Noam Chomsky*, p.89.
[19] Chomsky, *Logical Structure*, p.3.

spokesperson for American linguistics,"[20] but the lure of academic notoriety with all its perks conflicted, in many ways, with his social and political interests. The 1960s involved a period of tremendous student unrest on university campuses throughout the country. Chomsky spoke publicly as a voice for the alienated and oppressed sector of society. He spoke at rallies, forums, and conferences, addressing issues of pressing concern regarding the violation of fundamental human rights, American domestic and foreign policy, the ongoing embargo of Cuba, the arms race, American involvement in the Middle East and Latin America, and the moral responsibility of intellectuals to speak out against such atrocities. Yet, it was Chomsky's leading voice as a harsh critic of America's involvement in the Vietnam War that projected him into public attention. Chomsky's name became synonymous with protests against the Vietnam War to such a degree that he became a prime target for the political elite. At times, it appeared that Chomsky's promising university career and private life may be jeopardised by his political commitment to various causes. In fact, it reached the point where he had to consider the harsh reality that he would most likely be arrested and incarcerated for a lengthy period of time. Chomsky was willing to sacrifice both his career as a linguist and his family obligations for the cause of social justice. He states,

> I knew that I was just too intolerably self-indulgent merely to take a passive role in the struggles that were then going on. And I knew that signing petitions, sending money, and showing up now and then at a meeting was not enough. I thought it was critically necessary to take a more active role, and I was well aware of what that would mean. It is not a matter of putting a foot in the water, now and then, getting it wet and then leaving. You go in deeper and deeper. And I knew that I would be following a course that would confront privilege and authority.[21]

Chomsky continues,

> We confidently expected that I'd be in jail in a few years. In fact, that is just what would have happened except for two unexpected events: (1) the utter (and rather typical) incompetence of the intelligence services, which could not find the real organizers of resistance though it was transparent, and kept seeking hidden connections to North Korea, Cuba, or wherever we must have been getting our orders from, as well as mistaking people who agreed to appear at public events as "leaders"

---

[20] Barsky, *Noam Chomsky.*, p.102.
[21] Ibid., p.124.

and "organizers"; and (2) the Tet Offensive, which convinced American business that the game wasn't worth the candle, and led to the dropping of prosecutions.[22]

Incredibly, amidst the political turmoil of the sixties, and Chomsky's increasingly demanding schedule as a public intellectual, he found the time required to publish *Aspects of the Theory of Syntax* (1965), a more comprehensive theory of transformational grammar than was presented in *Syntactic Structures*.

In 1966, Chomsky was appointed the Ferrari P. Ward Professor of Modern Languages and Linguistics at MIT. He also became highly involved in draft resistance efforts, and the following year, was part of a massive march to the Pentagon. In a 1967 edition of the *New York Review of Books*, Chomsky reached out to the public with a "call to resist illegitimate authority."[23] A day prior to the march, a leaflet was freely distributed that promoted the march as "an act of direct creative resistance to the war and the draft,"[24] and was signed by Chomsky and others. All members of the resistance group were expected to turn in their draft cards. Representatives of the group went to the Office of the Attorney in the Department of Justice and informed officials of their plans to dodge the draft. In total, 994 draft cards were returned to the assistant attorney general. The following day, demonstrators marched to the Pentagon, but anyone who tried to enter the building was confronted by military police. Inevitably, Chomsky and many others were arrested and held in custody in a police station. Norman Mailer, in his book entitled *The Armies of the Night* (1968), recounts the march. He describes his encounter with Chomsky in the police cell. In a third-person voice, Mailer states,

> ... Noam Chomsky, a slim sharp-featured man with an ascetic expression, and an air of gentle but absolute moral integrity. Friends ... had wanted him [Mailer] to meet Chomsky at a party the summer before - he had been told that Chomsky, although barely thirty, was considered a genius at MIT for his new contributions to linguistics - he had an amateur's interest in the subject, no, rather, he had a mad inventor's interest, with several wild theories in his pocket which he had never been able to exercise since he could not understand what he read in linguistics books ...[Mailer] cleared his throat now once or twice, turned over in bed, looked for a preparatory question, and

---

[22] Ibid., p.126.
[23] Ibid., p.127.
[24] Ibid., p.128.

recognized that he and Chomsky might share a cell for months, and be the best and most civilized of cellmates, before the mood would be proper to strike the first note of inquiry into what was obviously the tightly packed conceptual coils of Chomsky's intellections. Instead they chatted mildly of the day, the arrests ..., and of when they would get out. Chomsky - by all odds a dedicated teacher - seemed uneasy at the thought of missing class on Monday.[25]

Mailer's reflection on the march highlights one of Chomsky's many special qualities as an academic and social activist. That is, even though he was incarcerated and his life plans were in jeopardy, nevertheless, like any truly great educator, he was worried about missing his upcoming class. I believe this reflects his completely authentic nature as a human being. Throughout these turbulent times, Chomsky was often threatened with lengthy jail terms and eventually made his way onto Richard Nixon's enemy list.

During the 1970s, Chomsky reached new heights in linguistics and also refined his skills as a political activist, vociferous muckraker, and public speaker. In 1971, for instance, Chomsky participated in a public debate with French philosopher Michael Foucault. They discussed the concept of human nature and its ethico-political implications, and it became rather obvious as the discussion unfolded that Foucault's historical materialist position would conflict with Chomsky's natural materialist understanding of what it means to be human. The crux of the debate revolved around the question of whether human nature is defined by external factors (historical, political, economic) or an internal, genetically predetermined disposition. The two participants discussed their particular understanding of human creativity. Foucault argued that creativity is a somewhat rare human activity, a cognitive act reserved for exceptional thinkers. For Chomsky, creative thinking is a crucial part of what it means to be human. He states,

> Creativity ... it's a normal act. I'm speaking of the kind of creativity that any child demonstrates when he's (sic) able to come to grips with a new situation: to describe it properly, relate to it properly, tell one something about it, think about it in a new fashion for him, and so on.[26]

---

[25] Ibid., p.129.
[26] Noam Chomsky and Michel Foucault, *The Chomsky-Foucault Debate on Human Nature* (New York: The New Press, 2006), p.19.

Even so, Chomsky appreciates the value of Foucault's understanding of human creativity. He acknowledges that the common creative thinking of a young child differs significantly from the creative insights of leading intellectuals. For Chomsky, this sort of creative thinking lies latent in young children, and is only developed fully under particular circumstances. He states,

> In fact, it may very well be *true* that creativity in the arts or the sciences, that which goes beyond the normal, may really involve properties of, well, I would also say of human nature, which may not exist fully developed in the mass of mankind (sic), and may not constitute part of the normal activity of everyday life.[27]

Chomsky relates creativity to human nature and then applies his thinking to the creation of a just society. He posits that a crucial element of human nature is "the need for creative work, for creative inquiry, for free creation without the arbitrary limiting effect of coercive institutions, then of course, it will follow that a decent society should maximize the possibilities for this fundamental human characteristic to be realized."[28]

In 1976, Chomsky was appointed to the coveted position of Institute Professor at MIT, a position normally reserved for Nobel laureates. He continued to speak publicly about issues regarding America's involvement in Vietnam, Cambodia, and the Middle East, and virtually anything to do with American domestic and foreign policy. He even addressed the role played by the media and other institutions in the manufacturing of consent in society. For Chomsky, freedom of thought and expression are crucial components of a truly democratic society. If the media and their corporate-funded allies attempted to filter out any information that conflicted with their business interests, then Chomsky would not hesitate to voice his concern.

For Chomsky, freedom of thought and expression are worthy of protection at all costs. Ideas should be exposed to the rigours of public debate, and either accepted or dismissed on rational grounds. Public sentiments and government interests should not determine whether or not someone chooses to express a particular idea. Chomsky does not agree "that the state, or any other system of organized power and violence, should have the authority to determine what people think or say."[29] This is clearly evident in the case of the Faurisson affair. Robert Faurisson, a professor of French literature at the University of Lyon, France, was removed from his teaching post because he

---

[27] Ibid., p.20.
[28] Ibid., pp.37-38.
[29] Barsky, *Noam Chomsky*, p.177.

denied the existence of gas chambers in Nazi Germany and questioned the overall historical presentation of the Holocaust itself. In 1979, Chomsky was asked to sign a petition related to Faurisson and in favour of freedom of expression. It states,

> Since he began making his findings public, Professor Faurisson has been subject to a vicious campaign of harassment, intimidation, slander, and physical violence in a crude attempt to silence him. Fearful officials have even tried to stop him from further research by denying him access to public libraries and archives.[30]

Chomsky signed the petition, and was later accused of holding similar views, even though, in 1969, he clearly stated that the Holocaust is "the most fantastic outburst of collective insanity in human history."[31] In his defence, Chomsky clarified the fundamental difference between supporting a person's right to freedom of expression and condemning harmful and historically inaccurate ideas. Even so, inevitably, people of a particular political slant have used Chomsky's commentary on the Faurisson affair to their own advantage and have claimed that he is an anti-Semitic and anti-Zionist zealot, a neo-Nazi, a supporter of the German National Socialist Party, and expresses an unwavering distrust of the governments of the United States and Israel. Such accusations have continued to haunt Chomsky in his endeavour to heighten people's awareness of the important role played by freedom of thought and speech in a democratic society.

In recent years, Chomsky has continued to lead the way in modern linguistics and social criticism. His career in linguistics seems to be a summation of many great accomplishments, including the theory of Universal Grammar (UG), Generative Grammar, the Chomsky Hierarchy, and the Minimalist Program (MP). He has received many honorary doctorates and is the recipient of innumerable awards, including the American Psychological Association's Distinguished Scientific Contribution Award (1984), the Kyoto Prize in Basic Science (1988), the National Council of Teachers of English's Orwell Award (1987, 1984), and the Killian Faculty Achievement Award (1991-92) - a highly prestigious faculty award that recognizes "extraordinary professional accomplishments by full-time members of the MIT faculty."[32] John Lyons, in his concise introduction to Chomsky's linguistics, captures the seismic impact of Chomsky's thought on ideas in modern linguistics. He states,

---

[30] Ibid., p.180.
[31] Ibid., p.186.
[32] Otero, *Chomsky*, p.3.

Chomsky's position is not only unique within linguistics at the present time but is probably unprecedented in the whole history of the subject. His first book … revolutionized the scientific study of language; and for many years he has spoken with unrivalled authority on all aspects of grammatical theory.[33]

Even though Lyons makes it clear that not all linguists accept Chomsky's ideas, he states,

Chomsky's theory of grammar is undoubtedly the most dynamic and influential; and no linguist who wishes to keep abreast of current developments in his subject can afford to ignore Chomsky's theoretical pronouncements. Every other 'school' of linguistics at the present time tends to define its position in relation to Chomsky's views on particular issues.[34]

In 2002, Chomsky retired from MIT as professor emeritus. However, in 2017, he joined the University of Arizona's Department of Linguistics as Laureate Professor of Linguistics, Agnese Nelms Haury Chair. Normally, when people approach retirement years, they tend to retreat from political activism, but this is not the case with Chomsky. At present, Chomsky is in his nineties and provides a continuous stream of political commentary in various forms of mainstream and alternative media.

At heart, Chomsky is an educator. Both his position as a Professor of Linguistics and his social activism embrace a search for truth. As a scientist, his approach to teaching and learning is cooperative in nature, in contrast to the far more common top-down approach practised in schools. Chomsky's passion for teaching is reflected in testimonies offered by his former students. Fundamentally, Chomsky treats his students with tremendous respect. He pays close attention to their questions, responds to them in a clear and thoughtful manner, and expands their limits of understanding. He "generates an atmosphere of intense rationality, a sense of discovery. Whatever he is thinking about is the leading edge of his discipline."[35] As a teacher, he offers "inspiring classes, brilliant insights,"[36] an "unmatched rapidity of comprehension … [and] theoretical imagination he routinely brings to bear on the subjects of his attention."[37] Chomsky has taught many graduate

---

[33] Lyons, *Chomsky*, p.9.
[34] Ibid.
[35] Barsky, *Noam Chomsky*, p.192.
[36] Otero, *Chomsky*, p.4.
[37] Ibid.

students, and they went on to teach in universities around the world. Endless personal testimonies attest to Chomsky's truly authentic character. He treats people with a degree of seriousness and sincerity that is rarely encountered in contemporary times. After public speeches or academic presentations, Chomsky always leaves plenty of time for questions. He listens attentively and responds intelligently to questions and inquiries, and often spends additional time after scheduled events discussing issues with members of the audience in a more informal manner. In 1996, for example, Chomsky gave a series of lectures in India. The lecture on language and mind delivered in Delhi was followed by a lengthy and insightful question-and-answer session, but time restraints in scheduling ensured that many questions submitted by members of the audience remained unaddressed by Chomsky. He agreed to respond to the questions as soon as he returned to MIT. Members of the Department of Linguistics at Delhi University collected the questions, sent them to Chomsky, and within a month, Chomsky sent back detailed responses to the questions. How many academics would go to such lengths with an audience? It highlights a level of human decency and authenticity rarely encountered in the academic community.

There is what Chomsky calls a 'tenuous thread' that unites his work as a linguist with his political ideas. This thread is explored in detail later on, but it is worth noting at the outset that what appears to be two apparently unrelated disciplines are, in fact, related in a tenuous fashion. As Lyons states,

> ... it should perhaps be emphasized here that his [Chomsky] theory of language and his political philosophy are by no means unconnected, as they might appear to be at first sight.[38]

For example, Lyons relates radical behaviourist approaches to learning, and Chomsky's vehement critique of them, to concerns highlighted by Chomsky in his political discourse. For instance, there are similarities between the radical behaviourism's overall project and, according to Lyons,

> ... sociologists, psychologists and other social scientists whose 'expert' advice is sought by governments: that they 'desperately attempt ... to imitate the surface features of sciences that really have significant intellectual content', neglecting in this attempt all the fundamental problems with which they should be concerned and taking refuge in pragmatic and methodological trivialities. It is Chomsky's conviction that human beings are different from animals or machines and that

---

[38] John Lyons, *Chomsky* (London: Fontana Press, 1991), p.13.

this difference should be respected both in science and in government; and it is this conviction which underlies and unifies his politics, his linguistics and his philosophy.[39]

In this manuscript, I explore this unifying thread in detail by exploring how Chomsky's understanding of human nature, grounded in his work as a linguist and political activist, along with his enlightened views on education, can play a key role in pedagogy and general educational discourse. Accordingly, James McGilvray states,

> His [Chomsky] work appears, then, to be divided between a narrow science for the few and broad political discussions for all. But a closer look hints at a way in which these apparently disparate intellectual interests are part of a more general project. Both his linguistics and his political works discuss and advance a view of human nature that suggests how his work as scientist is connected to his work as political analyst and advocate. This view of human nature may provide a way to forge a single, coherent intellectual project that ties together two poles.[40]

In the following chapter, I consider Chomsky's approach to linguistics and how it relates to human nature.

---

[39] Ibid., p.14.

[40] James McGilvray, *Chomsky: Language, Mind, and Politics* (Cambridge: Polity Press, 1999), p.2.

Chapter 2

Language and Human Nature

*It's a possibility that there's something we just don't fundamentally
understand, that it's so different from what we're thinking about
that we're not thinking about it yet.*

Leonard Krugelyak, *Nature* (2008)

The purpose of this manuscript, as mentioned above, is to develop a pedagogy based on Chomsky's thoughts on human nature and education. To do so, I begin this chapter by briefly exploring the developments and intricacies of Chomsky's linguistic theory. Then, I relate his findings in linguistics to his understanding of human nature. In a later chapter, I consider Chomsky's understanding of human nature from a political perspective, then use the combined findings to develop a dynamic approach to teaching and learning. But, before I begin, it is important to highlight a fundamental assumption upon which the entire manuscript's edifice is built.

It is assumed in the manuscript that an effective way to understand human nature is through a study of human language. It is often claimed that human beings are unique because of their capacity for language acquisition. Other animals communicate in many different ways, but human beings alone have a highly complex and articulate system of language. If this is the case, then surely the study of language acquisition has something significant to contribute to an understanding of what it means to be human. Fair enough, but it may be argued that there are other areas of study equally worthy of one's attention in an attempt to understand human nature. For example, one could quite easily focus one's attention on the fine arts, classical music, poetry, philosophy, or literature. Without a doubt, Mozart, Milton, Schopenhauer, and Tolstoy have explored the complexities of human nature in their own unique fashion, and it would be worth studying their works, but the focus in this manuscript is on Chomsky's thought, arguably an equally valid starting point. Also, even though these other areas of human creativity appear, on the surface, to be radically different from the study of language acquisition; nevertheless, it may be argued that they use similar cognitive structures and are the product of the same regions of the brain that are responsible for reasoning and analytical skills. In other words, one may initiate a study of human nature through the study of various expressions of human creativity - art, music, poetry, literature, philosophy, and language - but they are a product of a unique cognitive capacity and particularly well-developed region of the human brain. Besides, as I will highlight later, Chomsky has so many truly valuable insights on education, insights that one may not find in other areas of study, that it would be a shame to dismiss them outright solely because one wants to focus one's attention elsewhere. In his commentary on higher education, and especially his discussions about the specialisation of knowledge into departments and faculties, Chomsky suggests that the study of human nature should be an integral part of education. In fact, he argues that there should be a department of human nature similar in structure to other departments in schools and universities. A department of human nature would be interdisciplinary and bring together specialists in many different fields of study, including, I would imagine, creative thinkers in the fine arts, music, biology, cognitive science, linguistics, and philosophy. In any case, I concur with Lyons, who states,

> The significance of Chomsky's work for disciplines other than linguistics derives primarily, then, from the acknowledged importance of language in all areas of human activity and from the peculiarly intimate relationship that is said to hold between the structure of language and the innate properties or operations of the mind ... There are many scholars working now in the social sciences and the humanities who believe that this is so. For them, Chomsky's formalization of grammatical theory serves as a model and a standard.[1]

Associated with this assumption is a common argument that findings in science, and especially in the science of linguistics, cannot be applied effectively to a study of human nature because science deals with facts and the essence of human nature deals with values. At least, that is how the traditional argument is posited. But, it is often the case that there is a grey area in the debate, an area which may provide justification for another position. Chomsky seems to recognise the validity of both sides of the argument. In an interview conducted in 1981, he states, "the idea of trying to derive a system of beliefs concerning social change or social organization from principles of language, for example, seems to me too absurd to merit comment."[2] Even so, in 1976, at a conference on human equality at the University of Illinois, Chomsky posits,

---

[1] Lyons, *Chomsky*, p.12.
[2] Otero, *Chomsky*, p.372.

The question "What is human nature?" has more than scientific interest ... it lies at the core of social thought as well. What is a good society? Presumably, one that leads to the satisfaction of intrinsic human needs, insofar as material conditions allow. To command attention and respect, a social theory should be grounded on some concept of human needs and human rights, and in turn on the human nature that must be presupposed in any serious account of the origin and character of these needs and rights. Correspondingly, the social structures and relations that a reformer or revolutionary seeks to bring into existence will be based on a concept of human nature, however vague and inarticulate.[3]

In fact, Chomsky admits that there may be a "tenuous thread" that combines his world as a scientist with his political efforts. For instance, in 1981, Chomsky states,

I am constantly asked how my linguistic work relates to my endeavors in other domains, say, in opposing state violence or defending human rights. No doubt one can always find some links among the various activities in which a single individual is engaged, though in my case at least, the links seem to me tenuous indeed. If there is a point of contact, it is quite abstract; perhaps at the level of some concept of human nature involving a basic need for free, creative work and self-expression.[4]

Later, I will explore this tenuous thread in detail. I will identify how Chomsky's approach to linguistics and his political discourse are bound together, tenuously at least, by a fundamental understanding of what it means to be human.

Human Nature: Common Traits

I begin the investigation by clarifying what exactly I mean by the expression 'human nature'. The expression is often associated with distinctively human traits, qualities, characteristics, or attributes. It may be argued that a study of human nature highlights those traits that are a distinctive part of what it means to be human. People witness innumerable so-called unique human traits, including aggression, competitiveness, altruism, compassion, intelligence, rationality, and trustworthiness. I argue that, even though these traits may

---

[3] Ibid., pp.112-113.
[4] Ibid., p.372.

suggest something about human nature, language is what makes humans truly who they are; that is, language is a uniquely human trait. Even so, language itself is based on certain cognitive attributes that are not unique to the human species. This complicates the matter and raises some interesting questions regarding the origin of language. In order to support the claim that human nature and language acquisition are intricately related, that is, that the language faculty is what truly distinguishes human beings as a species, I will travel a somewhat perilous journey and consider findings in various disciplines of study. At times, this may appear to be a rather breathtaking and somewhat overwhelming venture. Clearly, the study of human nature is a vast subject, and its scope is far beyond the limits of this manuscript, so I will focus on a few key issues that relate, directly or indirectly, to education. Edward O. Wilson, in his *Sociobiology* (1975) discusses the importance of studying human nature and how it is a prevalent subject of interest in various disciplines. He states,

> The intuitive grasp of human nature has been the substance of the creative arts. It is the ultimate underpinning of the social sciences and a beckoning mystery to the natural sciences. To grasp human nature objectively, to explain it to the depths scientifically, and to comprehend its ramifications by cause-and-effect explanations leading from biology into culture, would be to approach if not attain the grail of scholarship, and to fulfil the dreams of the Enlightenment.[5]

In a popular film on Chomsky, entitled *Manufacturing Consent: Noam Chomsky and the Media* (1992), Chomsky discusses the topic of human nature. He states, "Humans have certain properties and characteristics which are intrinsic to them, just as every other organism does. That's human nature." For the purpose of this manuscript, I treat the expression 'human nature' simply as a set of traits unique to human beings. This may include some of the traits identified above, but it is worth noting that what are often considered to be unique human traits are frequently shared with other species. For instance, aggression, competition, altruism, and compassion are traits found commonly in human beings and other species. The study of human nature includes consideration of those particular traits that are unique to human beings. This is not an easy task, and a complete study would require an exhaustive analysis of ideas in many areas of study.

---

[5] Edward O. Wilson, *Sociobiology: The New Synthesis* (Twenty-Fifth Edition) (Cambridge: Massachusetts: The Belknap Press of Harvard University Press, 2000), p.vii.

A particularly challenging aspect associated with human nature is trying to determine which traits are either innate or a product of one's upbringing and environment. Fundamentally, at least for the sake of brevity, it will be understood that the nature side of the debate supports the idea that human nature is predominantly (not solely) genetically innate. That is, the traits that define human beings are, to a significant degree, inherited. Particular traits are prevalent because one or both of one's parents and/or grandparents portray similar traits. Nineteenth- and early twentieth-century eugenicists and some contemporary evolutionary psychologists extend the nature side of the debate to include some rather contentious conclusions. For instance, they argue that alcoholism, manic depression, and other traits are predominantly genetically-based, and that one's environment or upbringing plays an insignificant role in the final outcome. The nurture side of the debate defends the position that one's environment and upbringing play dominant roles in one's overall development as a person. Genetic inheritance plays a role, but environmental factors are far more important. As Otero suggests,

> When considering democracy-for-everyone and education-for-democracy, as when considering other aspects of human endeavor, the most fundamental question unavoidably focuses on the interaction of 'nature' and 'nurture', or, less misleadingly, the interaction between the genetic endowment of an individual and a particular cultural environment ... What has to be discovered, then, is the relative importance or weight of the respective contributions of the human brain and the environment"[6]

Common sense tends to suggest that both sides of the debate are correct to a degree. There are physical, social, and mental attributes that one inherits from one's parents. Nevertheless, members of the same family can be quite different in their physical appearance, mental capacities and overall temperament. Both genes and environment play key roles in this debate. As Otero suggests,

> It does not take a genius to see that it is not the environment that accounts for the fact that a human cannot fly like an eagle nor an eagle speak like a five-year-old child. But not everyone can readily see, even less help others see, that the environment cannot possibly provide a sufficient basis for any of the seemingly miraculous things a five-year-old can do. A quick look at what children have to know to be able to do

---

[6] Otero, *Chomsky*, pp.4-5.

what they do without giving it a second thought shows that their knowledge goes well beyond what the environment can provide."[7]

Even so, this distinction between nature and nurture, and the ongoing debate around it does not necessarily address the essence of the matter. It identifies two opposing or coexisting sides of the debate, but it does not identify the traits that are unique to human beings. If I can somehow settle this issue by identifying specifically unique human traits, then it is quite simple to develop a particular approach to education that recognizes these traits as key elements of an effective pedagogy.

The debate regarding human nature and unique human traits extends back to early Greek philosophy and ancient religious traditions. For Plato and Aristotle, the essence of human nature is the ability to reason. Humans share numerous traits with animals and plants, but their capacity to reason is what makes them unique. During the mediaeval period, Christian theologians used an emphasis on reason as justification for the position that humans alone are worthy of God's love. St. Thomas Aquinas argues that human beings have their origin in God, the Creator of the Universe. Humans bear the image of God, and all other sentient beings and the natural environment are there to serve the needs and desires of the Divine's special creation. Thus, the early Greek emphasis on reason as a uniquely human trait inevitably leads to expressions of anthropocentrism. Even so, early biblical scholarship also identifies the important role played by Adam's Fall. Rather than focusing on the capacity of human beings to reason, the story of Adam and Eve highlights the corrupt and sinful nature of human beings; that is, human beings have an innate capacity to sin. The vast majority of later thinkers in theology and philosophy followed suit. They emphasise the evil nature of human beings but also the corrective role played by reason. Rene Descartes sets in motion a philosophical and scientific tradition that emphasises the key roles played by innate capacities, especially reason, in human affairs. John Locke challenges Descartes's assumption about reason and puts forth an equally influential position based on the idea of a 'tabula rasa'. Locke posits that humans are born with a blank mind, or 'blank slate'. The environment provides sense impressions on the mind, and people come to know things accordingly. Even though rationalists and empiricists debate ferociously about human nature, and the roles played by reason and sense experiences; nevertheless, it is clearly obvious that both schools of thought favour some type of high-level cognition as a unique human trait.

---

[7] Ibid., p.5.

The common sentiment that reason is the essence of human nature remains an underlying assumption until Charles Darwin published *The Descent of Man* (1871), in which he shows clearly that many of the traits that are assumed to be unique to human beings are, in fact, shared with other sentient beings. The key point for Darwin is one of degree. The majority of creatures, including human beings, share a vast array of traits, but some creatures have a greater degree of particular traits than other creatures. For instance, human beings have a greater capacity to reason than other sentient beings, but apes, dogs, cats, and, according to Darwin, even worms have, to a degree, the capacity to reason and solve problems. The same argument applies to all human traits, including aggressiveness, competitiveness, and altruism. For example, even though Herbert Spencer emphasises the capacity of human beings to be overly aggressive, ruthless, and selfish; nevertheless, other contemporary evolutionary thinkers challenge Spencer's conclusions. Peter Kropotkin, the Russian geographer and anarchist, inspired by Darwin's *On the Origin of Species* (1859), travelled throughout Siberia and other regions for five years in an attempt to witness firsthand the competition in nature that was professed by Darwin and others. Interestingly, Kropotkin, in his *Mutual Aid* (1902), shows that, contrary to common belief at that time, nature does not live "red in tooth and claw"; rather, animals (including humans) of the same species tend to survive in greater numbers when they live in a cooperative manner. Cooperation, or what Kropotkin calls "mutual aid", is a key factor in evolution that challenges the dominant Darwinian "red in tooth and claw" position. Even so, Kropotkin's findings do not shed any light on the old debate about human nature. In fact, both Darwin and Kropotkin complicate the matter. They show clearly that apparently unique human traits are commonly found in other species. In a later chapter, I address this issue in more detail.

It is quite apparent that a consensus in this debate concerning human nature and unique human traits is highly improbable, especially because it extends into many areas of study, including evolutionary biology, cognitive science, psychology, linguistics, philosophy, and theology. In fact, the conclusions thus far lead some contemporary thinkers, including philosopher of science David Hull, to conclude that, inevitably, there is no such thing as human nature. There are no traits that are unique to human beings. He suggests that such "essential sameness in human beings" is "temporary, contingent and relatively rare" in biology.[8]

If this is the case, if there is no such thing as human nature, then how can educators justify their actions in the classroom? How can they defend their

---

[8] David Hull, "On Human Nature." *Proceedings of the Biennial Meeting of the Philosophy of Science Association*, 1986 (2): 3-13.

short-term and long-term goals if these goals are not based upon some sort of understanding of what it means to be human? Unfortunately, an educator with a clearly defined, well-articulated understanding of human nature is a rare find. But, this by no means implies the concept of human nature is meaningless, especially in educational discourse. Contrary to both the nihilist position adopted by Hull and the views posited by earlier thinkers, Chomsky presents a reasonably precise and accurate understanding of human nature, rooted in his interests in linguistics and politics, that can be used by educators as a foundational pedagogical principle.

What is Universal Grammar?

The study of language extends back for centuries, but it took root systematically in the nineteenth-century. Franz Boas, for instance, in his *Introduction to the Handbook of American Indian Languages* (1911, 1922), posited that every language has its own unique structure. This structuralist approach to the study of language differed significantly from earlier approaches that focussed primarily on the historical and comparative study of different languages. In the United States, Leonard Bloomfield's *Language* (1933) certified linguistics as an autonomous and scientific field of study. He shifted from earlier attempts to study languages within specific cultural environments to a systematic discipline isolated from any nonlinguistic influences. Even so, Bloomfield adhered to rigorous behaviourist principles and relied upon empirical descriptions. In the 1950s, Zellig Harris, who was a strong influence on Chomsky's early approach to linguistics, published his *Methods in Structural Linguistics* (1951) and followed a strict Bloomfieldian approach to the study of languages. But, a few years later, Chomsky detached himself from Harris's influence and developed an entirely revolutionary approach to linguistics.

From the late-1950s onward, Chomsky developed and modified various general theories of language. It is worth noting that there are two fundamental approaches to the study of grammar, that is, what is commonly referred to as E-language and I-language. An E-language (externalised) approach to linguistics studies the properties of various languages. Its focus is normally on the environment in which a particular language is spoken, and deals primarily with the *corpora*, or the vast collection of sentences actually produced in a specific language. An I-language (internalised) approach to linguistics considers the internal properties of language and its relation to the human mind. Chomsky's approach to the study of language favours the latter position. In fact, even though he recognises the value of studying the external similarities and differences between particular languages, it is, inevitably, "of no particular empirical significance, perhaps none at all."[9]

Fundamentally, Chomsky's approach to the study of language has remained fairly consistent throughout his career, only adding necessary refinements and modifications. His earliest attempts to articulate a UG occurred in *Syntactic Structures* (1957). In this work, Chomsky establishes an understanding of generative grammar and describes specific grammatical rules that underlie the structure of sentences. He differentiates between phrase structure rules and alterations or transformations of these rules that lead to what is called "transformational generative grammar" (TGG). In this earlier work, Chomsky clearly shows that syntax is independent of semantics. A second revolution in linguistics occurred with the publication of Chomsky's *Aspects of the Theory of Syntax* (1965). In this work, he develops ideas introduced in *Syntactic Structures* and introduces some new concepts, including the recognition of "deep" and "surface" structures in a sentence, and the difference between language knowledge and language use. In the 1970s, Chomsky introduced the Extended Standard Theory (EST) which, in 1981, was changed into the Government and Binding theory (GB). In the GB version of UG, Chomsky argues that human language is based on fundamental principles, regardless of the specific grammar, and certain parameters that permit a degree of variation between grammars. In the mid-1980s, the GB version was replaced by what is commonly referred to as a Principles and Parameters (P&P) theory.

Fundamentally, a UG suggests that all languages share the same underlying principles, but they also embody unique parameters, or limited choices between variables. In many respects, a UG acts like a computational or processing system, and coordinates the sound sequences of letters and words with meanings. In Chomsky's earlier works, he viewed this system, or "language faculty", as a distinct compartment or module of the human brain, something separate from other mental faculties, such as vision, logic, and numeracy. In the early 1990s, Chomsky, once again, modified his earlier theory and developed a Minimalist Program (MP) based on an article written in 1993 and his *Minimalist Program* (1995). The MP is not a theory of language per se. Rather, it is an ongoing programme that is based on some relatively new concepts. Chomsky acknowledges the overall tentative nature of the MP and suspects that it raises many challenging questions. He states,

Questions of this kind are not often studied, and might not be appropriate at the current level of understanding, which is, after all,

---

[9] V.J. Cook and Mark Newson, *Chomsky's Universal Grammar* (Third edition) (Malden, MA.: Blackwell Publishing, 2007), p.13.

still quite thin in a young and rapidly changing approach to the study of a central component of the human brain, perhaps the most complex object in the world, and not well understood beyond its most elementary properties.[10]

The fundamental idea of a UG provides clear insights into the understanding of language, knowledge, and the human mind. It is an innate structure of the human mind, often assumed to be related somehow to Broca's and Wernicke's areas of the brain, acts like a computational system, and allows a person to attach meaning to the sounds of letters and words. Rather than attending to the specific surface details of a particular language, UG provides one with a way to explore in a profound way what it means to be human.

Chomsky's earlier works in linguistics are highly technical, and what I offer here is merely a taste of his overall approach in order to grasp the relationship between his technical works, the human mind, and creativity. In the sections to follow, I discuss the innate quality of UG, followed by a practical illustration of its innateness. From a rather simplistic point of view, Chomsky's approach to linguistics is a window into the way the human mind works, or as Lyons says, "the structure and predispositions of the human mind."[11] For Chomsky, the term 'mind' implies "some level of abstraction of yet-unknown physical mechanisms of the brain."[12]

The Innateness of Universal Grammar

For the sake of brevity, I will leave it to professional linguists to debate the fine details of Chomsky's various grammars. Nevertheless, it is clear that Chomsky's analysis of the structure of languages has much to contribute to the study of the human mind and human nature. His earlier works are highly technical and focus primarily on the rules of grammar, but in later works, Chomsky moves beyond a focus on rules and treats linguistics as a branch of cognitive psychology. He explores its implications for an understanding of the structure and functioning of the human mind. For example, in *Rules and Representations* (1980), Chomsky states, "I would like to think of linguistics as that part of psychology that focuses its attention on one specific cognitive domain and one faculty of mind, the language faculty."[13] He reiterates the fact that UG is a property of human biological endowment but also distinguishes

---

[10] Quoted in Cook and Newson, *Chomsky's Universal Grammar*, p.242.

[11] Lyons, *Chomsky*, p.107.

[12] Chomsky, *Language and the Problems of Knowledge*, p.7.

[13] Noam Chomsky, *Rules and Representations* (New York: Columbia University Press, 1980), p.4.

between the parameters defined by genetics and the variance of language aptitude defined by environmental factors. It is well known, for example, that the parameters of intelligence quotient (IQ), shared with language acquisition in the same cognitive region of the brain, are determined by genetic inheritance, but the range of individual IQ scores is influenced by environmental factors. Similarly, the language faculty, at a deep level, is determined genetically, but its individual surface expressions are influenced by environmental factors. The genetic component, or what David Hume calls "the original hand of nature," is, as Chomsky suggests, "to be awakened by experience and to be sharpened and enriched in the course of the child's interactions with the human and material world."[14] In other words, language is not an activity that a child chooses to do or not to do. Rather, language is something that is inevitable; it is something that happens to the child, similar in fashion to the inevitable growth of arms and legs.

In *Language and Problems of Knowledge* (1988), Chomsky reiterates the dynamic relationship between innateness and the environment. He states,

> We must determine how the child comes to master the rules and principles that constitute the mature system of knowledge of language. The problem is an empirical one. In principle, the source of such knowledge might lie in the child's environment or in the biologically determined resources of the mind/brain that we may call the language faculty; interaction of these factors provides the system of knowledge that is put to use in speaking and understanding.[15]

Chomsky's P&P theory represents "a radical break from the rich tradition of thousands of years of linguistic inquiry."[16] The primary aim of the work is to show that, at a surface level, there are thousands of different languages, but at a deep level, the languages are based upon some "fixed principles under slightly varying conditions."[17] What appears to be apparent variations of languages are, in fact, merely surface-level "parameters" of the language faculty. Chomsky argues that the study of what he calls "generative grammar," that is, a finite grammar which generates an infinite set of expressions, which leads to an understanding of the "cognitive traits and capacities, a particular component of the human mind/brain."[18] The language faculty has an initial state, or UG, which is innate and, during early childhood, moves through a

---

[14] Chomsky, *Language and the Problems of Knowledge*, p.34.
[15] Ibid., p.15.
[16] Chomsky, *Minimalist Program*, p.5.
[17] Ibid., p.7.
[18] Ibid., p.12.

series of states to a final, relatively stable state "that undergoes little subsequent change, apart from the lexicon."[19] For Chomsky, the innate quality of UG is an underlying and important feature of human nature. It embodies a unique human quality, and clearly suggests that the language faculty plays a key role in the way we understand what it means to be human. Chomsky's emphasis on innate features of the mind is, for John Searle, the "most spectacular conclusion ... that Chomsky derives from his work in linguistics."[20] The UG is "in crucial respects a special characteristic of humans, with properties that appear to be unusual in the biological world."[21] Without a deep, foundational UG, "language acquisition becomes a miracle."[22] Granted, in recent years, psychologists have attempted to show that apes also have an innate capacity for language acquisition, but their attempts failed miserably. Chomsky reflects on similar arguments posited in earlier times. He states,

> During the lively eighteenth-century debates on whether apes have language, one proposal was that they do, but are smart enough to realize that if they manifested this capacity, humans would put them to work as slaves; so they prefer to keep quiet when people are around. I always liked that one.[23]

In the Delhi Lecture of 1996, Chomsky begins by highlighting some of the key assumptions associated with the MP but promptly moves beyond assumptions to facts. He posits that the earlier assumption that a language faculty exists is, in fact, true. There is ample evidence to support the truth statement that a unique human species property actually exists. The UG is no longer an assumption - it is a fact. Even so, people tend to resist the idea that language acquisition is innate. For some strange reason, the concept of innateness is rarely raised in contemporary discourse, almost as if it is taboo to do so. Granted, during the past century, ideas about innate capacities circulated among eugenicists, and its repercussions led to distorted pseudo-scientific and racial ideas during the Holocaust; nevertheless, one doesn't want to throw out the baby with the bathwater. The fact that human beings have arms rather than wings or two legs rather than four, surely suggests that innateness plays a crucial role in their development. Chomsky compares the difference between his granddaughter, a rock, and a rabbit. He states,

---

[19] Ibid.
[20] Searle, "Chomsky's revolution in linguistics," p.19.
[21] Barsky, *Chomsky Effect*, p.14.
[22] Chomsky, *Architecture*, p.13.
[23] Chomsky, Ibid, pp.48-49.

To say that "language is not innate" is to say that there is no difference between my granddaughter, a rock and a rabbit. In other words, if you take a rock, a rabbit and my granddaughter and put them in a community where people are talking English, they'll all learn English. If people believe that, then they believe that language is not innate. If they believe that there is a difference between my granddaughter, a rabbit and a rock, then they believe that language is innate ... There is no doubt that language is an innate faculty.[24]

Clearly, for Chomsky, the capacity for language acquisition is innate - it is part of our biological make-up. In 1983, Chomsky states,

You have to laugh at claims that heredity plays no significant role in language learning, because exactly the same kinds of genetic arguments hold for language learning as hold for embryological development ... In fact, language development should be called *language growth* because the language organ grows like any other body organ ... the onset of puberty may well vary over quite a range depending on childhood diet and all kinds of other environmental influences. Nonetheless, everyone takes for granted that the fundamental processes controlling puberty are genetically programmed ... all through an organism's existence, from birth to death, it passes through a series of genetically programmed changes. Plainly, language growth is simply one of these predetermined changes. Language depends upon genetic endowment that's on par with the ones that specify the structure of our visual or circulatory systems, or determine that we have arms instead of wings.[25]

Phrase Structure Analysis

Chomsky argues that the language faculty is most likely located in a relatively autonomous region of the mind and interacts through a vast neurological system with other modules in the brain. But, how does Chomsky actually arrive at this conclusion? That is, what can one take from UG to support the claim that language acquisition is innate? Even though a detailed analysis of Chomsky's UG is far beyond the scope of this manuscript, and virtually any interpretation offered here will most likely be susceptible to criticism from

---

[24] Ibid., pp.50-51.
[25] Otero, *Chomsky*, pp.45-47.

professional linguists; nevertheless, it is worth briefly considering one relatively simple principle that highlights UG's innate quality.[26]

Phrase structure analysis systematically dissects a sentence into smaller and smaller elements until, at the end of the process, one is left with individual words or morphemes. Chomsky highlights the fact that there exists particular sentences that do not strictly abide by the rules defined by phrase structure grammar or, as he states, fit "clumsily" within the defined framework. As a result, in later works, he modifies and refines his models to better suit the needs of an ever-growing consideration of sentences. Thus, Chomsky introduces a transformational grammar that "reflects better the 'intuitions' of the native speaker and is semantically more 'revealing' than phrase structure grammar."[27] A transformational grammar contains both transformational grammar rules and phrase structure rules, and permits a wider range of options, including various tenses and both singular and plural noun phrases. It transforms initial phrase markers by modifying, removing, and shifting elements. Therefore, instead of producing two individual phrase markers, one for an active mood and another for a passive mood, transformational grammar rules show how the two phrase markers are derived from the same underlying phrase marker. It is also important to note that languages vary in the way sentences are structured, so phrase structure and transformational rules change accordingly.

For Chomsky, phrase structure rules and transformational rules remained a constant in the field until, in the early 1980s, he introduced his P&P theory. At this stage, Chomsky moves away from earlier rules of grammar and proposes a more general approach that applies to all languages. The field of linguistics, at least in the study of UG, continues to develop and change. From the P&P theory to the MP, novel and highly creative ideas about generative grammar continue to enrich our understanding of human language. In MP, Chomsky states that "the field is changing rapidly under the impact of new empirical materials and theoretical ideas. What looks reasonable today is likely to take a different form tomorrow."[28] It is worth noting here that Chomsky, in his endeavour to use the tools of science to explore the intricate nature of language and its relation to human nature, treads carefully within the scientific domain. He acknowledges that the scientific method works effectively for simple

---

[26] The linguistic exposition to follow is based on the two chapters of Cook and Newson (2007) and Lyons (1991).

[27] Lyons, *Chomsky*, p.63.

[28] Noam Chomsky, *The Minimalist Program* (20th Anniversary Edition) (Cambridge, Massachusetts: The MIT Press, 2015), p.9.

problems, but "beyond the simplest structures it becomes very descriptive."[29] Even at the molecular level, science often embraces a degree of scepticism. Inevitably, when one moves into the complexities of language and human nature, the scientific method becomes far more descriptive in nature. As Chomsky suggests,

> The idea that deep scientific analysis tells you something about problems of human beings and our lives and our inter-relations with one another and so on is mostly pretence in my opinion - self-serving pretence which is itself a technique of domination and exploitation and should be avoided.[30]

In Chomsky's phrase structure analysis, sentences are reduced to elementary grammatical constituents, or morphemes. A sentence is a collection of phrases collected together. For instance, let's begin with the following sentence:

    1)   The boy kicked the ball.

This sentence consists of two different nouns, a verb, and an article used twice, and is structured according to specific rules that make the sentence comprehensible. These rules, which are first presented in Chomsky's *Syntactic Structures* (1957), include the following:

    2)   (i) $S \rightarrow NP + VP$

           (ii) $NP \rightarrow Det + N$

           (iii) $VP \rightarrow V + NP$

           (iv) $Det \rightarrow$ *the*

           (v) $N \rightarrow \{$ *boy, ball* $\}$

           (vi) $V \rightarrow \{$ *kicked, hit, ...}*

These rules suggest that a sentence (S) consists of a noun phrase (NP) and a verb phrase (VP). The NP contains a determinant (article) and a noun (N). The VP contains a verb (V) and an additional NP. These rules are expressed in the following tree diagram:

---

[29] Chomsky, *Architecture*, p.2.
[30] Ibid.

3)   Figure 2.1

```
                                    S
                    NP                           VP
            Det            N            V               NP
             |             |            |          Det        N
            The           boy        kicked        |          |
                                                   the        ball
```

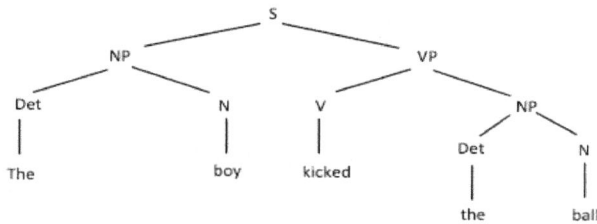

Clearly, few sentences in English are expressed in such a simple fashion.
Sentences are often quite complex and contain other constituent elements,
including adverbs, adjectives, and intransitive verbs, so the rules can be rather
complex. In addition, I can change the order of words in a sentence. For
instance, instead of (1), I could say:

4)   The ball was kicked.

In this case, the NP in the subject position, *the ball*, is interpreted as the
object. Therefore, a movement has occurred in the sentence to permit 'ball' to
move from VP to NP. Prior to the 1980s, Chomsky focused primarily on the
complexities of phrase structure and transformational rules that varied
between languages. In later years, with the inception of the theory of
principles and parameters, Chomsky moved away from a focus on specific
rules and highlighted principles, or general conditions, that are not restricted
by the limitations of a specific language but apply to all languages. I will
consider one specific principle, the Locality Principle (LP), and show how it
reflects, at least partially, the innateness of language acquisition.

The LP states that when constituents of a sentence move, they move within
specific limits, or else the sentence becomes completely ungrammatical. The
movement has to be short. For example, in the case of a subject-auxiliary
inversion, the use of auxiliary verbs, including 'will', 'can', 'may', and 'have',
change a sentence into a question. For instance:

5)   The boy will kick the ball.

I can move 'will' to the front of the sentence to make a question:

6)   Will the boy kick the ball?

If the sentence contains more than one auxiliary verb, the LP suggests that
only one constituent can move to the front of the sentence, and it has to be

the one that is the shortest distance from the front. One auxiliary verb cannot jump over another auxiliary verb; otherwise, the sentence is ungrammatical. For instance:

7)   The boy will have kicked the ball.

I can move 'will' to the front of the sentence, and it will remain grammatical.

8)   Will the boy have kicked the ball?

But if I move 'have' to the front of the sentence, then I am left with an ungrammatical sentence (indicated with the use of an asterisk).

9)   * Have the boy will kicked the ball?

Young children can easily recognise the difference between the grammatical nature of (8) and the ungrammatical nature of (9). But, how do they know the difference? Surely, family members and friends do not teach them how to move specific words in a sentence. It must be something that is unique in the human brain, that is, something which is innate. As Cook and Newson state,

> [P]rinciples such as Locality do not appear to be learnable by the same means that, say, children learn to roller-skate or to do arithmetic … In the absence of more definite evidence, the uniqueness of language principles such as Locality points to an autonomous area of the mind devoted to language knowledge, a 'language faculty', separate from other mental faculties such as mathematics, vision, logic, and so on. Language knowledge is separate from other forms of representation of the mind.[31]

Cook and Newson conclude that "the minds of human beings include the principle that movement is local; it is part of the common UG."[32] The Locality Principle must be pre-programmed into the human brain; that is, it must be a component of one's genetic inheritance. Needless to say, this is merely one of many principles, but it clearly highlights the innate capacity of UG and language acquisition.

---

[31] Cook and Newson, *Chomsky's Universal Grammar*, pp.45-46.
[32] Ibid., p.47.

Human Creativity

But, what is the relationship between the innateness of UG and human creativity? The structure and functioning of bodily organs are determined by a genetic inheritance, and, according to Chomsky, the "language organ" is simply another feature of our genetic endowment. Yet, creativity also fits into this particular discourse. Young children acquire and creatively use language. They display an incredibly creative use of words and sentences. If it is assumed that language is innate, then creativity, as an element of language, is a standard across our species and, as a result, a key component of human nature.

What exactly is meant by the term 'creativity'? A standard dictionary definition makes reference to a process of bringing something new into being. Poets, fiction writers, and scientists are often considered to be highly creative thinkers. Carl Rogers, in *On Becoming a Person* (1961), identifies specific conditions that are required in order to foster creative thinking. For instance, creativity requires openness to new experiences and an ability to manage conflicting and ambiguous messages. It involves the capacity for one to deal with concepts, ideas, hypotheses, and differing expressions of thought. Creative thought also requires a psychologically safe environment where one feels accepted by others and free to express one's ideas and sentiments. Creativity, in this sense, reflects what Karl Popper calls "critical imagination," that is, a "clash between ideas, or frameworks of ideas."[33] This includes a combination of factors, including an intense interest in a problem, a readiness to challenge presuppositions, and freedom to explore possible sources of error. From the perspective of linguistics, creativity means the capacity of human beings to produce and understand an incredibly large number of sentences that perhaps have never been uttered by anyone in the past. This particular understanding of creativity suffices for my analysis of Chomsky's linguistics, but later on, I consider how human creativity can be applied in a broader and more dynamic fashion, in a classroom setting.

Chomsky's understanding of human creativity begins with a simple observation. Infants can speak a language with perfect grammatical structure and in a highly imaginative fashion. Perhaps common sense suggests that they learn to speak because they are exposed continuously to family members and others who speak the same language. It is obviously true that a child who is raised, say, in an English-speaking environment will naturally learn to speak English, even with its regional accents and local peculiarities. Environmental

---

[33] Karl Popper, *Unended Quest: An Intellectual Autobiography* (New York: Fontana/Collins, 1982), p.47.

influences dictate the language a child learns, but it cannot explain how a young child, with minimal exposure to a language, can speak it in a grammatically perfect and creative manner. Obviously, parents do not actually instruct their young children in the complexities of syntax and morphology, and even if they did attempt to do so, this would not explain how young children are incredibly creative in their use of language. Often, they utter thoughts that reflect the pinnacle of human creativity and imagination. How is this possible? How can a young child with limited exposure to a language be so proficient in it? In an interview in 1983, and later published in *Language and Politics* (1988), Chomsky states,

> Take the sentence, "John believes he is intelligent." Okay, we all know that *he* can refer either to John or to someone else, so the sentence is ambiguous. It can mean either that John thinks he, John, is intelligent, or that someone else is intelligent. In contrast, consider the sentence, "John believes him to be intelligent." Here the pronoun *him* can't refer to John; it can refer only to someone else.

> Now, did anyone teach us this peculiarity about English pronouns when we were children? It would be hard even to imagine a training procedure that would convey such information to a person. Nevertheless, everybody knows it - knows it without experience, without training, and at quite an early age. There are a number of other examples that show that we humans have explicit and highly articulate knowledge that simply has no basis in linguistic experience.[34]

In the same interview, Chomsky cites another example that highlights the fact that it's impossible for young children to learn such complexities of language simply by listening to others in their immediate environment.

> English contains grammatical constructions that are called parasitic gaps. In these constructions, you can drop a pronoun and still understand the sentence in the same way as when the sentence contains a pronoun. Consider the sentence, "Which article did you file without reading it?" Notice that you can drop the pronoun '*it*' without changing meaning or grammaticality. You can say, "Which article did you file without reading?" But you can't say, "John was killed by a rock falling on," when you mean, "John was killed by a rock falling on him." This time omitting the pronoun destroys both meaning and grammaticality.

---

[34] Otero, *Chomsky*, p.47.

Constructions of this type - where you can and cannot drop the pronoun - are very rare. In fact, they are so rare that it is quite likely that during the period a child masters his native language (the first five or six years of life), he never hears any of these constructions, or he hears them very sporadically. Nonetheless, every native speaker of English knows flawlessly when you can and can't drop pronouns in these kinds of sentences.[35]

So, how does Chomsky explain this simple observation? Before I consider his insights on the matter, I believe it is important to address a theory of learning that was popular until the late 1950s and, unfortunately, remains a prevalent idea in educational discourse.

In 1957, American psychologist and behaviourist B. F. Skinner published his *Verbal Behavior*. For Skinner, human (and animal) behaviour can be modified according to various external stimuli and forms of reinforcement. Tactics of reinforcement encourage or discourage people from behaving in a certain way. For instance, praising a child, or giving a child a tangible reward for a completed task, are forms of positive reinforcement that are practised commonly in homes and classroom settings. Negative reinforcement acts in a similar way, but its primary function is the implementation of punishment as a way to deter particular patterns of behaviour. Teachers commonly use various forms of punishment to control the classroom setting. The behaviour of a loud, disruptive student can be controlled by the use of various forms of classroom management based primarily on a behaviourist model of human nature.

Chomsky argues that strategies aimed at modifying human behaviour are implemented, in many cases, to serve the needs and interests of particular parties. In a classroom setting, modified behaviour frequently serves the overall interests of the teacher but can, at times, also serve the interests of students. Behaviour modification works well with animals but, unfortunately, is often implemented in a classroom setting.

Chomsky's critique of radical behaviourism is twofold in nature. In accordance with his emphasis on the important role played by freedom of expression and creativity in the learning process, he argues that behaviourists are, in many ways, restricting the freedom of students and moulding them to some preconceived idea of good behaviour. This is the political critique of radical behaviourism, and I will explore it in detail later on. There is a second and, in my opinion, far more convincing critique of behaviourism, and it is the result of Chomsky's work in linguistics. Skinner's position is based upon a

---

[35] Otero, *Chomsky*, pp.47-48.

fundamental assumption posited by John Locke and later empiricists; infants are born with absolutely blank minds and come to know the world through sense experiences. Without sense experiences, a child is unable to know anything. Two years after the publication of Skinner's foundational work, Chomsky wrote a damaging critique of it in the journal *Language*. Chomsky denies the fundamental assumption posited by Skinner and other behaviourists regarding the primary source of human learning, and makes reference to recent developments in linguistics and cognitive science to support his position. Chomsky argues that infants at birth have a genetic disposition to learn at least one language. In fact, Chomsky goes one step further, and states unconditionally that behaviourism has absolutely no scientific basis. He suggests that a specific region of the brain is responsible for the acquisition of language, and that exposure to specific sense experiences - for example, a child's exposure to a specific language - simply explains the reason why a child learns to speak one language rather than another language, but it does not explain why a child has the ability to acquire a language in the first place. In other words, the innate capacity of a child to acquire a language implies that language acquisition itself is genetically predetermined. This leads Chomsky into a lengthy discourse on young children's incredible degree of creative use of language. They use strings of words in a coherent and highly creative fashion, and often, these sentences have never been uttered before in the child's immediate environment. This, for Chomsky, provides a firm foundation for the conviction that language acquisition, and creativity, as an essential (and biological) component of it, is a key element of human nature. Fundamentally, in his critique, Chomsky does not intend to attack Skinner personally; rather, he uses his acquired knowledge as a linguist and cognitive scientist to challenge the fundamental assumptions and conclusions of radical behaviourism, and the contentious ways that terms, such as 'reinforcement', 'stimulus', 'response', 'habit', and 'conditioning', are applied in concrete social settings. Even so, the tendency to control human behaviour implicit in a behaviourist approach to learning is often regarded as being rather abhorrent for someone who embraces a conception of human nature that recognises the value of human creativity in all facets of life.

Language Acquisition and Creativity

Any account of language acquisition or human learning that is based upon behaviourist/empiricist assumptions fails to account for what Chomsky calls 'Plato's problem' and 'Descartes' problem'. Plato's problem is highlighted by Bertrand Russell, who states, "How come that human beings, whose contacts with the world are brief and personal and limited, are nevertheless able to know as much as they do know."[36] For McGilvray, it addresses "how only a relatively short amount of time and some impoverished information are needed to develop certain very complicated and rich cognitive capacities."[37] That is, how can one know so much given one's extremely limited experiences in the world? Similarly, Chomsky asks, "How do we come to have such rich and specific knowledge, or such intricate systems of belief and understanding, when the evidence available to us is so meagre?"[38] That is, how is it that one is capable of generating incredibly creative, complex, and abstract uses of language with minimal exposure to experience? For Plato, such knowledge is remembered from an earlier form of existence, and it's rooted in the soul. Chomsky parts company with Plato when it comes to metaphysical speculations. Surely, argues Chomsky, one does not learn such complexities of syntax by listening to one's parents, because, in many cases, sentences are generated that have never been uttered or heard before. The solution is simple - this capacity must be rooted in an innate property of the human mind. The essence of human language is not something that has to be learned; rather, it is something that one grows into, similar in many respects to the way one grows into puberty. Chomsky also refers to Plato's problem as the poverty-of-the-stimulus argument, that is, the data stimulated by the immediate environment are far too limited to explain the knowledge constructed by the mind. Descartes' problem highlights the creative aspect of language and recognizes that words "need have little to do with the environment, and when we do say something that deals with the environment, we say any number of things and still have them be appropriate."[39] In fact, Descartes is often credited as the first person to recognize the creative aspect of language use.

Thus far, it is clear that Chomsky supports the position that language acquisition and its vast expressions of human creativity are part of one's biological makeup. But, how exactly did Chomsky arrive at these conclusions? How did he use his understanding of modern linguistics to arrive at an explanation about the innate capacity of language acquisition and creative aspect of human nature? What exactly did he accomplish in linguistics that made him such an authoritative and controversial figure in the scientific study of language? In order to address these questions, I will briefly consider some of the general ideas associated with generative grammar. Before doing so, I need to make a declaration of sorts and state unequivocally that, because of my lack of expertise in such a technical area of study, I merely raise for

---

[36] Smith, *Chomsky*, p.41.
[37] McGilvray, *Chomsky*, p.16.
[38] Quoted in Cook and Newson, *Chomsky's Universal Grammar*, p.55.
[39] Ibid.

consideration a few basic ideas that I feel contribute to the overall aim of the manuscript.[40]

In Chomsky's approach to linguistics, he often makes reference to a vast array of topics in numerous highly technical fields of study, including cognitive science, neuroscience, biology, philosophy, and psychology, and only someone well-trained in those areas is in a position to grasp what he has to say fully. In addition, in his foundational works, especially in LSLT, he uses logic and advanced mathematics as fundamental tools for analysis. This makes it rather challenging for someone not trained in these disciplines to fully comprehend the intricacies of his arguments. Therefore, as mentioned earlier, I will keep my comments brief and simple, and raise for consideration only those topics that have something to contribute to the overall aim of the manuscript.

Ever since his early years as a linguist, Chomsky has focussed his efforts on the issue raised above, that is, how a child acquires, with virtually no external stimuli, an extremely creative grasp of at least one highly technical language. This issue is rooted in the rationalist tradition, and includes philosophers and linguists from Descartes, Leibniz, Cordemoy, Cudworth, Humboldt, all the way back to Plato. Chomsky is firmly grounded in the Cartesian tradition. Linguists in this tradition posit that, in contrast to animal communication, in human languages, there is embedded an innate quality of creativity, and that it is not restricted by the influence and control of external stimuli. Chomsky frequently makes reference to rationalist thinkers, especially in his *Cartesian Linguistics* (1966), and shows how they relate the intricacies of language and the study of mind to concrete social reality. It is what McGilvray calls a "unified intellectual project"[41] and has been a primary focus of Chomsky's since his early years as a scholar. Chomsky highlights the similarities between his view of innate knowledge and ideas found in Plato's *Meno*, specifically, Plato's doctrine of *anamnesis*, or recollection. In this dialogue, a slave-boy who lacks formal instruction in arithmetic or geometry develops, through the prodding of Socrates, an understanding of the fundamental concepts used in the Pythagorean Theorem. Plato's point in this dialogue is that the boy had, in some way, already known these concepts, that they were innate by virtue of the mind's (or soul's) former existence, and that it only took some prodding by Socrates for the boy to remember or recollect the knowledge. A key part of

---

[40] For a detailed overview of Chomsky's ideas written by professional philosophers of language and linguists, I recommend V.J. Cook and Mark Newson, *Chomsky's Universal Grammar* (2007), James McGilvray's *Chomsky : Language, Mind, and Politics* (1999), and Neil Smith's *Chomsky: Ideas and Ideals* (1999).
[41] McGilvray, *Chomsky*, p.13.

Chomsky's project is to show that an empiricist view of learning and knowledge is unable to solve Plato's problem. It takes a rationalist approach to language acquisition to do so, and, more specifically, Chomsky's theory of UG. That is, language acquisition can only be explained if one assumes that children are born with a knowledge of what Chomsky calls "the universal principles governing the structure of human language."[42]

Early rationalist thinkers tried to establish a foundation that would highlight the mental processes involved in the utterance of sentences, and these efforts continued through the nineteenth-century with the works of Wilhelm von Humboldt. These initial efforts play a key role in Chomsky's development of transformational grammar, or a "mathematically precise description of some of the most striking features of language."[43] In his earlier works, Chomsky introduces the concept of a "Deep Structure," that is, at a profound level, all languages are the same. Contrarily, the concept of "Surface Structure" suggests that languages differ in significant ways. Fundamentally, what this means is that the principles of languages are the same at a deep level but are different at the surface level of sounds and use of words. A transformational grammar identifies the transformational rules that connect deep and surface structures. Inevitably, this leads to the idea of a UG, that is, the idea that all languages share certain structural properties. The approximately 10,000 languages in the world, despite their surface differences in grammar, share a common set of syntax rules and fundamental principles. The UG is innate, embedded somewhere in the circuitry of the brain, and represents "the set of linguistics principles we are endowed with at birth in virtue of being human."[44] The left hemisphere of the brain appears to be responsible for linguistic ability, similar to the way the right temporal lobe can incite mystical experiences. For Neil Smith, personality, moral judgement, numeracy skills, and face recognition are a product of cerebral modularity, that is, "[t]here appears to be an innate basis for virtually all our human activities."[45]

In concrete terms, this means that a native speaker of English who hears the sentence "John ball kicks a" will recognize that the sentence is not grammatically correct, even though its meaning can be deciphered. Conversely, let's consider a sentence often cited by Chomsky: "Colorless green ideas sleep furiously." The sentence is grammatically correct, but it is meaningless. As Lyons states,

---

[42] Lyons, *Chomsky*, p.164.

[43] Ibid., p.11.

[44] Smith, *Chomsky*, p.42.

[45] Ibid., p.182.

Chomsky has argued, in several of his publications, that the general principles which determine the form of grammatical rules in particular languages, such as English, Turkish or Chinese, are to some considerable degree common to all human languages. Furthermore, he has claimed that the principles underlying the structure of language are so specific and so highly articulated that they must be regarded as being biologically determined; that is to say, as constituting part of what we call 'human nature' and as being genetically transmitted from parents to their children.[46]

Linguists debate, at an abstract level, the innate nature of UG and the fundamentals of human language and mind. Chomsky provides plenty of linguistic evidence to support the innate quality of language acquisition. Perhaps it is better for me not to get too entangled in details and keep in mind that, as was mentioned earlier, there is a simple and quite practical explanation in support of innateness. In fact, every parent has witnessed it firsthand. Children acquire a language at approximately the same age. Generally speaking, children utter simple words during their first year and speak full sentences at approximately 18-24 months of age. The development appears to take place overnight. One day the child is babbling, then the next day he or she is connecting words and speaking grammatically correct sentences. And when this happens, there's no turning back. The child's use of language is full of richness and creativity. It's almost like the child wanted to speak earlier, but could not do so, but when the restrictions are removed, the endless string of wondrous and creative thoughts fill a room with glorious sounds.

Technicalities aside, Chomsky's view of language acquisition makes sense. Inevitably, there is far more to Chomsky's highly technical approach to linguistics than what has been discussed above. Even so, I believe that what has been considered is sufficient for the purposes of the manuscript. It provides one with a convincing, rational, and common-sensical argument about language acquisition, human learning, and creativity, an argument that, as I will show later, has tremendous value for classroom teachers. But, besides creativity, there is, according to Chomsky, a second key component of human nature, and this component is found in his political discourse. But, before I turn my attention to Chomsky's political works, I must address two issues that, in my mind, tend to linger unaddressed in much of the literature related to UG and the evolution of language.

---

[46] Lyons, *Chomsky*, p.11.

Chapter 3

Two Possible Bones of Contention

*Nevertheless the difference in mind between man and the highest
animals, great as it is, is certainly one of degree and not of kind.*

Charles Darwin, *Descent of Man*

There appear to be two unresolved problems or bones of contention, that
underlie the idea of a UG. I begin by reviewing what has been accomplished
so far. I assume that any approach to education is based on an understanding
of human nature. Therefore, in order to establish a solid foundation for an
adequate approach to pedagogy, I need to clarify what exactly it means to be
human. From a Chomskyan perspective, language is the one trait that
distinguishes humans from other species. Humans share numerous traits
with other creatures, but they alone have an innate UG, a language organ
located somewhere in the brain that incorporates a set of rules from which all
possible grammatical sentences can be derived from a given language. So far,
everything seems to make sense. A problem arises when one asks, Where
exactly is the language organ located? How did it get there? Is it the product of
a long evolutionary process through natural selection, or did it suddenly
appear by accident? If it is the product of evolution through natural selection,
then do other animals have rudimentary expressions of this trait? Marc
Hauser states,

> I find the search for human uniqueness particularly intriguing ... after
> discovering that a trait is unique, we should ask: Why did it evolve?
> What does this trait currently do for the individual and what might it
> have done for the individual when it originally evolved?[1]

Questions of this sort need to be addressed before I can move forward with a
Chomskyan approach to education because, if there are no convincing
arguments to support the idea that language is an innate and uniquely human
trait, then my attempt to develop a pedagogy based on Chomsky's ideas will
fail miserably.

---

[1] Marc D. Hauser, *The Evolution of Communication* (Cambridge, Massachusetts: The MIT
Press, 1997), p.31.

The first bone of contention is related to apparent leaps (or stumbles) in the evolutionary tree. There appears to be some sort of biological leap from the communication skills of non-human animals to the complexities of language acquisition by human beings. What are the origins of language? Did language evolve from the simple forms of communication of other animals, or did it somehow emerge spontaneously in human beings, perhaps as the product of a random form of genetic mutation? Is there at least one intermediate state between relatively simple forms of animal communication and the complexities of human language? How does one explain this apparent leap? From a particular point of view, Chomsky's UG appears to be a radical leap in the evolutionary process, and I need to explore this leap in detail in order to be convinced of the soundness of his position. The second bone of contention deals with Chomsky's claim that there exist particular traits unique to the human species, and these traits lead to an understanding of human nature. Darwin posits that the apparent differences between human beings and higher animals are merely differences of degree and not of kind. He considers in detail numerous so-called unique human traits, including cognitive abilities, moral faculties, and expressions of emotions, and argues with ample evidence that other creatures share these traits to varying degrees. Are there actually any specific traits that are unique to human beings? In earlier times, it was assumed that human beings alone were rational beings, so any discussions about human nature often began with this assumption. In modern times, this assumption has been severely challenged, and, as a result, a simple understanding of human nature has become highly complicated. If I cannot establish with a degree of certainty that there are unique human traits, then again, my effort to establish a sound pedagogy based on an understanding of human nature will fail.

Before I address these bones of contention, it is important to acknowledge that many of the findings I mention in the following discussion embrace a certain degree of speculation and uncertainty. Whether I am considering the evolution of human language, the functioning of the human mind, or the uniqueness of particular human traits, inevitably, I must tread with a degree of humility and trepidation. The deeper I delve into these challenging ideas, the more I appreciate how Alice must have felt as she tumbled down the rabbit hole. As I travel deeper, more doors open and stranger ideas seem to appear. It is also worth noting that because of the quantity and complexity of research over the past few decades in linguistics, evolutionary biology, and neuroscience, it is far beyond the scope of this manuscript to attempt anything beyond a brief and highly simplified overview of the key ideas. I am looking for general trends of thought, and I will leave the intricacies of debate to the specialists.

A Leap or a Stumble?

I begin with the issue of UG's apparent leap in the evolutionary process. Evolutionary biologists, anthropologists, philosophers, and members of other disciplines have speculated on the evolution of language, but linguists, for some reason, have remained, until quite recently, relatively silent. Even though they argue that language is unique to human beings and has a biological foundation; nevertheless, they also claim that its origin is unknowable. Cook and Newson are absolutely correct when they state, "The species-specificity of UG nevertheless raises difficult questions about how it could have arisen during evolution."[2] Similarly, Derek Bickerton claims that the "cognitive gap between humans and nonhumans is evolution's Achilles' heel."[3] In fact, as I will indicate later, it was only in the last two decades that Chomsky formally addressed the relationship between the language faculty and evolutionary biology.[4] Regardless, it definitely seems to be the case that some sort of leap occurred at some period in recent history that accounts for the rather sudden appearance of language. Until approximately 100,000 years ago, there was no evidence that a complex symbolic system of any sort existed in human beings. Then, quite suddenly, in evolutionary time, there was a dramatic shift in the way humans communicated. People began to express themselves creatively in art and other complex symbolic forms. As Chomsky suggests, "there doesn't seem to be any indication that it was there before, and it all seems to be the same after. So it looks as if - given the time involved - there was a sudden 'great leap forward.'[5]

Darwin has some interesting ideas about the origin and evolution of language, but it must be kept in mind that many of the findings of modern science remained dormant during his lifetime. He speculates that language originated by imitating and modifying "various natural sounds, the voices of other animals, and man's own instinctive cries."[6] Darwin claims that humans

---

[2] V.J. Cook and Mark Newson, *Chomsky's Universal Grammar: An Introduction* (Malden, MA: Blackwell Publishing, 2007), p.47.

[3] Derek Bickerton, *More Than Nature Needs: Language, Mind, and Evolution* (Cambridge, Massachusetts: Harvard University Press, 2014), p.5.

[4] I am making reference here to Chomsky's formal writing on the subject. In fact, as I discuss in the following section, Chomsky has been interested in the origin and evolution of language since the 1970s.

[5] Noam Chomsky, *The Science of Language: Interviews with James McGilvray* (Cambridge, Massachusetts: Cambridge University Press, 2012), p.13.

[6] Charles Darwin, *The Descent of Man.* In Edward O. Wilson (ed.), *From So Simple a Beginning: The Four Great Books of Charles Darwin* (New York: W.W. Norton & Company, 2006), p.810.

share many inarticulate sounds and gestures with other species, including cries of pain, fear, surprise, and anger. He states,

> Articulate language is, however, peculiar to man (sic), but he uses in common with the lower animals inarticulate cries to express his meaning, aided by gestures and the movements of the muscles of the face.[7]

Articulate language, for Darwin, means much more than merely mimicking sounds because parrots, for instance, can mimic words. Articulate language involves "connecting definite sounds with definite ideas; this obviously depends on the development of the mental faculties."[8] In addition, he posits that the quantitative difference in cognitive capacities between nonhuman primates and human beings is significantly less than the difference between various other species. Darwin states,

> We must also admit that there is a much wider interval in mental power between one of the lowest fishes, as a lamprey or lancelot, and one of the higher apes, than between an ape and man (sic); yet this immense interval is filled up by numberless gradations.[9]

Darwin identifies a relationship between language and the mental faculties but, at times, appears to be uncertain whether language is a product of intelligence or vice versa. For instance, he argues that what he refers to as "articulate language" is unique to human beings, but its ability to connect sounds with ideas "depends on the development of the mental faculties." Darwin argues,

> The mental powers in some early progenitors of man must have been more highly developed than in any existing ape, before even the most imperfect form of speech could have come into use; but we may confidently believe that the continued use and advancement of this power would have reacted on the mind by enabling and encouraging it to carry on long trains of thought.[10]

In this case, language, for Darwin, appears to be a product of the development of the human intellect, even though he claims "there is no fundamental difference between man (sic) and the higher mammals in their mental

---

[7] Charles Darwin, *The Descent of Man*. In Ibid., p.809.
[8] Ibid.
[9] Ibid., p.798.
[10] Ibid.

faculties."[11] It's merely a question of degree, of how human beings have a greater degree of intelligence simply because they had to develop certain cognitive capacities in order to survive. For Darwin, it explains why, for example, higher apes do not use their vocal organs for speech because speech is not needed for their survival, and also because it "no doubt depends on their intelligence not having been sufficiently advanced."[12] Contrarily, Darwin also argues, "Without the use of some language, however imperfect, it appears doubtful whether man's (sic) intellect could have risen to the standard implied by his dominant position at an early period."[13] In this case, he seems to support the idea that certain higher mental faculties develop as a product of language.

In either case, Darwinian thinking suggests that evolution occurs by a process of gradual descent through minute modifications. Small changes in a species take many generations. If this is the case, and the fact that humans as a species have remained the same for approximately 200,000 years, then it certainly appears to be the case that some sort of radical leap in evolution would be required to account for the development of language. True, Darwin denies the possibility that natural selection is the sole factor attributed to the modification of species. It is a factor, but not *the* factor of evolutionary change. Even so, a leap of this sort would clearly violate Darwin's fundamental principle, *natura non facit saltum.*

It is worth noting that not all scholars support a purely gradualist or continuity approach. For instance, Eric Lenneberg disagrees with the "continuity theories" associated with the Darwinian position, that is, that language originated in primitive forms of communication and is the product of a long, continuous process of evolution. For example, continuity theories posit that there is no essential difference between lower forms of communication and language. Human beings are more intelligent than other animals and, as a result, have access to a larger collection of words and sounds. In this case, argues Lenneberg, there exists a quantitative difference between animal communication and human language but not a qualitative difference. The problem with a continuity theory of this sort, argues Lenneberg, is that it is based upon the assumption that language acquisition is related somehow to intelligence. Evidence tends to suggest that language capacity correlates poorly with intelligence and that individuals with severely challenged cognitive abilities can still understand the intricacies and meanings of a spoken language. Lenneberg states,

---

[11] Ibid., p.798.
[12] Ibid., p.811.
[13] Ibid., p.910.

What is thought to be the beginning of language in parrots, monkeys, or dolphins, is empirically totally different from the beginnings of language in the human infant. At the most primitive stages of language acquisition, man does not imitate sounds, words, or sentences, but generates novel sound sequences that are recognized as speech and language because the rules of generation bear certain *formal* similarities to those of the standard language.[14]

Lenneberg also dismisses another type of continuity theory, one that recognises a qualitative difference between forms of animal communication and language, but, nevertheless, is 'a discernible and continuous history."[15] This continuous history has been disrupted by a series of fateful events, loss of species, unexpected off-shoots, and an accumulation of many missing links. In addition, Lenneberg is sceptical about the results of studies that compare the differences in brain structure between humans and other animals. Even though, as I will explore in more detail below, research in neuroscience and linguistics shows that a particular region of the human brain is responsible for the acquisition and development of language; nevertheless, this research does not address the evolution of language itself. Lenneberg disagrees with evolutionary theorists who claim that human brains evolved from smaller brains of other non-human primates and that with growth came higher cognitive skills and language. Lenneberg states,

It is tempting to relate the size of the brain to man's two most outstanding characteristics: his capacity for language and his general cognitive capacities. Intuitively, this relation may be reasonable. But it is important to remember that it rests on no more than just that: intuition. There is no way of demonstrating that cognitive or language capacities either required or resulted from a rapid increase in the number of brain cells.[16]

Even when I consider findings of this sort, there does appear to be an apparent leap in the overall process. The evidence suggests that language did not evolve through a slow process of gradual descent; rather, it seemed to appear on the scene in a meteoric fashion. Bickerton states,

---

[14] Eric Lenneberg, *Biological Foundations of Language* (New York: John Wiley & Sons, Inc., 1967), p.233.
[15] Ibid, p.230.
[16] Ibid., pp.258-259.

Either language as we know it sprang full-blown into the world, with all its complexities ... or it emerged originally in a much more primitive form. ... The first of these scenarios is inherently less likely. Evolution does not normally, if indeed ever, involve leaps of this magnitude.[17]

For Bickerton, this scenario leads to what he calls the "Continuity Paradox," that is, language must have evolved out of some earlier system, but there does not seem to be such a system out of which it could have evolved. That is, evolution suggests that language must have evolved from something, but there is no evidence to support it. Clearly, language has a biological basis and is written into the genetic code, but its origin appears to be incomprehensible.

Chomsky on the Evolution of Language

Bickerton claims that Chomsky did not address the issue of language evolution until quite recently. He argues that, for many years, "Chomsky had nothing to say about the evolution of language, except that there was nothing sensible that anyone could say about it."[18] Bickerton is partly correct. Even though Chomsky did not write systematically about the evolution of language earlier in his career; nevertheless, he has been interested in the topic for many years. In a recent correspondence with me, he states,

[I]n the 70s I was co-teaching grad courses on biology of language with Salvador Luria (Nobel laureate in evolutionary biology), and Eric Lenneberg, who really opened the topic for serious inquiry, was a close personal friend back to our grad student days in the early '50s. I didn't write much about it, because there was little to say ... Until the '90s, what was known about language had not reached a level of simplicity and depth that made it possible to say very much. That changed with the advent of the minimalist program, when Berwick and I started writing about the topic, separately and then together in our book, and publications since updating it.[19]

Chomsky argues that language is the product of a stumble, rather than a leap. A leap implies an intentional act, whereby a stumble is purely accidental. Even so, Chomsky is correct when he states that "Language does indeed pose

---

[17] Derek Bickerton, *Language & Species* (Chicago: University of Chicago Press, 1990), p.109.
[18] Derek Bickeron, *Adam's Tongue: How Humans Made Language, How Language Made Humans* (New York: Hill and Wang, 2009), p.170.
[19] Chomsky sent me this email correspondence after he reviewed my manuscript. The email is dated November 14, 2022.

a severe challenge for evolutionary explanation."[20] In his later works, Chomsky often speculates on the evolution of language. For instance, he argues that certain events occur by chance only once in the evolutionary record. In *Language and the Problems of Knowledge* (1988), Chomsky speculates,

> In some cases it seems that organs develop to serve one purpose and, when they have reached a certain form in the evolutionary process, became available for different purposes, at which point the process of natural selection may refine them further for their purposes.[21]

To support his position, Chomsky cites the example of some insects that, in their initial stages of development, have a problem with heat exchange and develop rudimentary wings to fan their bodies. Eventually, their bodies become too large for the fanning effect to be of any use, so the rudimentary wings develop into proper wings for flight, and the body is cooled by a constant flow of air. Possibly, according to Chomsky, "human mental capacities have in some cases evolved in a similar way."[22] Similarly, Ernst Mayr argues that a high degree of intelligence and language, as its natural by-product, is most likely an evolutionary anomaly. He claims that among the billions of species that have existed since the beginning of time, only human beings have acquired the level of intelligence required to establish complex civilizations. Mayr concludes that it requires a complexity "of rare, favorable circumstances to produce high intelligence."[23]

Chomsky acknowledges the fact that non-human animals portray vague similarities to the language faculty, but "if you get to organisms where there is relatively common evolutionary origin, say the primates, there is simply nothing with interesting similarities."[24] At the same time, he declares that it is theoretically possible "that higher primates, say gorillas or whatever, actually have something like a human language faculty but they just have no access to it."[25] Over the past two decades, Chomsky has proposed a new approach to the evolution of the language faculty that recognises the possible influence of Darwinian evolutionary biology. This approach, according to Cook and

---

[20] Robert C. Berwick and Noam Chomsky, *Why Only Us: Language and Evolution* (Cambridge, Massachusetts: The MIT Press, 2016), p.50.

[21] Noam Chomsky, *Language and the Problems of Knowledge: The Managua Lectures* (Cambridge, Massachusetts: The MIT Press, 1996) (eighth printing of original 1988 publication), p.167.

[22] Ibid.

[23] Ibid., p.29.

[24] Noam Chomsky, *Architecture of Language* (Oxford: Oxford University Press, 2000), p.4.

[25] Ibid., pp.17-18.

Newson, "seems to concede much of the ground to Chomsky's opponents and leave very little that is peculiar to language … the broad language faculty … is no longer unique and much of it may be shared with the animal kingdom."[26] Theoretical possibilities aside, Chomsky clearly favours the idea that a language faculty is the preserve of human beings alone, but acknowledges that its origin is best explained by a fairy tale. He states,

> [I]t is almost as if there was some higher primate wandering around a long time ago and some random mutation took place, maybe after some strange cosmic ray shower, and it reorganized the brain, implanting a language organ in the otherwise primate brain. That is a story, not to be taken literally. But it may be closer to reality than many other fairy tales that are told about evolutionary processes, including language.[27]

Recently, Chomsky has produced three fundamental works that have specifically addressed the evolution of language. In many respects, these works have, once again, systematically shifted the overall focus and direction of biolinguistics. I will provide a brief overview of these works, in part because of their seismic effect in the study of language acquisition, but also because one of them involves a rather exciting union of two often disparate thinkers, that is, Chomsky and an evolutionary biologist.

In 2002, Chomsky, Marc Hauser, and Tecumseh Fitch published a paper in the prestigious journal *Science*.[28] The (HCF) paper is significant for two reasons. First, it presents Chomsky's clearly articulated exposition of ideas on the evolution of language. Second, and perhaps even more interesting for many biologists and linguists, the paper brings together two leading opponents in the evolution of language debate. Hauser is an evolutionary biologist who subscribes wholeheartedly to the modern synthesis of neo-Darwinism. For Bickerton, to see Chomsky and Hauser as co-authors is "almost as great as what you'd expect if, on opening a back issue of some political journal, you found a position paper on the Middle East coauthored by Yasser Arafat and Ariel Sharon."[29]

The HCF paper begins by differentiating between language as a system of communication and the computational process that underlies it. It is worth recalling that in P&P, Chomsky assumed that the language faculty evolved as a

---

[26] Cook and Newson, *Chomsky's Universal Grammar*, p.48.
[27] Ibid.
[28] Hauser, Marc, Chomsky, Noam, and Fitch, W. Tecumseh. "The faculty of language: What is it, who has it, and how did it evolve? *Science* (2002) 298:1569-79.
[29] Bickerton, *Adam's Tongue*, p.171.

whole, without any evolutionary precursors in other species and also without any connections to other non-linguistic domains. More recently, Chomsky identifies Merge as the core computational mechanism. Merge contains the central recursive property of language and two distinct interfaces: sensory-motor interface and conceptual-intentional interface. Thus, language is regarded as an interfacing mechanism. The language contains two interfaces and a recursive link between them. In the HCF paper, the authors argue that, initially, the computational capacities evolved for non-communicative purposes, most likely for advantages provided by the use of symbolization and reasoning, and that only later were they deployed for communication purposes. Animal communication systems lack the recursive property, that is, "the rich expressive and open-ended power of human language."[30] Recursion, in this sense, has the capacity to take a finite set of elements (words) and generate a potentially infinite array of discrete expressions (sentences). This is what Chomsky refers to as 'discrete infinity'. Animals have the capacity to differentiate sounds and generate a meaning system, but they lack the internal, recursive, computational system that is the basis of human language. The faculty of language in the broad sense (FLB) includes the phonological, semantic, and internal computational systems, but the faculty of language in the narrow sense (FLN) is represented by the internal computational system alone, and its core property is recursion (or Merge). Therefore, FLN is a subset of FLB.

Inevitably, the clear distinction between FLB and FLN raises a few interesting questions, and this is where evolutionary biology and biolinguistics unite. Which features of FLB have been inherited unchanged by humans? Which features of FLB have been subjected to minor changes? Which features are unique to humans, and how did they evolve? And most interestingly, did FLN evolve initially for non-communicative reasons? The authors of HCF state,

> Comparative work has generally focused on animal communication or the capacity to acquire a human-created language. If, however, one entertains the hypothesis that recursion evolved to solve other computational problems such as navigation, number quantification or social relationships, then it is possible that other animals have such abilities ... If we find evidence for recursion in animals, but in a noncommunicative domain, then we are more likely to pinpoint the

---

[30] Larson, Richard, Deprez, Viviane, and Yamakido, Hiroko (eds.), *The Evolution of Human Language: Biolinguistic Perspectives* (Cambridge: Cambridge University Press, 2011), p.16. This volume contains the HCF paper and more recent work in the area of biolinguistics.

mechanisms underlying this ability and the selective pressures that led to it. This discovery, in turn, would open the door to another suite of puzzles: Why did humans, but no other animals, take the power of recursion to create an open-ended and limitless system of communication?[31]

It is interesting to note how Chomsky has become more receptive to the views of evolutionary biologists. Even recursion, the key element of the internal computational system, may have been used initially for non-communicative purposes, and its earlier remnants may be found in components of FLN shared with other animals. I suspect this is where Hauser and Chomsky find common ground. In any case, it is clearly apparent that the study of the evolution of language has moved in a new direction. As Hauser suggests,

[T]he study of language evolution has entered into a new phase, with different theoretical approaches, experimental procedures, and test population, and significantly, far less speculation and far more empirical evidence.[32]

In 2005, Chomsky published an article in which he clarifies and expands upon some of the key ideas posited in the HCF paper. He considers, once again, whether or not recursion is unique to the language faculty and concludes that it is not so. He states that the "evolution of language required some innovation to provide instructions for Merge to operate."[33] Language, therefore, and especially recursion (Merge), evolved through traits shared with other animals for non-communicative purposes. But, how did recursion evolve from apparently non-recursive traits? Chomsky states,

Within some small group from which we are all descended, a rewiring of the brain took place in some individual, call him *Prometheus*, yielding the operation of unbounded Merge … The capacity would then be transmitted to offspring.[34]

In 2016, Chomsky co-authored a book with computer scientist Robert Berwick on language and evolution. He confirms his belief that Merge may have arisen

---

[31] Ibid., p.37.
[32] Marc Hauser, "On obfuscation, obscurantism, and opacity: evolving conceptions of the faculty of language." In Ibid., p.99.
[33] Noam Chomsky, "Some simple evo devo theses:how true they might be for language?" In Ibid., p.53.
[34] Ibid., p.59.

from a rewiring of the brain and provided individuals with many advantages, including "capacities for complex thought, planning, interpretation, and so on. The capacity would presumably be partially transmitted to offspring, and because of the selective advantage it confers, might come to dominate a small breeding group."[35]

It may be true, as Hauser suggests, that modern biolinguistics involves less speculation and more empirical study. Even so, it is rather apparent, at least to me, that Chomsky's current position on the evolution of language still embodies a high degree of speculative thought. The idea that recursion is a crucial component of human language and the human mind remains a provocative and speculative hypothesis. Even so, Fitch suggests, "if this hypothesis *is* falsified (as most strong hypotheses eventually are in science), it will be by empirical study, not by clever arguments."[36] Clearly, the recursion argument still begs a fundamental question: If many components of recursion and the FLB are present in other species, and these components evolved initially to solve non-linguistic problems, including navigation and social relationships, then why is it that humans alone have developed the capacity to acquire a language, something unique in the evolutionary record? It may be true, as Chomsky posits, that an accidental rewiring of the human brain occurred millions of years ago and acted as the catalyst for language acquisition, but suggestions of this nature remain at the level of speculation.

Speculations Abound

It is worth noting here that not everyone agrees with Chomsky's saltationist view on the evolution of language, that is, a view which claims that the production of new species is discontinuous and sudden, perhaps even an accidental stumble. For Michael Ruse, such a position is completely implausible. In his defence, Ruse makes reference to the evolution of the vocal passage, a reference also found in Darwin's *The Descent of Man* (1871), and states,

> Reconstructing the shape of the vocal passage from skulls, we find that, up to *Homo sapiens*, the passage was much as one encounters in today's apes. Then, we get a gradual lengthening of the supralaryngeal tract, until some 30,000 years ago the modern human form was fully

---

[35] Berwick and Chomsky, *Why Only Us*, p.80.
[36] W. Tecumseh Fitch, "Three meanings of 'recursion': key distinctions for biolinguistics." In Larson et al (eds.), *Evolution of Human Language*, p.75.

developed. This coincides with the beginning of the explosive growth of human culture.[37]

Similarly, Darwin argued that with an increased use of the voice, "the vocal organs would have been strengthened and perfected." For Ruse and other evolutionary thinkers, language is the product of a slow evolutionary process, a gradual development of a particular organ, rather than the result of a random leap or stumble.

But, how exactly did language originate? How is it, for example, that humans share approximately 99% of their DNA with chimpanzees, but these non-human primates can do no more than manipulate a few simple symbols while humans can express thoughts and ideas through complex and highly creative languages? Humans can stand back from the world, contemplate, critique, evaluate, and judge, but other creatures appear to live forever in the present, restricted by the confines of their immediate environment. How did humans arrive at this particularly unique position in the evolutionary tree?

The responses to these questions embrace various hypotheses. If, on the one hand, one believes that humans are the product of special creation and that language acquisition originated as the result of an act of divine intervention from a Supreme Being, then the matter is resolved promptly. God created humans with language, and they alone are His special creation. If, on the other hand, one considers the abundance of evidence that supports the fact that humans, as a species, evolved through a natural process, then speculations abound regarding the evolution of language. Beyond strictly theistic interpretations, it is generally accepted as fact that our ancestors shared a few common branches of the evolutionary tree with other primates and that our closest living relatives include chimpanzees and gorillas. It could be argued that language developed through a combination of environmental factors and the simple grunts of communication. Perhaps humans share with their ancestors a common cognitive infrastructure. Indeed, this might be the case, and a number of psychologists and linguists, in their attempts to teach apes to speak, have devoted their careers to this idea. Even so, it must be acknowledged that there is a significant difference between teaching a chimpanzee to point to specific symbols on a board and the complex structure of a language. The vocabulary of Nim, Sherman, Austin, Washoe, and other non-human primates is restricted to a few hundred symbols, and they are incapable of producing genuine sentences. Even so, studies with apes provide some interesting insights into how young children begin their life-

---

[37] Michael Ruse, *Taking Darwin Seriously: A Naturalist Approach to Philosophy* (New York: Prometheus Books, 1998), p.133-134.

long adventure with language. For instance, Bickerton compares the utterances of an infant to the symbols used by an ape.[38] When I consider the results, I find it difficult to distinguish between the two respondents.

Respondent 1: toothbrush there, me toothbrush; sleep toothbrush; red, me eat (sees picture of tomato); berry, give me, eat berry; come … there; give eat there, Mary, me eat; give me berry; afraid, hug; Mary afraid, hug; play; pull, jump; tired, sleep, brush teeth, hug.

Respondent 2: rock? (rocks chair); rock; chair; chair; chair; house? Chair; get up (asked if want to get up); get; please? (asked if wants juice); please (given juice); thank-you; thank-you; apple (it is apple juice); fan; fan; T.V.; T.V.; T.V. (dog's name mentioned); puppy; switch.

Clearly, both respondents rely solely on one-word responses. In fact, the over-abundant use of one-word responses would seem to suggest that the latter respondent is the signing ape, when, in fact, it is the young child. The findings are interesting, and one may be tempted to conclude that language evolved from the communicative skills of apes. In fact, the findings suggest virtually nothing about the origin of language, and simply support Chomsky's overall understanding of language acquisition. Chomsky argues that young children do not "learn" a language; rather, they "grow" into it. Granted, the surface structure of a specific language, with its use of words, sounds, and unique accents, is learned through social interaction, but the foundations of language are innate. Initially, toddlers use simple one-word utterances, but they quickly grow into the use of a complex language structure. So, once again, how did language originate? Bickerton speculates that it has something to do with a combination of evolutionary accidents, and that language is fundamentally a "change in neural organization that caused us to slot meaningful symbols into formal structures."[39] Bickerton might be correct. Even though language acquisition is based on cognitive capacities that are shared, to varying degrees, with other animals, it is reasonable to speculate that something occurred within the structure of the human brain, in order for the innate language faculty to appear. Perhaps, Bickerton and Lenneberg are on the right path. It is feasible to suggest that findings in the neurobiology of language acquisition may contribute something significant to the debate.

An underlying assumption often associated with a neurobiological approach to language is that language is a biological system that evolved through phylogeny, that is, it followed a specific evolutionary course. Language is, in part, an expression of various cognitive capacities, including some capacities,

---

[38] Bickerton, *Language & Species*, pp.110-111.
[39] Ibid., p.256.

such as memory, attention, and associative learning, that are shared with other animals. Language also includes an innate faculty that is unique to human beings. Language acquisition, a distinctive feature of human nature, is a combination of both cognitive capacities and an innate language faculty. The difference between human and non-human primate brains is fundamentally the structure of those areas of the brain that constitute the language network in humans. Angela Friederici states, "cross-species analyses of those brain regions that are responsible for language in humans, as well as those fiber bundles that connect these regions, reveal crucial differences between human and non-human primates."[40] There are brain regions in the left hemisphere that are primarily responsible for language acquisition and the processing of words and sentences, especially Broca's area and Wernicke's area. Initially, it was believed that Broca's area of the brain was responsible for language production and Wernicke's area focussed on language comprehension. As a result of modern imaging techniques, it is now believed that Broca's area promotes grammatical processes during production and comprehension, and Wernicke's area assists lexical-semantic processes. It is argued that a highly complex and intricate language network exists in both hemispheres of the brain. Different regions of the brain are connected by fibre bundles that create pathways for the transmission of information between specific regions. Friederici asserts that there is a white matter dorsal fibre tract that connects a specific area of Broca's area (BA 44) to the posterior temporal cortex, and that this "fiber tract could be seen as the missing link which has to evolve in order to make the full language capacity possible."[41]

The fundamental difference between human and non-human primate brains, and especially the way specific brain areas are connected by white matter fibre tracts, is an important finding in the overall debate. What, in fact, is the function of these white matter fibre tracts? Different fibre tracts are responsible for different language functions, but all fibre tracts transfer information from one area of the brain to another. White matter fibre tracts, according to Friederici, are the "backbone of language processing."[42] In the left hemisphere, for example, dorsal fibre tracts process complex sentences, but ventral fibre tracts promote semantic processing. Similar pathways are found in the right hemisphere, and there are also cross-hemisphere pathways that transfer information between the two hemispheres.

---

[40] Angela D. Friederici, *Language in the Brain: The Origins of a Uniquely Human Capacity* (Cambridge, Massachusetts: The MIT Press, 2017), p.3.
[41] Ibid., p.ix.
[42] Ibid., p.103.

It is interesting to compare the brain structure of humans to non-human primates. For instance, the cerebral cortex in a human brain is more than three times greater in size than in a chimpanzee brain. It appears that significant differences in white matter in the prefrontal cortex between human and non-human primates play an important role in our understanding of the evolution of seemingly complex cognitive abilities in humans. There are also differences between humans and chimpanzees when one considers the maturation rate of prefrontal white matter - the former mature at a much faster rate than the latter - and this may suggest why humans develop complex cognitive structures early in life. In addition, differences occur between human and non-human primates when one considers the structure in Broca's area of the brain. For instance, in human brains, there is a leftward asymmetry in Broca's area in the inferior frontal gyrus, but non-human primates do not portray this particular asymmetry. Also, there are also differences between human and non-human primate brains when one considers the dorsal connections between BA 44 in Broca's area and the superior temporal cortex. For Friederici, these findings indicate that "These structures may have evolved to subserve the human capacity to process syntax, which is at the core of the human language faculty."[43]

Clearly, recent findings in biology and neuroscience shed some light on the evolution of language. Even so, speculations abound, and consensus is rarely achieved. Friederici's findings might be moving in the right direction, but other equally valid hypotheses are also embraced by the scientific community. For example, Philip Lieberman, in his *Toward an Evolutionary Biology of Language* (2006), argues that Chomsky's insistence on the existence of an innate language organ is inconsistent with the principles and findings of evolutionary biology and neuroscience. Rather than focussing on one specific organ, Lieberman suggests language originated through the development of neural circuits that regulate motor control with memory and higher cognitive functions. For instance, in *Human Language and Our Reptilian Brain* (2000), Lieberman claims that the idea of an innate language faculty, a UG, is not supported by biological facts. He argues that a functional language system (FLS), which is comprised of the neocortex - the most recent evolutionary aspect of the mammalian brain, the subcortical basal gangliaIn - reptilian brain, and a complex neural network, might suggest something about the origin of human language and cognition. It is true that the neural capacity of the FLS is unique to human beings, but its anatomy and physiology evolved from structures and systems in other animals. In fact, Lieberman posits that "human linguistic and cognitive ability can be traced back to the learned

---

[43] Ibid., pp.217, 219.

motor responses of mollusks."[44] In Lieberman's earlier work, *The Biology and Evolution of Language* (1984), he suggests that language is the result of many evolutionary compromises, small changes in the structure of the vocal tract and in perceptual mechanisms in the brain. He speculates that perhaps cognitive systems that organise non-linguistic activities in non-human primates evolved with minor changes to create language. In this case, the origin of language is not a qualitative leap from non-human animal forms of communication; rather, it is merely a product of a long natural process of adaptations and modifications in order to cope with the world. He states,

> There seems to be no compelling reason to accept theories that propose discontinuities, that human language suddenly appeared full-blown from a 'protolanguage' by means of a unique biological process … Darwinian processes that appear to account for the evolution of communication in other species can account for the evolution of the proposed functional language system and many of its properties … The roots of our present linguistic ability probably go back to our distant ape-human ancestor … When speech or complex syntax came into being probably will never be known, but some of the necessary neural and anatomical prerequisites were present from the start of hominid evolution.[45]

Lenneberg's *Biological Foundations of Language* (1967), the first systematic description of the complex field of biolinguistics, initiated a rich and speculative tradition of research, and the tradition continues to grow. Clearly, speculation abounds when it comes to theories about the evolution of language. Indeed, the speculative nature of the subject tends to suggest that, inevitably, it will remain a mystery, something beyond the cognitive capacities of human beings to comprehend.

Language may have originated as a product of a well-developed larynx, neural system, the existence of white matter fibre tracts, a combination of random compromises or evolutionary accidents, a highly developed cognitive capacity, or the spontaneous emergence of other features that enhanced the earliest pre-modern hominid ancestors to utter what Bickerton calls a "protolanguage". If this is the case, then it would seem more accurate to describe the evolution of language as a stumble, rather than a radical leap. There definitely appears to be a completely random and accidental element

---

[44] Philip Lieberman, *Human Language and Our Reptilian Brain: The Subcortical Bases of Speech and Thought* (Cambridge, Massachusetts: Harvard University Press, 2000), p.2.
[45] Ibid., pp.155-156.

associated with the evolution of language. If these plausible speculations do not solve the problem of leaps or stumbles, at least they are oriented in the right direction.

Human Traits Revisited

A second problem arises when Chomsky claims that particular traits are unique to human beings. As was noted earlier, reasoning skills and other higher cognitive capacities are often regarded as uniquely human traits. Even so, in his *Descent of Man and Selection in Relation to Sex* (1871) and *The Expressions of the Emotions in Man and Animals* (1872), Darwin clearly shows that traits often considered to be found solely in the human domain are often shared, to varying degree, with other species. For instance, Darwin rejected the commonly accepted assumption that intelligence is unique to the human species. He declares that there is no qualitative difference between human beings and some other animals in their cognitive capacities. Darwin states,

> Of all the faculties of the human mind, it will, I presume, be admitted that *Reason* stands at the summit. Few persons any longer dispute that animals possess some power of reasoning. Animals may constantly be seen to pause, deliberate, and resolve. It is a significant fact, that the more the habits of any particular animal are studied by a naturalist, the more he (sic) attributes to reason and the less to unlearned instincts.[46]

Animals share with humans the entire spectrum of feelings and emotions. They experience a vast array of emotions, including contentment, fear, sadness, anxiety, jealousy, curiosity, and love. The issue here is one of degree. Animals, humans and non-humans alike, share particular traits, but some animals have developed them to a greater degree. Granted, humans are more intelligent than apes or cows, but apes and cows also express a degree of intelligence. And the same argument extends to all the so-called human traits. Interestingly, as I mentioned earlier, in his last book entitled *The Formation of Vegetable Mould Through the Action of Worms* (1881), Darwin extends this argument to the study of the lowly earthworm. Darwin states,

> As I was led to keep in my study many months, worms in pots filled with earth, I became interested in them, and wished to learn how far they acted consciously, and how much mental power they displayed. I was the more desirous to learn something on this head, as few observations of this kind have been made, as far as I know, of animals

---

[46] Edward O. Wilson (ed.), *From So Simple a Beginning*, p.804.

so low in the scale of organisation and so poorly provided with sense organs, as are earth-worms.[47]

The primary purpose of the study was to show that the upper crust of soil, or vegetable mould, is created by worms. Soil passes through the intestines of worms and is regurgitated to form the upper crust of fertile soil. In his glass display of worms, Darwin noticed that worms have the mental capacity required to turn around spiky leaves before dragging them into the soil for consumption rather than gripping them clumsily by the stalks or in the middle. They would also use leaves for plugging up their burrows. These activities, according to Darwin, display a degree of intelligence.

Similarly, one often assumes creative thinking is a uniquely human trait. Higher degrees of creativity are the result of a more developed cognitive structure in the brain. Even so, creativity is a trait humans share with other creatures. Once again, the varying expressions of creative thought between humans and other sentient beings are merely a difference of degree rather than a difference of kind. True, human beings have a greater capacity to think creatively, but this does not negate the fact that other sentient beings have, to a lesser degree, a similar capacity.

Creativity means the ability to produce or use ideas, alternatives, possibilities, and objects that are original and meaningful and to view things in new ways or from a different perspective. For naturalist Edward O. Wilson, creativity is the unique and defining trait of humans. Nevertheless, one may argue that other species exhibit varying degrees of creative thinking skills. Both birds and primates tend to be highly innovative thinkers. Anthropologists recognise that the advent of tool use accompanied a significant increase in intelligence and the development of creative thinking. For example, chimpanzees make spears for hunting and use sticks for foraging army ants; crows craft twigs into tools and even drop stones into vessels to raise the water level inside; elephants intentionally plug up water holes with boulders and tree trunks; when it rains, orangutans make their own umbrellas; capuchin monkeys crack cashew nuts with rocks; cockatoos bend pipe cleaners and make a hook to extract food from a tube. In his study of worms, Darwin showed that even worms have a slight capacity to solve problems in a slightly creative fashion. There seems to be an abundant amount of evidence in nature to support the argument that creativity is not a uniquely human trait.

Clearly, Darwin's discourse on what one often assumes to be human traits raises for critical consideration many of the issues associated with human

---

[47] Ibid., p.134.

nature. For instance, the vast majority of traits, including intelligence, are not an all-or-nothing affair. Rather, they are shared, to varying degrees, amongst many species. As James Rachels suggests,

> Man (sic) is not *the* rational animal; he is merely more rational than the other animals, who have 'a certain amount of reason' also. What better way to demonstrate the continuities in nature, from the lowest creatures to the highest, than by finding a modicum of intelligence even in the earthworm?[48]

In light of the findings cited above, it appears to be the case that the classical argument that humans alone are rational beings should be revisited. This also extends into similar arguments about other cognitive and affective traits. Even though humans share various traits, to a degree, with other animals; nevertheless, one may state with complete confidence that language is a uniquely human trait. Humans do not share language, to varying degrees, with other creatures. Humans alone have the innate capacity to speak a language, and this is a unique human trait. So far, scientists have not provided any evidence to support the fact that other sentient beings have moved beyond simple forms of communication to the use of complex languages. Language is a reflection of the mind, so it can be safely assumed that human beings have more complex minds than other creatures. Language, as opposed to animal grunts, is the product of a highly developed cognitive structure. From a Darwinian perspective, this cognitive structure developed as a species-specific survival mechanism. True, Darwin posits that evolution occurs through gradual changes or slight modifications, and language acquisition in human beings appears to be a dramatic leap (or stumble) from the grunts of other sentient beings, but, as noted above, recent findings in the neurobiology of language seem to provide a reasonable response to the apparent leap. Non-human animals rely on speed, agility, or strength as survival mechanisms, but through natural selection, human beings use well-developed brains and complex forms of thinking and communication. Stephen Jay Gould states,

> Yes, the brain got big by natural selection. But as a result of this size, and the neural density and connectivity thus imparted, human brains could perform an immense range of functions quite unrelated to the original reasons for increase in bulk. The brain did not get big so that we could read or write or do arithmetic or chart the seasons - yet

---

[48] James Rachels, *Created From Animals: The Moral Implications of Darwinism* (Oxford: Oxford University Press, 1990), p.136.

human culture, as we know it, depends upon skills of this kind ... [T]he universals of language are so different from anything else in nature, and so quirky in their structure, that origin as a side consequence of the brain's enhanced capacity, rather than as a simple advance in continuity from ancestral grunts and gestures, seems indicated."[49]

I contend that, even though humans may share a capacity to think creatively with other sentient beings, their creative capacity is so advanced relative to, say, a monkey or a worm, that it is almost justifiable to treat it as a different kind of thinking altogether. I agree with Gould's claim that human language is different from anything else in nature. Consequently, the cognitive structure of language, including one's capacity for complex creative thought, is also different from anything else in nature. It is on a completely different scale and can be treated justifiably as being a unique human trait.

In light of what has been discussed above, it appears that any viable solution to problems related to the evolution of language embraces a certain degree of speculation.[50] It seems to be the case that language originated as a product, accidental or otherwise, of growth in human intelligence. For whatever reason, as the human brain developed, something occurred - a genetic mutation, accidental neural reconfiguration, a random stumble - and the primary networking components of the so-called language organ developed and evolved. In any case, one can posit with complete confidence that language itself is a uniquely human trait. Its evolution may embrace speculation, but its uniqueness is fact. If one agrees on these points, then an articulated understanding of human nature is possible.

Through an exposition of Chomsky's ideas in linguistics, along with some current speculations on the evolution of language, I have shown that language is a human trait, and, moreover, that creativity, as an important part of language acquisition, is an essential component of human nature. But, according to Chomsky, freedom is also an important part of what it means to be human, and this is best exemplified in his political works. It is to Chomsky's political works that I now turn my attention.

---

[49] Quoted in Daniel C. Dennett, *Darwin's Dangerous Idea: Evolution and the Meaning of Life* (New York: Touchstone, 1995), p.390.

[50] It is worth mentioning that Chomsky disagrees with most of the literature I review in this chapter, except the foundational work of Lenneberg, and the recent works of Berwick and Friederici. In his review of my manuscript, he states that the important "matters are ignored in the literature you cite (Friederici aside). More reason why it is telling us little about evolution of language ... But almost all of what you review bears only marginally on the topic." (correspondence dated November 14, 2022).

Chapter 4

Politics and Human Nature

It requires a very unusual mind to undertake the analysis of the obvious.

Alfred North Whitehead, *Science and the Modern World*

Now, it is time to turn to an analysis of freedom, the second element in Chomsky's understanding of human nature. Even though the creative element of human nature is established through a consideration of Chomsky's linguistics, the element of freedom is most easily identified in his political discourse. Nevertheless, Chomsky, once again, highlights the tenuous thread between linguistics and politics and states the "intensive study of one aspect of human psychology - human language - may contribute to a humanistic social science that will serve, as well, as an instrument for social action."[1]

Chomsky's political view is rooted firmly in a tradition that includes the Enlightenment, classical liberalism, libertarian socialism, progressive contemporary thought, and even some scientific thinkers in the seventeenth century. His political work often includes references to Adam Smith, Wilhelm von Humboldt, Rene Descartes, Jean-Jacques Rousseau, Peter Kropotkin, Michael Bakunin, Rudolph Rocker, John Dewey, Bertrand Russell, and a vast array of other thinkers. Even though they differ in the specific details related to social change, these thinkers share a common vision of the way society should be organised: a society that stresses the importance of democracy, diversity, freedom of speech, and creativity, and is free of oppression and coercion from concentrated forms of power, whether the concentrated power is in the hands of Church authorities, the State, corporations, slave-owners, or feudal lords. In 1994, in a personal correspondence with Robert Barsky, Chomsky states,

> I think there is an important and detectable thread (to borrow your term) that runs from Cartesian rationalism through the romantic period (the more libertarian Rousseau, for example), parts of the enlightenment (some of Kant, etc.), pre-capitalist classical liberalism (notably Humboldt, but not Smith), and on to the partly spontaneous tradition of popular revolt against industrial capitalism and the forms

---

[1] Neil Smith, *Chomsky: Ideas and Ideals* (Cambridge: Cambridge University Press, 1999), p.189.

it took in the left-libertarian movements, including anti-Bolshevik parts
of the Marxist tradition.[2]

Chomsky's political works span over many decades and cover a vast array of
subjects. Initially, it can be quite daunting for one to grasp the overall aim of
his political discourse, but after some familiarity with it, one can identify
some common themes which appear frequently over time. Actually, at a
fundamental level, Chomsky simply applies Cartesian common sense to
political issues, and he invites others to do the same. He states,

> [I]t does not require very far-reaching, specialized knowledge to perceive
> that the United States was invading South Vietnam. And, in fact, to take
> apart the system of illusions and deception which functions to prevent
> understanding of contemporary reality [is] not a task that requires
> extraordinary skill or understanding. It requires the kind of normal
> skepticism and willingness to apply one's analytical skills that almost
> all people have and that they can exercise. It just happens that they
> exercise them in analyzing what the New England Patriots ought to do
> next Sunday instead of questions that really matter for human life,
> their own included.[3]

In this chapter, I explore various themes in Chomsky's political discourse and
show that freedom, as a key element of human nature, underlies the entire
spectrum of his work. I focus my efforts on the following five themes:
libertarian socialism, the critique of American foreign policy, manufacturing
consent, the responsibility of intellectuals, and intellectual self-defence.
Before I do so, I need to explain what is meant by the term 'freedom', and
identify how it is interpreted in the context of Chomsky's political analysis.

Freedom is a slippery term. It is used commonly in society in many different
ways. Everyone seems to have their own particular understanding of the word.
The Oxford English Dictionary presents the many ways freedom is understood
in common discourse. For example, freedom can mean the state or fact of
being free from servitude, constraint, or inhibition; release from slavery or
imprisonment; liberation from the bondage or dominating influence of sin,
spiritual servitude, worldly ties; not being subject to despotic or autocratic
control, or to a foreign power; and the state of being able to act without
hindrance or restraint. In Chomsky's political works, he often refers to these

---

[2] Robert Barsky, *The Chomsky Effect: A Radical Works Beyond the Ivory Tower* (Cambridge:
MIT Press, 2007), p.119.
[3] Barsky, *Noam Chomsky*, p.114.

varied interpretations of the word. Essentially, though, when Chomsky refers to freedom, he is referring to some sort of individual or social emancipation from the oppressive socio-political and economic forces in society. In part, this includes the important role played by freedom of thought and expression in a democratic society. Chomsky is a self-proclaimed anarchist or, synonymously, a libertarian socialist or anarcho-syndicalist. I will explore these terms shortly. What is worth noting at this time, is that, contrary to what is often read in the media, anarchism is a highly developed social philosophy based predominantly on the concept of freedom. Even though he was not an anarchist, Humboldt, for instance, claims that "freedom and variety are the preconditions for human self-realization."[4] He states,

> Nothing promotes this ripeness for freedom so much as freedom itself. This truth perhaps may not be acknowledged by those who so often use this unripeness as an excuse for continuing repression, but it seems to me to follow unquestionably from the very nature of man (sic). The incapacity for freedom can only arise from a want of moral and intellectual power. To heighten this power is the only way to supply the want, but to do so presupposes the freedom which awakens spontaneous activity. And those who do not comprehend this may justly be suspected of misunderstanding human nature and wishing to make men (sic) into machines.[5]

Unlike in Chomsky's works in linguistics, where he explicitly associates creativity with language acquisition and human nature, in his political works, he rarely addresses, in a direct fashion, the link between human nature and freedom. Even so, it is an underlying current in his discourse and is implicitly implied in all his political works. This is normally accomplished when he makes reference to other thinkers who address the concept of freedom. For example, in *Deterring Democracy* (1991), Chomsky uses approvingly the expression 'an instinct for freedom' by the nineteenth-century Russian anarchist, Michael Bakunin. Fundamentally, the way Bakunin uses the word 'instinct' is what Chomsky means by a key component of human nature. Chomsky suggests that this instinct for freedom "inspired Rousseau's classic lament that people are born free but are everywhere in chains, seduced by the illusions of the civil society that is created by the rich to guarantee their plunder."[6] Even so, there are precious gems in Chomsky's work where he explicitly discusses the relationship between human nature and the instinct

---

[4] Otero, *Chomsky*, p.137.
[5] Ibid.
[6] Noam Chomsky, *Deterring Democracy* (New York: Hill and Wang, 1991), p.397.

for freedom. For instance, he highlights the fact that "[t]here have been efforts to ground the instinct for freedom in a substantive theory of human nature. They are not without interest ... (but this instinct) remains a regulative principle that we adopt, or reject, on faith. Which choice we make can have large-scale consequences for ourselves and others."[7] Similarly, in an earlier essay, Chomsky states that "the essence of human nature is human freedom and the consciousness of this freedom."[8]

Earlier, I considered Plato's problem, that is, how one knows so much with so little external stimuli. Conversely, in his political works, Chomsky introduces the idea of 'Orwell's problem', which addresses the question, "How can we remain so ignorant when the evidence is so overwhelming?" That is, how is it that people accept the messages propagated by concentrated forms of power in society when it is clearly evident that these messages contradict common sense and are at variance with the overall well-being of society. According to Edward Herman,

> Freedom ... in this post-Orwellian age, *means* the ability of the large economic interests to operate without constraint. As democracy and other legal rights for ordinary citizens might be constraining, freedom requires non-freedom in a political-social-economic sense for the majority.[9]

What Herman is alluding to is Chomsky's concept of the 'Fifth Freedom'. During the Second World War, President Roosevelt proclaimed that the Allies were fighting to protect four fundamental freedoms: freedom of speech, freedom of worship, freedom from want, and freedom from fear. According to Chomsky, the Four Freedoms and the Atlantic Charter, signed by Roosevelt and Churchill, were nothing more than "lofty sentiments ...to maintain domestic cohesion during the difficult war years, and were taken seriously by oppressed and suffering people elsewhere, who were soon to be disabused of their illusions."[10] Chomsky added a crucial fifth freedom to this list, that is, the freedom of the corporate sector and its supporters "to rob and to exploit."[11]

---

[7] Ibid.

[8] Peck (ed.), *Chomsky Reader*, p.143.

[9] Edward Herman, *The Real Terror Network: Terrorism in Fact and Propaganda* (Boston: South End Press, 1982), p.9.

[10] Noam Chomsky, *Turning the Tide: The U.S. and Latin America* (Montreal: Black Rose Books, 1987), p.45.

[11] Ibid., p.47.

Infringements of the four official freedoms in enemy territory always evokes much agonized concern. Not, however, in our own ample domains. Here, as the historical record demonstrates with great clarity, it is only when the fifth and fundamental freedom is threatened that a sudden and short-lived concern for other forms of freedom manifests itself, to be sustained for as long as it is needed to justify the righteous use of force and violence to restore the Fifth Freedom, the one that really counts.[12]

It is quite apparent from these brief introductory comments on Chomsky's view of freedom that it extends far and wide and may, at an initial glance, appear to be rather complicated, if not entirely overwhelming. Even so, with a degree of reasoning and basic common sense, along with a reasonable understanding of some of the key themes that underlie his political thought, it is relatively easy to anticipate Chomsky's general response to a vast array of political issues. It is to these themes that I now turn my attention.

Libertarian Socialism

The political philosophy that most accurately describes Chomsky's political views is what he calls libertarian socialism. In essence, libertarian socialism is a combination of the positions found commonly under the rubrics of anarchism and Marxism. He favours the anarcho-syndicalist expression of anarchism found in the works of thinkers like Michael Bakunin and also representatives of the left-wing Marxist tradition. In fact, he sometimes refers to himself as a "derivative fellow traveller"[13] of the anarchist tradition. The matter becomes somewhat more complicated when one considers the various expressions of both strands of political discourse. Anarchism comes in many forms, and contrary to a contemporary misuse of the word in the media and the general public, anarchists are not members of lunatic fringe groups with a tendency to incite violent acts. In fact, non-violence is a common theme promoted throughout most of the anarchist tradition. For instance, both Gandhi and Tolstoy are self-proclaimed anarchists who promote non-violent forms of social change. The individualist type of anarchism embraced by Stirner and Thoreau is radically different to the community-oriented positions supported by Kropotkin and Bakunin. Essentially, the basis of all expressions of anarchist thought is freedom, but it's the fine details about how to achieve freedom that differentiate one form from another. In any case, there is no fixed goal in anarchism; rather, it is an ongoing, dynamic process, and its

---

[12] Ibid.
[13] Barry Pateman (ed.), *Chomsky on Anarchism* (Oakland: AK Press, 2005), p.135.

flexibility permits it to adjust to various socio-political and economic forces. As Rudolf Rocker states, anarchism "is not a fixed, self-enclosed social system but rather a definite trend ... a tendency towards freedom that expresses itself in different ways at different times."[14] In addition, Chomsky often refers to various Marxist thinkers. He regards the early Marx as an extremely important figure in history and also a true revolutionary thinker. There are various strains of Marxism, and Chomsky avoids wholeheartedly the authoritarian, Statist, dictatorship strain. Chomsky acknowledges the value of Marx's critique of capitalism and favours a non-authoritarian Marxist position found commonly in the works of Pannekoek, Luxemburg, and others.

It is worth noting that not all anarchist thinkers embrace Chomsky's use and interpretation of anarchism. For example, American social ecologist Murray Bookchin, and George Woodcock, the Canadian writer and self-proclaimed anarchist, are rooted firmly in the anarchist tradition and express concerns regarding Chomsky's tendency to reach far beyond the traditional anarchist boundaries. Even though Bookchin came from a strong Marxist background; nevertheless, in the latter part of his life, he based his social ecology on a firm anarchist tradition, especially the works of Russian anarchist Peter Kropotkin and French anarchist Elisee Reclus. Woodcock regards Chomsky as a sympathetic outsider who tries to use anarchism to support his own doctrines. Woodcock tends to express a rather orthodox understanding of anarchism; that is, one is either completely in or completely out. In light of anarchism's nineteenth-century battle with Marx, it is understandable that some anarchists do not seek support from Marxist thinkers, but anarchists like Chomsky tend to disagree with this particular stance.

A figure who appears frequently in Chomsky's political works is the Russian anarchist Michael Bakunin. This radical figure and vociferous opponent of Karl Marx, describes himself as a "fanatic lover of liberty, considering it as the unique condition under which intelligence, dignity and human happiness can develop and grow."[15] For Bakunin, true freedom, as opposed to a State-defined expression of freedom, is "the only kind of liberty that is worthy of the name, liberty that consists in the full development of all of the material, intellectual and moral powers that are latent in each person; liberty that recognizes no restrictions other than those determined by the laws of our own individual nature."[16] He warned the public numerous times that the Red bureaucracy proclaimed by Marx would prove to be "the most vile and terrible

---

[14] Milan Rai, *Chomsky's Politics* (London: Verso, 1995), p.94.
[15] Ibid., pp.95-96.
[16] Ibid. p.96.

lie of the century."[17] In a passage that Chomsky claims is one of the few accurate predictions in the social sciences, Bakunin states,

> Take the most radical revolutionary and place him (sic) on the throne of all the Russias or give him dictatorial power, and before a year is past he'll (sic) become worse than the czar himself.[18]

In other words, as Martin Buber suggests, "One cannot in the nature of things expect a little tree that has been turned into a club to put forth leaves."[19]

For Chomsky, these libertarian ideas are rooted in Enlightenment thought, especially in Rousseau's *Discourse on Inequality* (1755) and even Humboldt's *The Limits of State Action* (1852). As noted earlier, Chomsky has been an ardent anarchist or libertarian socialist since his early teenage years.[20] His fundamental political position has not changed since his early days in New York City with radical elements of his extended family. For Chomsky, one of the many attractive features of anarchism or libertarian socialism is its applicability to modern times. He states,

> What attracts me about anarchism personally are the tendencies in it that try to come to grips with the problems of dealing with complex organized industrial societies within a framework of free institutions and structures.[21]

A view portrayed commonly in both Bakunin's anarcho-syndicalism and Chomsky's libertarian socialism is a vision of a future society with its emphasis on the democratic control of one's productive life, which includes, more specifically, "a network of workers' councils, and at a higher level, representation across the factories, or across branches of industry, or across crafts, and on to general assemblies of workers' councils that can be regional and national and international in character."[22] In essence, in this sort of social structure, the workers themselves are the decision-makers, and they control the production and distribution of goods without coercive management that reaps the reward. In *Radical Priorities* (1981), Chomsky states,

---

[17] Otero, *Chomsky*, p.134.

[18] Ibid., p.135.

[19] Ibid.

[20] See, for example, an interview with Chomsky conducted in 1995 entitled "Anarchism, Marxism and Hope for the Future." In Pateman (ed.), *Chomsky on Anarchism*, pp.178-189.

[21] Rai, *Chomsky's Politics*, p.97.

[22] Ibid., p.98.

Anarchism can be conceived as a kind of voluntary socialism, that is, as libertarian socialist or anarcho-syndicalist or communist anarchist, in the tradition of, say, Bakunin and Kropotkin and others. They had in mind a highly organized form of society, but a society that was organized on the basis of organic units, organic communities. And generally they meant by that the workplace and the neighborhood, and for these two basic units there could derive through federal arrangements a highly integrated kind of social organization, that might be national or even international in scope. And these decisions could be made over a substantial range, but by delegates who are always part of the organic community from which they come, to which they return and in which, in fact, they live.[23]

Even though the social context of political thinkers to whom Chomsky often makes reference is radically different to today's reality of the concentration of power in a handful of transnational corporations, corporate-driven internal trade agreements, senior investors, banking executives, and powerful corporate lobbying agencies; nevertheless, their insights and fundamental vision of a better world have something significant to contribute to contemporary political discourse.

In light of what I considered earlier, it is apparent that Chomsky's understanding of the role of creativity in human nature, with its anti-behaviourist tendencies to resist external efforts to mould human minds and its emphasis on the value of rich intrinsic mental structures, is related, in many ways, to his relationship between freedom and human nature. The concept of freedom, best articulated through the libertarian socialist tradition, presupposes that external influences are minimised in one's effort to become an autonomous, rational, creative, and free human being. As Otero states,

If our minds are richly structured biological organisms and furthermore there is no evidence (or only conflicting evidence) that we are biologically programmed to obey our superiors in a hierarchy which is genetically determined ... then it is a rational conclusion that no one has a right to control someone else's life and character and mode of thought, or to "externalize" anyone's mind, or to impose external constraints on anyone's freedom of thought and expression.[24]

---

[23] McGilvray, *Chomsky*, p.197.
[24] C.P. Otero (ed.), *Noam Chomsky: Language and Politics* (Montreal: Black Rose Books, 1988), p.51.

The task ahead is to determine if the other themes discussed below also relate directly to Chomsky's understanding of freedom and, directly or indirectly, to his overall understanding of human nature.

Critique of American Foreign Policy

Any attempt to summarise Chomsky's critique of American foreign policy is incomplete. His voluminous output in this area is awe-inspiring, to say the least. He has documented in intricate detail the many ways the U.S. government has intervened in the affairs of other nations, often in a brutally violent fashion, with the sole purpose of protecting its exclusive Fifth Freedom and serving its own interests. Needless to say, such forms of violence, or what Chomsky often calls forms of "wholesale terrorism," are accomplished with a complex support system that includes the corporate sector, senior bank officials, government lobbyists, trade agreements, the mainstream media, and other elements of an elite network. I use the expression 'corporate sector' in a quite specific way. The corporate sector is composed mainly of CEOs of major transnational corporations, the same corporations one finds commonly, for example, in the maquiladora region of northern Mexico. These companies exploit the cheap labour of production workers south of the U.S. border and take advantage of well-established international trade agreements to ensure their products can be shipped tax-free to the rich consumers north of the border. In this way, CEOs pay little in actual human labour and reap massive profits.

Ever since the mid-1960s, Chomsky is best known throughout the world for his voluminous production of political books, especially his books related to American foreign policy. Often, his works in linguistics are written for an audience well-read in the technicalities of that particular science, but his political works are completely comprehensible for anyone willing to exercise reason and common sense.

Even though Chomsky addresses a vast array of issues related to American foreign policy and pays particularly close attention to American interests in Southeast Asia, Latin America, East Timor, Palestine, Israel, Iran, Iraq, and virtually every other country on the planet; nevertheless, his focus is always from an American point of view. This is because Chomsky feels that, as an American tax-paying citizen, he has a moral responsibility to address, first and foremost, his own government's foreign policies. In other words, he is tending to his own garden.

In this section, in an effort to grasp the way Chomsky approaches U.S. involvement in geopolitics, I focus my efforts on one region of the world - Latin America. I use Chomsky's commentary on this part of the world to highlight some of the key ideas in his political discourse and also to show that his understanding of freedom, as discussed above, plays a significant role in his general political analysis. Even though I refer to many of Chomsky's works; nevertheless, in order to remain relatively focused on the issue at hand, I concentrate primarily on the first three chapters of *Turning the Tide: The U.S. and Latin America* (1987). True, the socio-political and economic situation in Latin America has changed, for better or for worse, since the 1980s, but regardless of the fine details, the overarching structural relationship between the U.S. and Latin American countries remains fundamentally the same.

In Chomsky's political work, he argues forcefully that people have a moral obligation to remove the veils of distortion and illusion and "see a world that is rather different from the one presented to us by a remarkably effective ideological system, a world that is much uglier, often horrifying … (and) that our own actions, or passive acquiescence, contribute quite substantially to misery and oppression, and perhaps eventually global destruction."[25] If that does not motivate someone to action, then I suppose nothing will! But there is hope in this grim picture. People in the so-called developed part of the world live in a relatively free and open society, a part of the world that grants them "ample opportunities to discover the truth about who we are and what we do in the world."[26] Chomsky considers the many ways elite members of society perpetuate a veil of illusion to keep the masses in a state of ignorance and a sense of powerlessness and that "striking and systematic features of our international behavior are suppressed, ignored or denied."[27] As a result, "our role in perpetuating misery and oppression, even barbaric torture and mass slaughter, is not only significant in scale, but is also a predictable and systematic consequence of longstanding geopolitical conceptions and institutional structures."[28]

But, how does Chomsky support his thesis that our acquiescence contributes to the suffering of people in other parts of the world? Even if this is the case, what, in reality, can an individual do about it? Governments, transnational corporations, banks, international trade agreements, geopolitical structures - these are mammoth institutions that seem to be impenetrable. Is it not true that, in this case, ignorance is bliss? Well, argues Chomsky, this is actually what the elite want people to think so they may continue to rob and exploit. In *Turning the Tide*, one can see clearly how American foreign policy functions in

---

[25] Chomsky, *Turning the Tide*, p.1.
[26] Ibid.
[27] Ibid.
[28] Ibid., p.2.

Latin America, identifies its interests and long-term goals, and implements policies and procedures to support them.

The U.S. government and its business financiers have had an interest in Latin America since the early part of the twentieth century. American-supported banks, oil companies, rail and steamship companies, along with direct military intervention, have plagued the region for decades, and have left in their wake a bloody trail of torture, oppression, and poverty. Thus, claims Chomsky,

> We naturally look to the Central America-Caribbean region, then, if we want to learn something about ourselves ... The picture we see is not a pretty one. The region is one of the world's most awful horror chambers, with widespread starvation, semi-slave labor, torture and massacres by US clients. Virtually every attempt to bring about some constructive change has been met with a new dose of US violence.[29]

To support his position, Chomsky provides massive amounts of first-hand accounts of life in the region, references to local and international human rights reports, and also official documents that support the interests of the U.S. elite and its clients. For instance, according to the San Salvador's Human Rights office of the Archdiocese, 8,062 people were murdered "for political reasons, not in military confrontation, but as a result of military operations by the Army, Security Forces, and paramilitary organisations coordinated by the High Command of the Armed Forces."[30] Chomsky also cites the case of a former U.S. pilot in Vietnam, who, after being forced to spend some time in a psychiatric hospital because he refused to fly any more missions, eventually, in the early 1980s, made his way to a small village in El Salvador. He witnessed firsthand the brutal assault by the U.S.-supported war against *campesinos*, "many of [whom] have been tortured and mutilated by tormentors who have been trained in the sophisticated tactics of violence - often by our own military advisers."[31] He witnessed assaults on villages by American-funded helicopters, aeroplanes, and artillery, the complete destruction of villages, and the annihilation of crops and livestock to ensure a level of starvation unprecedented in the region. Chomsky states,

---

[29] Ibid., pp.4-5.
[30] Ibid., p.15.
[31] Ibid., pp.5-6.

As is the regular pattern, the worst atrocities were carried out by US-trained elite battalions (Atlacatl, Ramon Belloso) and by air and artillery units employing tactics designed by the US in Vietnam and taught by US advisors.[32]

Commonly, the assaults include the use of napalm, gasoline bombs, and white phosphorous rockets and also involve torture and rape. The first-hand testimonies are often graphic in detail. Chomsky states,

> He heard the stories of people whose families had been hacked to death by National Guardsmen or who had crawled from under a pile of bodies of trapped civilians cut to pieces with machetes and mutilated by US-trained troops, or who had themselves been subjected to horrifying tortures receiving no medical aid, since physicians were unwilling to "endanger their lives by treating someone who had been tortured by the security forces." Using a US-made scanner, he could hear the voices of American advisers directing troops on their mass murder missions.[33]

In Nicaragua, it's the same story. Arturo Cruz, a *Contra* political spokesman, claims "it was 'a delicate thing' to persuade rebel fighters to respect the lives of prisoners and pro-Sandinista civilians without demoralizing the fighters."[34] Chomsky states,

> And we can learn of a 14-year-old girl who was gang-raped and then decapitated, her head placed on a stake at the entrance to her village as a warning to government supporters; of nurses who were raped, then murdered; a man killed by hanging after his eyes were gouged out and his fingernails pulled out; a man who was stabbed to death after having been beaten, his eyes gouged out and a cross carved in his back after he fled from a hospital attacked by the *contras*; another tortured then skinned; another cut to pieces with bayonets by *contras* who then beheaded her 11-month-old baby before his wife's eyes; others who were raped to a background of religious music; children shot in the back or repeatedly shot "as though she had been used for target practice."[35]

---

[32] Ibid., p.6.
[33] Ibid.
[34] Ibid., p.12.
[35] Ibid.

Such testimonies can be duplicated many times over, and Chomsky includes them in his work, but one should note that similar testimonies can be found in other regions of the world. Atrocities and brutality have no limits, and, as Chomsky makes clearly evident, they are often funded by American taxpayers, executed under the direction of American-trained officials, and tactfully ignored by U.S. mainstream media. I consider in detail, in another section, the key role played by the mass media in American-funded atrocities in the world, but for now, it is worth citing Chomsky, who states,

> Through 1980 and beyond, the US press generally kept to the Party Line, though it was subsequently conceded that "Under the Carter Administration, United States officials said security forces were responsible for 90 percent of the atrocities," not "'uncontrollable' right-wing bands" - so that the assertions in the Human Rights Report and other public statements were deliberate lies, reiterated as conscious deception by the media.[36]

During the years of the Reagan Administration, "the US has provided direct military assistance to Guatemala, first in round-about ways, then more directly, helping to facilitate the torture, murder and general brutality."[37] This is what Chomsky refers to as "wholesale terrorism," as opposed to small, incidental expressions of "retail terrorism." The fellow who blows up a building and injures or kills a few innocent people is a retail terrorist, but governments and their corporate allies are wholesale terrorists. They do not injure or kill a few people - their killing is on a completely different scale. For instance, the U.S. often resorts to indirect infiltration of a particular region through the use of well-trained proxies, such as the Argentine neo-Nazis, the neo-fascist National Security states of South America, and even U.S.-trained Israeli paramilitary units. In 1987, Chomsky states,

> The careful observer will find that the worst atrocities have regularly been conducted by elite battalions fresh from their U.S. training. Salvadoran officers who admit their participation in death squad killings describe their service under CIA control and the training sessions on effective torture conducted by U.S. instructors. The significance of these facts cannot, however, be perceived in the West.[38]

---

[36] Ibid., p.15.
[37] Ibid., p.33.
[38] Noam Chomsky, *On Power and Ideology* (Montreal: Black Rose Books, 1987), p.59.

In 1980, Oscar Romero, Archbishop of El Salvador, sent a letter to President Carter. In this letter, Romero highlights some of the atrocities occurring in his country and requests that the President stop sending military aid to the country-led junta because this sort of aid "would be used to 'sharpen injustice and repression against the people's organizations which were struggling 'for respect for their most basic human rights' (hardly news to Washington, needless to say.)"[39]

Nevertheless, Chomsky shows clearly that the "striking correlation between US assistance and barbarism in Central America has its roots in deliberate planning, both in global terms and in specific application to this region."[40] He cites a USAID report (1967) that highlights the U.S. programme to train the National Guard and the National Police. The report states,

> authorities have been successful in handling any politically motivated demonstrations in recent years ... With the potential danger that exists in a densely populated country where the rich are very rich and [the] poor extremely poor El Salvador is fortunate that the Guard and Police are well trained and disciplined ...[41]

In this report, Chomsky is careful to distinguish between the general population in El Salvador, who by no means benefits from the actions of the Guard and the Police, and "those who own and rule the country, those whom we dare not disturb by trying to inhibit their pleasure in torture and mass murder."[42] Chomsky refers to Allan Nairn's detailed study,

> U.S. complicity in the dark and brutal work of El Salvador's Death Squads is not an aberration. Rather, it represents a basic bipartisan, institutional commitment on the part of six American Administrations - a commitment to guard the Salvadoran regime against the prospect that its people might organize in ways unfriendly to that regime or to the United States.[43]

This common tune, that is, the implementation of brutal policies and programmes funded by American tax-payers, that violate fundamental human rights and serve the interests of the U.S. government and wealthy business leaders, both within specific regions and in the international

---

[39] Noam Chomsky, *What Uncle Sam Really Wants* (Berkeley: Odonian Press, 1993), p.34.
[40] Chomsky, *Turning the Tide*, p.36.
[41] Ibid.
[42] Ibid., p.37.
[43] Ibid., pp.98-99.

community at large, almost plays like a broken record. The title of the tune is 'The Fifth Freedom'. The Fifth Freedom, as noted earlier, is the freedom of governments, funded by and serving the interests of the corporate and business sectors, to rob and exploit. Clearly, infringements of Roosevelt's other four freedoms are absolutely irrelevant to the interests of the elite. In fact, "the internal record of planning reveals a guiding geopolitical conception: preservation of the Fifth Freedom, by whatever means are feasible."[44] In essence, the function of Latin America is to "'fulfil its function as a source of raw materials and a market' for the industrial capitalist societies."[45] As Chomsky suggests,

> Much of what US governments do in the world can be readily understood in terms of this principle, while if it remains obscured, acts and events will appear incomprehensible, a maze of confusion, random error and accident … this principle is an invariant core, deeply rooted in the basic institutions of American society.[46]

Chomsky refers to a study by economist Edward Herman in which he explores the relationship between U.S. aid programmes and human rights violations and finds that U.S. funding increases in regions where human rights are neglected. In addition, he conducts a second study to analyse the correlation between U.S. funding and investment climate and finds that "US-controlled aid has been positively related to investment climate and inversely related to the maintenance of a democratic order and human rights."[47] Fundamentally, "US aid has tended to flow disproportionately to Latin American governments which torture their citizens."[48]

This brief overview of Chomsky's critique of American foreign policy suffices for my particular purpose. Clearly, there is a conflict between the interests of governments and their corporate sector allies and the fundamental human rights of private citizens. People want a life free from harm, intimidation, cruelty, and violence. They want to earn an honest living, and be able to support their families in a safe environment. Surely, this is not the case for the majority of people living in Latin America. But, what can people do about it? In an interview in 1981, Chomsky was asked a question about the role human rights plays in American foreign policy. He responds to the question with a question of his own.

---

[44] Ibid., p.47
[45] Chomsky, *What Uncle Sam Really Wants*, p.12.
[46] Chomsky, *Turning the Tide*, p.47.
[47] Ibid., p.158.
[48] Chomsky, *What Uncle Sam Really Wants*, p.29.

Should we attempt to influence this policy in the direction of concern for human rights, or should we renounce any such concern, thus abandoning foreign policy to other concerns such as the climate for business operations and control over resources? Properly put, the question reduces to this: Do we care about the human consequences of our actions (or inactions)?[49]

Granted, people may abhor oppression and violence, but, fundamentally, and this is a key point in Chomsky's analysis, "we participate in them - willingly or blindly, depending on our degree of sophistication - insofar as we tolerate the contribution of the United States to the plague of terror and torture that has spread over Latin America (and not there alone) in the past several decades."[50]

Even though a crucial element in American foreign policy is an effort to obscure these simple facts; nevertheless, Chomsky's political discourse is aimed at removing obscurity from the debate, and seeing the facts as they appear in real life. In doing so, it becomes clear that human freedom lies at the heart of the matter. On the one hand, governments and allied interest groups seek their fortune by restricting or eliminating fundamental human rights. On the other hand, small peasant community-based groups, Church groups, and others fight for a sense of freedom, human dignity, and self-worth.

Manufacturing Consent

Edward Herman and Chomsky wrote a ground-breaking book on the role of the mainstream, agenda-setting media in society, entitled *Manufacturing Consent: The Political Economy of the Mass Media* (1988). The book is dedicated in memory of Alex Carey, an outspoken intellectual, humanist, professor, and author of *Taking the Risk Out of Democracy* (1995). In the Foreword, Chomsky quotes Carey and his recognition of three features of the twentieth century.

The twentieth century has been characterized by three developments of great political importance: the growth of democracy, the growth of corporate power, and the growth of corporate propaganda as a means of protecting corporate power against democracy.[51]

---

[49] Otero, *Noam Chomsky: Language and Politics*, p.303.
[50] Ibid.
[51] Alex Carey, *Taking the Risk Out of Democracy* (Sydney: University of New South Wales Press, 1995), p.vi.

As Chomsky proclaims, democracy is feared by "'the masters of mankind', who understand that it can only impede the pursuit of their 'vile maxim' 'All for ourselves, and nothing for other people (Adam Smith)."[52]

Herman and Chomsky highlight in intricate detail how the news one receives from the major media streams is carefully selected to enhance a manufactured sense of truth, and "to mobilize support for the special interests that dominate the state and private activity."[53] Needless to say, the only way the atrocities associated with American foreign policy, as discussed above, are tolerated by the American public, is because the mainstream media have selected, emphasised, and omitted news to coincide with the interests of corporate advertisers and government agencies who fund them. In other words, the media do not select news by using unbiased professional and objective criteria; rather, the news is selected to manage and control public opinion about the issues that really matter to the business sector, and this selection process is what Chomsky calls the 'manufacturing of consent.'

Herman and Chomsky consider the media coverage in numerous conflict zones in the world, and show clearly that "the observable pattern of indignant campaigns and suppressions, of shading and emphasis, and of selection of context, premises, and general agenda, is highly functional for established power and responsive to the needs of the government and major power groups."[54] It is worth stating, at this point, that even though Herman and Chomsky mainly address the important role played by newspaper firms in promoting a specific agenda, and the newspaper industry is now a dwindling enterprise; nevertheless, other and perhaps even more powerful forms of media have become easily accessible to the general public.

The Propaganda Model, developed by Herman and Chomsky, incorporates five filters designed to manufacture a high degree of obfuscation in the general public regarding certain political and economic issues. The model promotes social consent, so that the elite may continue their global exploits. As Smith suggests, the filters

> "narrow the range of news" that becomes accessible to the public, blocking the aspirations of the weak and the poor, and conspiring to guarantee that the media propagate the views of big business under whose control they remain.[55]

---

[52] Ibid., p.vii.
[53] Ibid., p.xi.
[54] Edward Herman and Noam Chomsky, *Manufacturing Consent: The Political Economy of the Mass Media* (New York: Pantheon Books, 1988), p.xv.
[55] Smith, *Chomsky*, p.199.

The model ensures that the only news fit to print is the news that is sifted through five filters. The model itself is based on three presuppositions, or what McGilvray calls "three orders of prediction."[56] According to Chomsky, first, it serves "the interests of state and corporate power, which are closely interlinked, framing their reporting and analysis in a manner supportive of established privilege and limiting debate and discussion accordingly."[57] Second, "the media debate will be bounded in a manner that satisfies these external needs [of corporate and state power], thus limited to the question of the alleged adversarial stance of the media."[58] Third, concerns about the freedom of the press and its lack of bias "will be ignored or bitterly condemned, for it conflicts with the needs of the powerful and privileged."[59] In 1984, Chomsky stated,

> For those who stubbornly seek freedom, there can be no more urgent risk than to come to understand the mechanisms and practices of indoctrination. These are easy to perceive in the totalitarian societies, much less so in the system of "brainwashing under freedom" to which we are subjected and which all too often we serve as willing or unwitting instruments.[60]

The first filter of the Propaganda Model is related to the size, ownership, and profit-orientation of the media. Say, for example, one submits to a mainstream media giant an article on human rights violations in Latin America from the point of view of the marginalised and oppressed. It will most likely be filtered out at this early stage. A relatively influential agenda-setting newspaper owned, in part, by members of the corporate elite with business interests in Latin America will inevitably remove the article from its list of possible fit-to-print pieces. Herman and Chomsky identify the top 24 media giants in the U.S. These companies "are large, profit-seeking corporations, owned and controlled by quite wealthy people. It can be seen ... that all but one of the top companies for whom data is available have assets in excess of $1 billion ... and the median size is $2.6 billion ... (and) that approximately three-quarters of these media giants had after-tax profits in excess of $100 million, with the median at $183 million."[61] Often, these media

---

[56] McGilvray, *Chomsky*, p.210.
[57] Noam Chomsky, *Necessary Illusions: Thought Control in Democratic Societies* (Concord: Anansi, 1991), p.10.
[58] Ibid., p.153.
[59] Ibid.
[60] Peck (ed.), *Chomsky Reader*, p.136.
[61] Herman and Chomsky, *Manufacturing Consent*, p.5.

giants are controlled by even bigger and more powerful corporations. For example, at the time of their publication, Herman and Chomsky noted that NBC was owned by General Electric and Westinghouse, two corporate giants "with boards of directors that are dominated by corporate and banking executives."[62] In addition, the powerful media rely on governmental support, in return for their efforts to manufacture consent. Corporations like General Electric and Westinghouse rely on government subsidies to fund their "nuclear power and military research and development, and to create a favorable climate for their overseas sales."[63] As a result,

> The media giants, advertising agencies, and great multinational corporations have a joint and close interest in a favorable climate of investment in the Third World, and their interconnections and relationships with the government in these policies are symbiotic.[64]

It's a great relationship. The media giants manufacture consent in the general population, ensure it is docile and receptive to manufactured messages, and, at the same time, financially support specific political candidates and parties. In return, governments funnel public funds to support the parent companies of media giants in their global ventures.

The second filter of the Propaganda Model is related to advertising. Let's go back to the article submitted to a media giant on human rights violations in Latin America. If, by some sort of a miracle, or simply by human error, the article makes it through the first filter, then it is confronted by further obstacles before the article sees the light of day. The mass media rely on revenues from advertising in their papers. An article that directly attacks General Electric's military research programmes, or its involvement in the production of napalm during the Vietnam War, will not be fit-to-print, solely because General Electric and its affiliates most likely spend millions of dollars in newspapers to advertise their fridges and stoves (but not their military hardware). The owners or shareholders of a giant media outlet will not bite the hands that feed them.

Once again, if, for some reason, the article passes through the second filter, then no doubt someone will be held accountable. Herman and Chomsky cite the case of WNET.

---

[62] Ibid., p.8.
[63] Ibid., p.13.
[64] Ibid., pp.13-14.

Public-television station WNET lost its corporate funding from Gulf + Western in 1985 after the station showed the documentary "Hungry for Profit," which contains material critical of multinational corporate activities in the Third World ... The chief executive of Gulf + Western complained to the station that the program was "virulently anti-business if not anti-American," and that the station's carrying the program was not the behavior "of a friend" of the corporation.[65]

The third filter of the Propaganda Model addresses the issue of sourcing. It's important that the mass media have access to a steady flow of reliable material, and time restraints restrict them from exploring every piece of news. Therefore, they rely on particular sources that conform to their overall interests. Federal government sites, private corporations, local city halls, and police departments are valuable official sources because they "turn out a large volume of material that meets the demands of news organizations for reliable, scheduled flows."[66]

Sourcing also includes the use of so-called experts, that is, the use of former government officials, university faculty, and members of conservative think tanks, that is, individuals who have a vested interest in the corporate sector and can be trusted to assess the facts accordingly. For instance, Herman and Chomsky identify the so-called experts on terrorism who appeared on the McNeil-Lehrer News Hour in the mid-1980s. While the majority of participants were government officials, a significant minority came from conservative think tanks, and the "largest number of appearances in the latter category was supplied by the Georgetown Center for Strategic and International Studies (CSIS), an organization funded by conservative foundations and corporations, and providing a revolving door between the State Department and CIA and a nominally private organization."[67]

It is inevitable, with armed sources at hand, that an article on human rights violations in Latin America will not pass the conservative sources. If the article offers a position contrary to the views expressed by the poor, and condones American involvement in the region, then, undoubtedly, the sources may claim the article fit-to-print; otherwise, it is fit for the trash can.

The fourth filter of the Propaganda Model incorporates what Herman and Chomsky refer to as "flak." It is a form of reprimand directed to the media by leaders of the corporate elite when something is published which does not conform to their particular interests. Flak often takes "the form of letters,

---

[65] Ibid., p.17.
[66] Ibid., p.19.
[67] Ibid., p.24.

telegrams, phone calls, petitions, lawsuits, speeches and bills before Congress, and other modes of complaint, threat, and punitive action."[68] The government is a key producer of flak. It closely monitors the activities of the media and does not hesitate to assail, threaten, or redirect the media in an attempt to keep it aligned with the established order.

The fifth and final filter of the Propaganda Model addresses what Herman and Chomsky refer to as the ideology of anti-communism as the ultimate control mechanism. At the time of its publication in the 1980s, communism was still a threat to the business sector. It offered people an alternative way to live, a way which did not conform to the prevailing corporate ideology. In the West, the term 'communism' was a fully loaded term; it was the absolute pinnacle of insults, at least according to the mainstream media. If one supported a peasant uprising in southern Mexico, or expressed anger over the assassination of priests and nuns in El Salvador, or even served food at a local soup kitchen, it was most likely assumed by the elite that that person was sympathetic to the communist movement. For example,

> In the cases of the U.S. subversion of Guatemala, 1947-54, and the military attacks in Nicaragua, 1981-1987, allegations of Communist links and the Communist threat caused many liberals to support counterrevolutionary intervention, while others lapsed into silence, paralyzed by the fear of being tarred with charges of infidelity to the national religion.[69]

Perhaps, in today's post-communist era, in a world where a Red scare is no longer an effective mechanism to polarise "us" from "them", a better term would be 'anti-terrorism', because the term 'terrorism' in contemporary times carries the same weight that communism did a few decades ago. The terms of reference may have changed, but the polarising effect has remained the same.

Contemporary corporate ideology contends that democracy (at least the Fifth Freedom) is threatened by terrorist groups and embraces a similar ideology to that professed during the Communist era. In earlier times, according to Chomsky in *Necessary Illusions* (1989), the standard perception embraced by the elite was that "democracy is threatened by the organizing efforts of those called the "special interests,' a concept of contemporary political rhetoric that refers to workers, farmers, women, youth, the elderly, the handicapped, ethnic minorities, and so on - in short, the general

---

[68] Ibid., p.26.
[69] Ibid., p.30.

population."[70] In today's rhetoric, one can add the term 'terrorist' to this list of special interest groups.

The Propaganda Model acts as a preventive measure; that is, it prevents the rabble from having a voice in what is assumed to be a democratic society. Actually, they may be able to voice their concerns in small, relatively insignificant media outlets but will not be granted access to the mainstream, agenda-setting media giants. Interestingly, in many ways, the internet offers people a powerful tool to combat the corporate sector and establish a sense of true democracy. Prior to the internet, small groups often felt isolated and powerless, but, in recent times, with relatively easy access to the internet, small groups throughout the world with similar interests and concerns can join in solidarity and work together for social change. In effect, the internet allows the powerless to bypass the five filters in their efforts to establish a truly human way to live.

Responsibility of Intellectuals

The word 'intellectual' is another one of those words that is used and understood in many different ways. In normal parlance, the noun 'intellectual' usually means a relatively well-schooled individual who enjoys learning and is interested in ideas, that is, a person with a superior and engaging intellect. Intellectuals are usually associated with particular professions, including education, research, journalism, and law. Commonly, intellectuals are portrayed as inquisitive and creative thinkers, or perhaps dispassionate critics, who hide away in an office or a library and generate fascinating ideas. From this perspective, intellectuals work in relative isolation, are negligent of daily affairs, and are detached from any particular institutional or governmental ideology. Their sole responsibility is the creation of ideas, and their span of accountability does not extend far beyond the library or lecture hall.

Chomsky discards this common view of intellectuals as isolated subjects, merrily on their way to the pursuit of truth. Granted, it is obvious that intellectuals are, at least to a degree, interested in ideas and often use the channels of teaching and publishing to express their ideas. This is a given fact and something Chomsky will not dispute. Even so, for Chomsky, the romanticised vision of intellectuals as isolated scholars is rejected on two grounds. First, it distorts the general nature of research and teaching. Academics, especially scientists, work in collaboration with others. True, there are times when intellectuals work in isolation, but the general thrust of

---

[70] Chomsky, *Necessary Illusions*, p.3.

scientific progress is a collaborative one. Second, it dismisses outright the moral accountability associated with an intellectual's position in an institution of teaching and research. Universities, schools, and research centres are funded by and serve the interests of governments that, as I noted earlier, serve powerful international corporate interests. For Chomsky, then, there are moral implications associated with intellectuals that are often neglected in public discourse.

It is worth emphasising here that intellectuals also include teachers and others involved in schools. In fact, the different categories of intellectuals mentioned in this section incorporate the various roles and responsibilities adopted by classroom teachers. What, then, are the roles performed by intellectuals in modern society that cause concern for Chomsky? To address this question, he reflects on insights provided by Bakunin, who regards intellectuals as a "new class" with the ability to control technical knowledge and inevitably to use it to control socio-political and economic forces. Bakunin states

> the reign of *scientific intelligence*, the most aristocratic, despotic, arrogant and elitist of all regimes. There will be a new class, a new hierarchy of real and counterfeit scientists and scholars, and the world will be divided into a minority ruling in the name of knowledge, and an immense ignorant majority. And then woe unto the mass of ignorant ones.[71]

Bakunin concludes that privileges are granted to "the shrewd and educated" while "regimented workingmen and women will sleep, wake, work, and live to the beat of a drum."[72] Bakunin's understanding of intellectuals embodies what Stanley Aronowitz and Henry Giroux refer to as either "accommodating intellectuals" or "hegemonic intellectuals." Accommodating intellectuals surrender to and support the dominant socio-political ideology and its ruling groups. Hegemonic intellectuals are far more entrenched than their accommodating counterparts. They completely define themselves through the prevailing ideology and overtly support the socio-political power structures. The result, according to Gregory Baum, is "a complex intermeshing of technocratic depersonalization and immobility, economic domination and

---

[71] Noam Chomsky, *Towards a New Cold War: Essays on the Current Crisis and How We Got There* (New York: Pantheon Books, 1982), p.61.
[72] Ibid., p.62.

exploitation, racial exclusion and inferiorization, and other forms including the subjugation of women."[73]

This view of intellectuals contrasts with the optimistic view posited by mainstream thinkers. For Daniel Bell, advances in a post-industrial society "will be rooted in the intellectual and scientific communities."[74] He points out that there has been a decisive shift in the nature of work, a shift from the traditional blue-collar worker in the labour force to the professional and technical occupation category. Similarly, John Kenneth Galbraith recognises that, over time, power was transferred from landowners to "the composite of knowledge and skills which comprises the technostructure."[75] For Galbraith, intellectuals as a "technocratic class" gain status and income through education and professional expertise and include,

> [P]eople who manage or otherwise staff the middle and upper reaches of the great financial and industrial firms, independent business -men and -women and those in lesser employments whose compensation is more or less guaranteed. Also the large population - lawyers, doctors, engineers, scientists, accountants and many others, not excluding journalists and professors - who make up the modern professional class.[76]

David Bazelon argues that these "working intellectuals" desire a privileged standard of living that includes the ownership of property for personal security or "general economic sweetening," but are generally job holders, or "the cream of the proletariat."[77] Similarly, for Barbara Hargrove, intellectuals have the "ability to manipulate and change systems in order to accomplish more social and economic good."[78]

In 1966, early in his career as a linguist and public intellectual, Chomsky published an essay entitled "The Responsibility of Intellectuals". This essay would prove to be the foundation both of his general perspective on

---

[73] Gregory Baum, *Religion and Alienation: A Theological Reading of Sociology* (New York: Paulist Press, 1975), pp.218-219.

[74] Ibid., p.63. Also refer to Daniel Bell, "Labour in the Post-Industrial Society," *Dissent* (Winter, 1972), pp.163-189.

[75] Chomsky, *Towards a New Cold War*, p.63.

[76] John Kenneth Galbraith, *The Culture of Contentment* (Boston: Houghton Mifflin Company, 1992), pp.15-16.

[77] David Bazelon, *Power in America: The Politics of the New Class* (New York: The New American Library, Inc., 1963), p.20.

[78] Barbara Hargrove, *The Emerging New Class: Implications for Church and Society* (New York: The Pilgrim Press, 1986), p.93.

intellectuals and, more specifically, of his own personal responsibility as an intellectual. In fact, Chomsky's interest in the responsibility of intellectuals goes back to his early years with radical and highly intellectual members of his extended family. They provided him with a completely different understanding of what it means to be an intellectual. Even as a high school student, Chomsky pondered the moral responsibility of intellectuals. He read a series of articles in *Politics* by American cultural critic Dwight Macdonald that addresses the issue of war guilt. More specifically, Macdonald wants to know, "to what extent were the Germans or Japanese people responsible for the atrocities committed by their governments? And quite properly, he then asks, "To what extent are the British or American people responsible for the vicious terror bombings of civilians, perfected as a technique of warfare by the Western democracies and reaching their culmination in Hiroshima and Nagasaki, surely among the most unspeakable crimes in history?"[79]

It should be clear by now that Chomsky's understanding of the responsibility of intellectuals is radically different from and more profound than the commonly held view. For Chomsky, intellectuals "perform as they are expected to by giving a tolerably accurate description of reality that conforms with the interests of the people who have wealth and power - the people who own these institutions that we call schools and in fact own the society generally."[80] Chomsky cites Harold Rosenberg's reference to intellectuals as a "herd of independent minds," and suggests that they are normally attached to their own political state and "have devoted themselves to lauding its alleged achievements (sometimes real) and concealing its abuses and crimes."[81] At the same time, intellectuals are masters of obfuscation. They make rather simple matters appear to be extremely complicated, far beyond the capacities of most people, and, thus, need specialists to decipher the complexities of the matter for the public at large. Also, intellectuals tend to be subservient to the elite, "disseminate propaganda concerning the evil practices, real or fabricated, of current enemies of the state,"[82] and conveniently neglect to mention similar evil practices of their own state. For Chomsky, "one can only be appalled at the willingness of American intellectuals, who, after all, have

---

[79] Peck (ed.), *Chomsky Reader*, pp.59-60.
[80] Donaldo Macedo (ed.), *Chomsky on Miseducation* (London: Rowman & Littlefield Publishers, 2000), pp.17-18.
[81] Noam Chomsky and Edward Herman, *After the Cataclysm: Postwar Indochina & the Reconstruction of Imperial Ideology* (Montreal: Black Rose Books, 1979), p.23.
[82] Ibid., p.24.

access to the facts, to tolerate or even to approve of this deceitfulness and hypocrisy."[83] What an intricate web they weave!

Nevertheless, Chomsky argues that intellectuals, normally in positions of privilege, have a moral responsibility "to expose the lies of government, to analyze actions according to their causes and motives and often hidden intentions."[84] In many cases, intellectuals of this sort reflect what Aronowitz and Giroux, in their analysis of teachers as intellectuals, call "transformative intellectuals". In this case, teachers regard pedagogy and the entire schooling process as forms of political struggle. They state,

> Thus schooling becomes a central terrain where power and politics operate out of a dialectical relationship between individuals and groups, who function within specific historical conditions and structural constraints as well as within cultural forms and ideologies that are the basis for contradictions and struggles.[85]

Thus, teachers as transformative intellectuals involve themselves critically in various aspects of the schooling process and take a personal responsibility in its overall purpose. They raise for critical discourse the prevailing ideological and economic conditions and their impact on education. Chomsky argues that intellectuals in many parts of the world have the freedom of expression, access to information, and ample leisure time to "speak truth to power", that is, "to seek the truth lying hidden behind the veil of distortion and misrepresentation, ideology, and class interest through which the events of current history are presented to us." Chomsky states,

> The issues that Macdonald raised are as pertinent today as they were twenty years ago. We can hardly avoid asking ourselves to what extent the American people bear responsibility for the savage American assault on a largely helpless rural population in Vietnam ... As for those of us who stood by in silence and apathy as this catastrophe slowly took shape over the past dozen years, on what page of history do we find our proper place?[86]

---

[83] Otero, *Chomsky*, p.267.

[84] Peck (ed.), *Chomsky Reader*, p.60.

[85] Stanley Aronowitz and Henry Giroux, *Education Under Siege: The Conservative, Liberal and Radical Debate Over Schooling* (Massachusetts: Bergin & Garvey Publishers, Inc., 1985), p.36.

[86] Ibid.

The responsibility of intellectuals as moral agents, argues Chomsky, "is to try to bring the truth about matters of human significance to an audience that can do something about them."[87] This is a mammoth task, especially because intellectuals, like people more generally, often easily dismiss any moral sentiments when wealth and power are in their grasp. Even so, the key point Chomsky is trying to make is that truth must be directed to those people who are receptive to the message and can act accordingly. As an example, Chomsky cites the time he was arrested alongside other pacifists, including a group of Quakers. In an attempt to disrupt illegitimate authority, the Quakers adopted "the slogan 'Speak truth to power.' I strongly disagree. The audience is entirely wrong, and the effort is hardly more than a form of self-indulgence. It was a waste of time and a pointless pursuit to speak truth to Henry Kissinger or the CEO of General Motors, or others who exercise power in coercive institutions - truths that they already know well enough, for the most part."[88] For Chomsky, to address people who wield tremendous power in the world is like addressing "the worst tyrants and criminals who are also human beings, however terrible their actions."[89]

Chomsky's essay explores in intricate detail the many ways intellectuals in recent times have blatantly ignored or simply dismissed the moral truism of speaking the truth and exposing lies. The details are beyond the scope of this manuscript, but he concludes with a further reflection on Macdonald and then raises a question.

> The question "What have I done?" is one that we may well ask ourselves as we read, each day, of fresh atrocities in Vietnam - as we create, or mouth, or tolerate the deceptions that will be used to justify the next defense of freedom.[90]

Chomsky is not so naive to believe that intellectuals in a university setting will embrace his truism. In fact, he is fully cognizant of the fact that universities rely on corporate funding and that the salaries of professors are determined, in part, by this funding. Inevitably, to expect members of what Isaiah Berlin calls the "secular priesthood" to bite the hand that feeds them would be extremely naive, to say the least.[91] Nevertheless, for people who are willing to do so, Chomsky suggests that they should focus their efforts "in areas where

[87] Noam Chomsky, *Powers & Prospects: Reflections on Human Nature and the Social Order* (Boston: South End Press, 1996), p.56.
[88] Ibid., pp.60-61.
[89] Ibid., p.61.
[90] Peck (ed.), *Chomsky Reader*, p.82.
[91] Referenced by Chomsky and Herman in *After the Cataclysm*, p.24.

we have a responsibility for what is happening and the opportunity to mitigate or terminate suffering and violence."[92] This explains why he focuses primarily on American domestic and foreign policy. At times, Chomsky makes reference to the policies in other countries, but normally this is done in an attempt to highlight a fact or issue in the American domain.

Chomsky reminds people that to speak truth and expose lies "is not a particularly honourable vocation."[93] In addition to the fact that it requires an almost fanatical devotion of one's free time to research, writing, publishing, and speaking publicly, activities that are normally accomplished in tandem with work, family obligations, and other facets of regular life; nevertheless, there is an additional factor that deters people from this vocation, that is, the tremendous abuse that they normally receive from individuals in positions of power and authority. Chomsky cites the case of Bertrand Russell, who spoke publicly about his pacifist tendencies during World War I, and also against the Vietnam War and the proliferation of nuclear arms. For his earlier efforts, "for integrity and honesty."[94] Russell was removed from his teaching position at Cambridge University and, in later years, endured abuse and ridicule. Chomsky compares the public treatment of Russell to the treatment received by Albert Einstein. They both agreed that the proliferation of nuclear weapons may eventually destroy the species and even signed a joint statement to that effect. Then, according to Chomsky,

> Einstein went back to his office ... Russell, on the other hand, went out in the streets. He was part of the demonstrations against nuclear weapons. He became quite active in opposing the Vietnam War early on, at a time when there was virtually no public opposition. He also tried to do something about that, including demonstrations and organizing a tribunal. So he was bitterly denounced. On the other hand, Einstein was essentially a saintly figure. They essentially had the same positions, but Einstein didn't rattle too many cages. That's pretty common. Russell was viciously attacked in the *New York Times* and by Secretary of State Dean Rusk and others in the 1960s. He wasn't counted as a public intellectual, just a crazy old man.[95]

Chomsky also cites the case of Alex Carey, the outspoken public intellectual and author of a lucid and compelling account of the overwhelming influence

---

[92] Rai, *Chomsky's Politics*, p.142.
[93] Chomsky, *Powers & Prospects*, p.61.
[94] Ibid., p.69.
[95] Barsky, *Chomsky Effect*, pp.208-209.

that corporate propaganda has had on Western democracy. Carey lectured at the University of New South Wales, but in his attempts to speak the truth and expose lies, he became "the target of obloquy and vilification by the 'voluntary' commissars."[96]

It is clear that Chomsky's understanding of the responsibility of intellectuals extends far beyond the norm and includes a strong moral component. The role of an intellectual, at least in the sense portrayed by Chomsky, and embraced by Russell, Carey, and many others, is a risky business. It means risking one's career, professional reputation, and even personal freedom. And the probability of some degree of success is quite low. The powerful forces are well prepared for any assaults. Nevertheless, one's moral worth as a human being is measured by honesty, dignity, and self-worth.

Intellectual Self-Defence

People often feel overwhelmed after hearing a presentation by Chomsky, and his books sometimes reinforce an overall sense of powerlessness. It seems to be an impossible task to effectively challenge the power elite and their far-reaching propaganda machine, but, in fact, Chomsky's intentions are quite different. For example, he states, "*Turning the Tide* was meant to be a more positive book - hence the title. But it just didn't come out that way."[97] The main thrust of his argument is that, if people have well-refined intellectual tools at hand, then they are in a position, both individually and collectively, to confront the dominant forces in society. In essence, what Chomsky is proposing is what he calls 'intellectual self-defence'. He states,

> If the schools were doing their job, which of course they aren't, but they could be, they would be providing people with means of intellectual self-defence ... so that people growing up in a democratic society would have the means of intellectual self-defence against the system.[98]

The primary element of intellectual self-defence is an awareness of the issues at hand. It involves becoming aware of the intricate details surrounding the corporate sector's involvement in public affairs. This takes time, and, as a result, is often a deterrent for people who work all day. This self-defence mechanism reflects, in many ways, what Brazilian educator Paulo Freire calls 'conscientization'. Freire developed a highly effective pedagogy to teach adults to read and write, and also to read the signs of the times, that is, to become

---

[96] Chomsky, *Powers & Prospects*, p.69.
[97] Rai, *Chomsky's Politics*, p.49.
[98] Ibid., p.50.

politically literate. Conscientization represents the "development of the awakening of critical awareness"[99] that leads to an understanding of prevalent social, political, and economic contradictions in society. In a similar fashion, Chomsky suggests that intellectual self-defence requires that people become aware of the various forces that define a corporate hegemony, cut through "the mass of misrepresentations and fraud to the hidden nuggets,[100]and penetrate the "veil of propaganda."[101] Unfortunately, this requires tremendous discipline, hard work, the ability to read widely, and the time to meet in community with others with similar interests and concerns. Chomsky posits,

> There's no way to be informed without devoting effort to the task, whether we have in mind what's happening in the world, physics, major league baseball, or anything else. Understanding doesn't come free.[102]

Needless to say, there is a consensus among most members of the public that such work is far beyond their capacities and time constraints. In part, this sort of self-defeating thinking is a product of the way schools have become sites of specialised knowledge. It is best to leave economics to the economists and political issues to political scientists. This approach leaves the majority of people with an authentic sense of powerlessness. They are not "specialists" in any branch of knowledge, so how can they possibly grasp what is happening in the world? This is precisely the attitude Chomsky attempts to combat. In fact, it is a simple venture, assuming one has the available time and resources. Chomsky states,

> I frankly don't think that anything more is required than ordinary common sense ... A willingness to use one's own native intelligence and common sense to analyze and dissect and compare the facts with the way in which they're presented is really sufficient.[103]

Indeed, what often appears to be a rather complicated and obscure issue is usually quite simple to understand. It is worth recalling that this is part and parcel of the elite's obfuscation agenda and their attempt to manufacture consent by making things appear complex and far too profound for the average person to understand. The elite demand a passive, acquiescent

---

[99] Paulo Freire, "Education as the Practice of Freedom." In Freire, *Education for Critical Consciousness* (New York: Continuum, 1971), p.19.
[100] Rai, *Chomsky's Politics*, p.51.
[101] Otero, *Chomsky*, p.271.
[102] Ibid. p.270.
[103] Rai, *Chomsky's Politics*, p.53.

population. Leave the big problems to us, they say, and get back to your sports programmes and shopping!

A responsible intellectual is normally confronted with three closely related tasks. The first task is to envision a world that "conforms to the exigencies of human nature."[104] The second task is to "analyze the nature of power and oppression in our present societies."[105] The third task is to join in solidarity with others. In fact, communities of concerned citizens play an absolutely essential role in social change. Intellectual self-defence sounds like a daunting venture for one to pursue in isolation, but as part of a community, the work is distributed among its members, critical dialogue is encouraged, and feasible solutions are proposed and implemented. If people are part of a support network, then their actions become a natural and gratifying part of the process. Chomsky states, "If you want to learn something, it'll take work. And the chances of success, or useful success, are greatly magnified by cooperative interchange and effort."[106]

Clearly, Chomsky's understanding of freedom as an essential part of human nature extends into a vast array of subjects found commonly in his political work. In conjunction with earlier commentary on language acquisition and creativity, it is obvious, at least for one receptive to Chomsky's ideas, that freedom and creativity play crucial roles in an understanding of what it means to be human. Even so, critics of Chomsky's position on human nature put forth the argument that human beings are extremely complex sentient beings, and other elements, besides freedom and creativity, may reflect, in a better way, the essence of what it means to be human. For instance, they may posit that altruism, a sense of wonder, or even the love of music is what distinguishes human beings from other species. I suspect Chomsky would respond in the following fashion. First, he would wholeheartedly agree with critics that human beings are highly complex creatures. In fact, he often mentions the fact that scientists struggle to understand the nature of a simple insect, so the pronouncement of an infallible position regarding human nature must be treated with a degree of scepticism. In addition, Chomsky would agree that other elements of human nature raised by critics are also important parts of what it means to be human, but, as noted earlier, these elements may not be unique to human beings. Peter Kropotkin, for instance, shows that mutual aid is a trait found commonly in all species.[107] Granted,

---

[104] C.P. Otero (ed.), *Noam Chomsky: Radical Priorities* (Montreal: Black Rose Books, 1981), p.19.
[105] Ibid.
[106] Otero, *Chomsky*, p.275.
[107] Peter Kropotkin, *Mutual Aid: A Factor of Evolution* (Montreal: Black Rose Books, 1989).

whales and dolphins may not reflect profoundly on their existence in a vast ocean, but they do have the capacity to reflect, and they respond in rather unique ways to various types of music. Darwin's study of worms shows clearly that even worms have the capacity to solve simple problems (turning a leaf around on the surface before pulling it downward into the soil), and non-human primates envelop incredible problem-posing skills. So, once again, these elements, as important as they are for human beings, are shared with members of other species and, thus, are not fundamental to what it means to be human. It is also worth noting that Chomsky approaches the study of human nature from the perspective of a linguist. He is concerned with the way infants acquire the capacity to speak the complexities of a language in a highly creative, grammatically correct fashion at approximately the same age. How is this possible? I feel Chomsky is standing on firm ground here. His point of departure is the study of language, and that alone is probably the best place to investigate human nature. Human beings alone have a capacity for language acquisition, so language itself must have something to do with the study of what it means to be human. If this is the case, then it is feasible to construct an approach to education that is based on human nature's two primary components, that is, freedom and creativity. To do so, I begin by considering in some detail Chomsky's perspective on education and then compare it to approaches proposed by other progressive and libertarian educators. To that task I now turn my attention.

Chapter 5

Libertarian Education

A hundred children - a hundred beings who are human - not at some time in the future, not just tomorrow, but now ... right now ... today.

Janusz Korczak, The Child's Right to Respect

Noam Chomsky has been a part of educational institutions since he was two years of age. From his early years in a Deweyite school to his teaching career at MIT and the University of Arizona, Chomsky has spent his entire life in schools. With such a vast array of experience, as both a student and a teacher, and many works devoted, in part, to the subject, it only makes sense that one interested in education would want to study Chomsky's views on the process of teaching and learning. In this chapter, I consider Chomsky's libertarian approach to education and compare it to the views proposed by anarchist educators, libertarian educators, and other progressive educators who participated directly in alternative schools. In this way, I am in a position to evaluate Chomsky's insights in light of their practical value. It is one thing to profess fancy ideas, but it is something completely different to apply them effectively in a classroom setting. As will become apparent, the "tenuous thread" that unites these educators is their emphasis on the importance of freedom and creativity in the teaching and learning process. Before I examine Chomsky's views on education, it is important to differentiate between anarchist education and libertarian education. Needless to say, the two approaches to education share many similar views, but there are some key philosophical differences that make them fundamentally unique contributors to alternative schooling.

Libertarian Education or Anarchist Education?

The terms 'libertarian education' and 'anarchist education' are often used interchangeably, but the failure to distinguish them can lead to confusion. Even though the anarchist schools considered below embrace libertarian values; nevertheless, there is a key difference between the two approaches to education.

According to Judith Suissa, libertarian education refers to approaches to education that reject traditional models of teacher authority and hierarchical school structures.[1] Libertarian educators advocate maximum freedom for the individual learner, student autonomy, a non-hierarchical teaching and learning environment, cooperation, rationality, creativity, and equality. The focus in libertarian education tends to be on the individual learner. In this sense, libertarian education would include various forms of alternative schooling, including Leo Tolstoy's school at Yasnaya Polyana, John Dewey's Laboratory School, Bertrand Russell's Beacon Hill School, and even alternative ideas such as Ivan Illich's 'learning webs'. In all of these alternative models, the primary focus is on the intellectual and moral growth of the individual learner. It is worth noting that Chomsky's experiences in a Deweyite alternative elementary school continue to influence his approach to education.

Anarchist education also incorporates many of the values and practices found commonly in libertarian education, but anarchist education has an overt political overtone. Even though Colin Ward and other contemporary anarchists argue that there is no such thing as anarchist education; nevertheless, I argue that anarchist education tends to be grounded in a clearly postulated anti-State and anti-Church political stance. The values inherent in libertarian schools are commonly promoted in anarchist schools, but the motivation is to create a non-hierarchical socio-political form of society. This will become clearly evident when I consider the educational ideas and practices of the Spanish anarchist Francisco Ferrer.

Chomsky and Libertarian Education

Ever since his early years at MIT, Chomsky has expressed a sincere interest in the function of schools in society. In fact, in many ways, this interest brings together in a dynamic fashion his extensive work both as an academic and as a social activist. Chomsky's commentary on education clearly portrays how freedom and creativity are integral to individual and social development. As Otero suggests,

> [T]he roots of Noam Chomsky's interest in education go well beyond his formative experiences, even beyond his experiences as an educator and, more generally, beyond his work as a student of culture and an activist. They are at the very core of his inquiries as a scientist and a philosopher.[2]

---

[1] Judith Suissa, *Anarchism and Education: A Philosophical Perspective* (Oakland, CA: PM Press, 2010).
[2] Otero (ed.), *Chomsky*, p.2.

It is safe to say that two of Chomsky's greatest inspirational figures in education are John Dewey and Bertrand Russell. Throughout his vast commentary on schools, Chomsky consistently makes reference to these two public intellectuals. They are foundational elements in his view on education. The humanistic conception of education proposed by Dewey and Russell actually extends back to the Enlightenment, anti-authoritarian Marxism, and various expressions of libertarian socialism. In essence, as Chomsky highlighted in 1971, this conception regards the learner "as a gardener regards a young tree, that is, as 'something with a certain intrinsic nature, which will develop into an admirable form, given proper soil and air and light.'"[3] Chomsky's libertarian approach to education embraces the sentiments found in a humanistic model and opposes an authoritarian approach to teaching and learning. He posits that the foundation of authentic education is rooted in a concept of human nature that encourages the development of freedom and creativity. In 1971, in an essay on the humanistic conception of education, Chomsky states,

> [T]he goal of education should be to provide the soil and the freedom required for the growth of this creative impulse; to provide, in other words, a complex and challenging environment that the child can imaginatively explore and, in this way, quicken his intrinsic creative impulse and so enrich his life in ways that may be quite varied and unique.[4]

In an interview with David Barsamian, Chomsky contrasts the naturally curious and creative aspects of a child's character with the often highly authoritarian and submissive features of contemporary schooling. Young children enter the formal schooling process with an open mind, but it is often the case that by the end of high school, the vast majority of students have completely lost the ability to ask questions or think in a creative and critical fashion. He states,

> Anyone who has had any dealings with children knows that they're curious and creative. They want to explore things and figure out what's happening. A good bit of schooling is an effort to drive this out of them and fit them into a mold, make them behave, stop thinking, not cause any trouble. It goes right from kindergarten … People are supposed to be obedient producers, do what they're told, and the rest of your life is supposed to be passive consuming. Don't think about things. Don't

---

[3] Ibid., 163.
[4] Ibid., p.164.

know about things. Don't bother your head with things … Just do what you're told, pay attention to something else and maximize your consumption.[5]

There is a fundamental difference between trying to convince students to think a certain way or not to think at all and challenging them to think through issues for themselves. The complicated nature of human affairs suggests that, in most cases, there is not a simple solution to any particular problem. Often, any feasible solution is the product of a lot of hard work. As Chomsky suggests, "you can compile evidence and you can put things together and look at them from a certain way. The right approach … is simply to encourage people to do that."[6]

Chomsky, in full agreement with Russell, reminds us that a humanistic conception of education is dictated by "a spirit of reverence and humility: reverence for the precious, varied, individual, indeterminate growing principle of life; and humility with regard to aims and with regard to the degree of insight and understanding of the practitioners."[7] Interestingly, this particular emphasis on reverence and humility is rarely mentioned in educational discourse. In fact, it is virtually nonexistent in the history of education and mentioned sporadically by progressive thinkers in the late nineteenth- and early twentieth centuries.

Chomsky's libertarian conception of education is based on the assumption that freedom and creativity are crucial components of the educational process, that is, "about the centrality to that intrinsic nature of a creative impulse … if these assumptions are indeed correct, much of contemporary American educational practice is rationally as well as morally questionable."[8] In essence, as indicated earlier, freedom and creativity are the central features of human nature to which Chomsky refers. He agrees with Dewey and Russell that libertarian educational theories inevitably lead to a new social order "in which productive, creative work would be freely undertaken as a part of normal, healthy life."[9] This understanding of work contradicts with the contemporary view that regards workers and human labour as a commodity to be sold on the market. In this case, workers lose their sense of self-worth and merely work as cogs in a wheel designed and operated by the corporate world. As a result, self-worth is defined by what one owns and how much one

---

[5] Barsky, *Chomsky Effect*, pp.205-206.
[6] Ibid., p.202.
[7] Otero, *Chomsky*, p.164.
[8] Ibid.
[9] Ibid., p.165.

consumes. A central theme in Dewey's works is that "the ultimate aim of production is not production of goods but the production of free human beings associated with one another on (sic) terms of equality. "[10] Clearly, an approach to education and work that promotes this sort of a human being contradicts the essential nature of what it means to be human. It requires a special kind of training or indoctrination, because, in essence, its assumptions contradict human nature. Schools become training centres, sites where students prepare themselves to become obedient, productive members of a consumer-based society. The idea of a free and creative thinker with a desire, as Humboldt says, "to inquire and to create,"[11] is replaced by a rigid, well-structured system of conditioning. Granted, education is, in most cases, a preparatory ground for work that, in turn, often offers one the freedom to live a consumer lifestyle. But, this "idea is, of course, repugnant to one who accepts Russell's humanistic conception of human nature."[12] Education, like work, becomes repulsive, something one has to do in order to earn the money required to play the consumer game. According to the American Poet Laureate Edwin Markham, it leads to a life of drudgery and nothing more.

> Bowed by the weight of centuries he leans
> Upon his hoe and gazes on the ground,
> The emptiness of ages in his face,
> And on his back the burden of the world.
> Who made him dead to rapture and despair,
> A thing that grieves not and that never hopes,
> Stolid and stunned, a brother to the ox?[13]

Chomsky agrees with Ivan Illich and other deschooling critics that the solution to the current problem in education is not to get rid of schools; rather, it is to redefine what educators are trying to do. Are teachers conditioning students to become future consumers or providing them with a challenging learning environment in which they can think in a creative and critical manner? That is, are teachers dumbing them down or raising them to unforeseen intellectual and moral heights? Often, progressive teachers feel powerless to make any changes in a system entrenched in a powerful tradition. They feel like they are merely pouring "official truth" into empty vessels. For Macedo, this "education for domestication, which borders on

---

[10] Ibid., p.26.
[11] Ibid., p.128.
[12] Ibid.
[13] Quoted in Sir William Osler, *The Student Life and Other Essays* (London: Constable's Miscellany, 1928), p.51.

stupidification,"[14] embraces what Freire calls "banking education," as opposed to "problem-posing education."[15] For Freire, banking education is similar to someone making a deposit in a bank. The money is deposited into the account, and, in a similar fashion, the teacher "makes deposits which the students patiently receive, memorise, and repeat."[16] In this case, students are kept in a passive and receptive state to preclude the questioning process and to avoid the development of "critical consciousness which would result from their interaction in the world as transformers of that world."[17] As a remedy to the problem, Freire proposes a problem-posing education that encourages students to be critical, praxis-oriented thinkers, individuals who can see through the veils of distortion in society. For Freire,

> Problem-posing education bases itself on creativity and stimulates true reflection and action upon reality, thereby responding to the vocation of men (sic) as beings who are authentic only when engaged in inquiry and creative transformation.[18]

Similarly, Chomsky states.

> An approach to education which emphasizes such values as punctuality and obedience is very well suited for training factory workers as tools of production. It is not suited at all to the humanistic conception of creative and independent individuals, which brings us back again to those assumptions concerning human nature and the social forces and educational practices that give due regard to intrinsic human capacities.[19]

A university, for instance, if emancipated from corporate control, could "preserve its independence as an institution committed to the free exchange of ideas, to critical analysis, to experimentation, to the exploration of a wide range of ideas and values, to the study of the consequences of social action or scientific progress and the evaluation of these consequences in terms of values that are themselves subject to careful scrutiny."[20] Unfortunately, it is often the case that university research is based upon grants provided by the

---

[14] Macedo (ed.), *Chomsky on Miseducation*, p.5.
[15] Paulo Freire, *Pedagogy of the Oppressed* (New York: Continuum, 1987)
[16] Ibid., p.58.
[17] Ibid., p.60.
[18] Ibid., p.71.
[19] Otero (ed.), *Chomsky*, p.171.
[20] Ibid., p.278.

private sector, and those grants are compatible with a narrow range of interests and ideologies. Universities are "economically parasitical" and "depend upon government subsidies and often on corporate funding,"[21]and the "natural conservatism of the faculty will combine with the political conservatism imposed by external pressures to set up barriers to free inquiry." [22] Chomsky raises a valid question:

> [H]ow many study projects at political science departments are concerned with the questions of, say, how poorly armed guerillas can withstand a fantastic military force by an outside aggressive power [sic], or how many political programmes are concerned simply with the problems of mass politics or revolutionary development in third-world countries, or, for that matter, in our own society? The answer is obvious in advance.[23]

A libertarian approach to schools is undoubtedly confronted by many challenges from the status quo. Traditionally, public schools were designed as institutions of indoctrination, with the sole purpose of providing factories with obedient workers, and this model remains in place as an underlying assumption in schools today. Education, it is commonly argued, is preparation for work. Bertrand Russell warns us,

> The gospel of work teaches man (sic) that what matters is the resulting product, but not the style displayed during its production. We build houses without beauty in which we eat meals that merely nourish, and beget children without love whom we subject to an education that destroys spontaneity and grace.[24]

Students are often rewarded for obedience and passivity rather than for creative and independent thought. The national state, dominant social institutions, and the corporate sector work in harmony to preserve the traditional role of schools. For Chomsky, this is "a serious threat to the liberatory and subversive function that is their [universities] responsibility to undertake in a free and healthy society."[25] In order to implement progressive or libertarian ideas into the school system, educators must expect opposition

---

[21] Rai, *Chomsky's Politics*, 130.

[22] Otero (ed.), *Radical Priorities*, p.229.

[23] Rai, *Chomsky's Politics.*, p.126.

[24] Bertrand Russell, *Mortals and Others: American Essays 1931-1935* (New York: Routledge, 2009), p.22.

[25] Otero (ed.), *Chomsky.*, p.201.

from these various powerful social and political influences. Even so, after reflecting on his experiences in a progressive Deweyite school, Chomsky states,

> Such schooling is fundamentally subversive, in the best sense, and therefore rarely undertaken, but it is possible even within the institutional constraints of our societies as they now exist, and the effort to create and expand such possibilities merits much effort and struggle. This is most important within the state educational system, where the overwhelming majority of the population is educated, or dis-educated.[26]

In the section to follow, I consider how the array of ideas mentioned above are implemented by educators in alternative schools. Some of the educators are self-proclaimed anarchists, and others are either libertarian socialist or progressive thinkers. It is worth noting at this point in my investigation that anarchist educators tend to distance themselves from other progressive and liberatory schools of thought. Fundamentally, anarchists argue that human nature is malleable, and defined, in large part, within a specific socio-political context. They disagree with Chomsky and other libertarian thinkers who relate human nature to innate human capacities. It's a fine distinction, but one worthy of consideration as I compare various views on education. Even so, they share particular features associated with Chomsky's libertarian approach to education; namely, they reject the traditional view of teachers as authority figures and schools as hierarchical structures of power, and advocate freedom for the individual child within a creative educational process.

Concord Academy

In 1838, Henry Thoreau and his brother, John, founded Concord Academy in Concord, Massachusetts. John was the preceptor of the school and taught young children, and Henry taught a variety of subjects to older students, including mathematics, natural philosophy, Greek, Latin, French, geography, grammar, and writing composition. Even though it is rather difficult to locate with any accuracy Thoreau's place in the anarchist and libertarian socialist political spectrum, his focus on individual freedom, experiential learning, simplicity, autonomy, equality, anti-slavery, and, to a degree, anti-statism situates him firmly within the liberatory tradition. As a result of its overall success, Concord Academy is regarded as "one of the most important of the nation's early educational experiments, combining intellectual rigor and a

---

[26] Otero (ed.), *Language and Politics*, p.394.

demanding curriculum."[27] The school itself is divided into two rooms, and the brothers place an emphasis on literacy skills, especially on writing composition. Students complete weekly compositions and present their creative ideas to the class. A student at the Concord Academy recorded his daily schedule in a journal entry:

> I study in the morning. I did Geometry, Geography and grammar and in the afternoon read, spell or say definitions from the reading lesson, say Latin & Algebra. I write every other morning. Saturday is given to writing compositions.[28]

Thoreau detests the common practice at that time of corporal punishment in schools. He also rejects the more traditional emphasis on rote memorization and recitation and favours a more experientially-based approach to teaching and learning. Even so, Thoreau is aware that educators who emphasise the experiential aspect of education often eschew tradition and its emphasis on learning through the use of books. Thoreau's approach to pedagogy highlights the important role played by both personal experiences and a traditional emphasis on the use of books, especially classical Greek and Latin literature, because "books are the society we keep."[29] As Jonathan Kozol states,

> Thoreau's pedagogic views, as dedicated as he was to freedom and to individual and practical experience for children and adults alike, did not exclude some rigorous instructional approaches that contemporary libertarians have tended to dismiss and even ridicule ... The notion that a child often learns "by doing" is confused too frequently with the calamitous idea that children *never* learn by reading.[30]

Kozol raises an extremely important point. The traditional-experiential divide is often quite wide, and each side tends to neglect the positive elements found in the other side. Nevertheless, as I will highlight later in the manuscript, there is a fundamental difference between regarding tradition as a collection of historically rich texts and viewing it as an authoritarian approach to teaching. Thoreau favours the former but abhors the latter. He believes that a liberatory

---

[27] Laura Dassow Walls, *Henry David Thoreau: A Life* (Chicago: University of Chicago Press, 2017), p.97.

[28] Walls, *Henry David Thoreau*, p.100.

[29] Robert F. Sayre (ed.), *Henry David Thoreau: A Week on the Concord and Merrimack Rivers, Walden, The Maine Woods, Cape Cod* (New York: The Library of America, 1985), p.78.

[30] Martin Bickman (ed.), *Uncommon Learning: Thoreau on Education* (Boston: Houghton Mifflin Company, 1999), p.viii.

approach to schooling should not neglect a systematic study of the classics in their original languages. For instance, he avoids the use of translations in the classroom and argues that reading and studying classical works in their original languages offers students a rich and profound learning experience. He states,

> The modern cheap and fertile press, with all its translations, has done little to bring us nearer to the heroic writers of antiquity. They seem as solitary, and the letter in which they are printed as rare and curious, as ever. It is worth the expense of youthful days and costly hours, if you learn only some words of an ancient language ... To read well, that is, to read true books in a true spirit, is a noble exercise, and one that will task the reader more than any exercise which the customs of the day esteem.[31]

Students in Concord Academy study Homer or Aeschylus in Greek and Cicero or Virgil in Latin, "works as refined, as solely done, and as beautiful almost as the morning itself."[32] This approach to teaching literature enriches the students' overall learning experiences.

As a graduate of Harvard College and an enthusiastic voice for lifelong learning, Thoreau promotes the idea that learning does not begin and end in a formal classroom setting; rather, learning should be pursued throughout life in different learning environments. In this sense, education is not regarded as a means to an end, a preparatory ground for employment, but is cherished as something intrinsically valuable. In a letter to Bronson Alcott, Thoreau embraces sentiments later expressed by Freire and other liberatory pedagogues. He states,

> I would make education a pleasant thing both to the teacher and the scholar. This discipline, which we allow to be the end of life, should not be one thing in the schoolroom, and another in the street. We should seek to be fellow students with the pupil, and should learn of, as well as with him, if we would be most helpful to him.[33]

Even though Thoreau's curriculum is rigorous, he balances it with field trips and experiential learning. For instance, to complement a lesson on geography or botany, he often escorts students outdoors to explore the immediate

---

[31] Ibid., p.13.
[32] Sayre (ed.), *Henry David Thoreau*, p.405.
[33] Ibid., xviii.

landscape with its woods, ponds, and fields. Students visit museums and local shops to speak with local craftsmen. Sometimes, in the evening, Thoreau takes his students to the lyceum to listen to a speaker. Field trips encourage students not only to appreciate the beauty of nature but also to relate experiences in nature to content learned in the classroom. Thoreau constantly promotes a praxis-oriented approach to schooling. Learning, for Thoreau, is far more than an accumulation of memorised facts; it implies an active and practical component, that is, applying classroom-based knowledge in the real world. In this sense, Thoreau can be regarded as a precursor to Dewey's experiential approach to teaching and learning.

The tendency to identify Thoreau as an anarchist thinker comes primarily from the publication of his essay entitled "Civil Disobedience" (1849) and the emphasis he places on individual freedom. In 1846, he was arrested and spent one night in jail for refusing to pay an overdue poll tax. Thoreau was aware that taxes were used, at that time, to support a hard and bloody war declared by the U.S. against the United Mexican States. Two years later, Thoreau explained to the public why he refused to pay his taxes, and his response was published a year later as "Resistance to Civil Government," later entitled "Civil Disobedience." The essay begins with the resonance of a true anarchist. In support of his friends in the "No-Government" movement, he claims, "That government is best which governs not at all,"[34] but then, later in the essay, modifies his position in line with a libertarian socialist position. He proclaims,

> But to speak practically and as a citizen, unlike those who call themselves no-government men (sic), I ask for, not at once no government, but at once a better government. Let every man (sic) make known what kind of government would command his respect, and that will be one step toward obtaining it.[35]

Thoreau argues that citizens have a moral right to speak out against state-sponsored violence that, in his case, condones slavery, kills Mexicans, and steals precious land from indigenous groups. For Thoreau, one of the best expressions of discontent and civil disobedience is one to refuse to pay one's taxes. Taxes, he argues, are the sign of citizenship, and each citizen has two choices - either pay the taxes or refuse to pay them. Either choice has to be the product of a deliberate and conscientious thought process.

---

[34] Elizabeth Hall Witherell (ed.), *Henry David Thoreau: Collected Essays and Poems* (New York: The Library of America, 2001), p.203.
[35] Ibid., p.204.

The underlying current of Thoreau's essay on civil disobedience and, in many ways, the focus of all his educational discourse is the importance of individual freedom. In a journal entry in 1858, Thoreau asks, "Men (sic) talk of Freedom! How many are free to think? Free from fear, from perturbation, from prejudice?"[36] Even so, his concept of freedom does not suggest that students have the absolute freedom to do whatever they wish in school. In fact, Thoreau's school operated under strict rules regarding behaviour and study habits. The freedom promoted in his school is inner freedom, that is, the freedom to explore ideas and express them creatively. Education, according to Thoreau, often "makes a straight-cut ditch of a free, meandering brook."[37] It restricts freedom of expression and creative, independent thought. It is worth noting that Thoreau's interest in education extends far beyond the walls of Concord Academy. He also promotes the idea of personal freedom in the broader Concord community. His pioneering efforts in adult education encourage adults to take advantage of their relative freedom to pursue lifelong learning. In his *Walden* (1854), Thoreau promotes the idea of "uncommon schools," that is, grassroots efforts by citizens to pool their resources for scholarly advancement. In his own school, Thoreau avoids approaches to teaching and learning that promote rote memory, institutional inertia, and blind authoritarianism. Thoreau's emphasis on experientially-based and critically reflective forms of pedagogy acts as a precursor to the ideas of later libertarian and progressive educators, but it is worth reiterating the emphasis placed by Thoreau on the role of tradition in education. As noted earlier, this is an often neglected element in liberatory forms of education but an absolutely essential part of an effective approach to teaching and learning. In fact, in my opinion, the greatest value of Thoreau's liberatory approach to education, besides his emphasis on personal freedom - a concept that is found commonly in libertarian discourse - is the way he highlights the dynamic relationship between a more traditional, book-focussed form of learning and the richness of experiential education. In fact, in some ways, his approach to pedagogy is merely a reflection of his own character. As Kozol suggests,

> In the long run, it is healthy to remind ourselves that Thoreau's most abiding legacy to educators … is the spirit of the man, the freshness and merriment, the sheer delight he takes in mischievous self-contradiction,

---

[36] Jeffrey S. Cramer (ed.), *The Quotable Thoreau* (Princeton: Princeton University Press, 2011, p.96.
[37] Bickman, *Uncommon Learning*, p.xiii.

the defiant humor, and the ultimate irreducible morality of his existence that remain the gift of joy and courage he has left to us.[38]

In 1841, the doors of Concord Academy closed permanently. John became extremely ill with tuberculosis, was unable to fulfil his teaching responsibilities, and Henry was unable to operate the school alone. Nevertheless, Thoreau's legacy as a liberatory educator is well-established and is often treated as a foundational element in a long tradition of alternative schools.

Yasnaya Polyana

In 1859, Leo Tolstoy, the great Russian novelist, established a free, non-compulsory school on his estate, Yasnaya Polyana, in order to teach the children of his peasant serfs how to read and write. Tolstoy's school is one of the earlier attempts to implement libertarian ideas into an educational setting. In his later years, he adopted a socio-political position often referred to as Christian anarchism, that is, a combination of an almost literal interpretation of the gospels and a strict, non-violent, non-authoritarian political stance. For Tolstoy, the gospels should be read without any reference to the supernatural or miraculous. They merely represent an ethical tract and one that professes both love of God and love of one's neighbour. Tolstoy's educational writings and, in fact, his entire corpus of fiction and non-fiction are imbued with this spirit of love for one's neighbour. Inevitably, with a strictly ethical and pacifist interpretation of the gospels, Tolstoy became a vociferous opponent of any institutional power - government, Church, education - that either restricts one's individual freedom or promotes violence. Although he places significant emphasis on self-development, and also uses specific Christian teachings as a basis for his particular pedagogy; nevertheless, he repeatedly highlights the importance of freedom from state authorities and the Church hierarchy, and promotes non-violent means of social change. As a result, traditional anarchists normally embrace him as one of their own.

In any case, Tolstoy's strictly anarchist tendencies did not develop until after his conversion experience in the early 1880s. Prior to that period, he embraced a progressive, free-thinking approach to socio-political issues, including education. Nevertheless, he remained highly critical of hierarchical social and political structures, authoritative members of government, and ecclesial leaders, and this did not sit well with others. Tolstoy was a powerful man in Russia. He was one of the wealthiest men in his country, and his works, including *War and Peace* (1869) and *Anna Karenina* (1878), two of the

---

[38] Bickman, *Uncommon Learning*, p.x.

world's greatest novels, brought him worldwide fame. The authorities could not touch him, but they did not trust him, especially after he founded his school. For years, Tolstoy expressed sympathy for the down-trodden and oppressed peasants in Russia. He also wrote about the powerful, intricate, and often corrupt relationship between the state and the Church. He held office for a time as a rural judge, and this position facilitated his launching and supervising of fourteen schools in the district. As a result, the authorities were concerned that Tolstoy's radical sentiments would eventually initiate some sort of revolutionary change in society. An incident in 1862 reflects the severity of the matter.

> A body of armed police, therefore, taking advantage of his [Tolstoy] absence ... descended in force on his home, surrounded it to forestall escapes, and carried out a comprehensive search. They ran through his manuscripts, read his private diary and letters, making a note of the names of his correspondents, broke locks, and tore off curtain linings. Outside, they prised up flagstones and dragged the ponds. Finding nothing, because his aunt and sister had managed to hide some material that would have got him into trouble, they extended the search to the schools, seized the children's notebooks and arrested the student helpers. Still they found nothing.[39]

In 1859, the school at Yasnaya Polyana was located in a two-storied stone building. Tolstoy explains,

> Two rooms are given up to the school, one is a cabinet of physical curiosities, and two are occupied by the teachers. Under the roof of the porch hangs a bell with a rope ... Half an hour after ringing the bell, there appear in the mist, in the rain, or in the oblique rays of the autumnal sun, dark figures, by twos, by threes, or singly ... The children have nothing with them - neither reading books nor copy-books ... nothing but their impressionable natures, and their convictions that today it will be as jolly in school as it was yesterday.[40]

He taught Russian, arithmetic, religion, history, and geography. After the first year, Tolstoy travelled to Western Europe to study various educational systems. In Berlin, he attended classes for artisans and also visited a school in Leipzig that emphasised compulsion and included "[a] prayer for the king,

---

[39] David Redfearn, *Tolstoy: Principles for a New World Order* (London: Shepherd-Walwyn, 1992), pp.43-44.

[40] Victor Lucas, *Tolstoy in London* (London:Evans Brothers Limited, 1979), pp.90-91.

beatings, everything by heart, frightened, morally deformed children." [41] He told Julius Froebel, nephew of the famous educator, that social progress in Russia would be achieved through popular education based on principles of a liberating pedagogy. In Marseilles, Tolstoy visited schools where children spent their days memorising facts, in a fashion similar to Charles Dickens's Mr. Thomas Gradgrind, the notorious school board Superintendent in *Hard Times* (1854) - "Now, what I want is Facts. Teach these boys and girls nothing but facts." Before he travelled to London, Tolstoy concluded, "I could have written whole books about the ignorance which I have witnessed in the schools in France, Switzerland and Germany."[42] Mechanical instruction, rote memory, punishment, and rigid didactics were the norm in these schools. In London, Tolstoy spent six weeks visiting schools and left the country with a favourable impression of education, especially the English private school system.

Upon his return to Russia, Tolstoy initiated an educational journal, *Yasnaya Polyana*, and twelve issues were published between 1861 and 1862. The primary aim of the journal was to explicate Tolstoy's key principles of education and some practical educational matters pertaining to his school. In particular, he differentiated between education and training. Education, for Tolstoy, "is the sum total of all those influences which ... give him (sic) a broader outlook and new knowledge ... Books, work, study ... art, science, life ... all these educate. As do playground games, and also the suffering of children from unfair punishment inflicted upon them."[43] In contrast, training "is the influence exercised by one man (sic) on another for the purpose of making him (sic) adopt certain moral habits."[44] For Tolstoy, training and teaching are completely different activities. Whereas training involves imposition and coercion from above, teaching "is the influence exercised ... for the purpose of leading [the student] to acquire certain accomplishments ... [and] are exercised without compulsion."[45] The tsarist secret police paid close attention to Tolstoy's entries in his educational journal, and led the Minister of the Interior to state,

> The careful reading of the educational review *Yasnaya Polyana*, edited by Count Tolstoy, leads to the conclusion that this review, in preaching new methods of tuition and principles of popular schools, frequently spreads ideas which, besides being incorrect, are injurious in their teaching. ... I consider it necessary to draw the attention of your

---

[41] Daniel Murphy, *Tolstoy and Education* (Dublin: Irish Academic Press, 1992), p.55.
[42] Ibid., p.57.
[43] Lucas, *Tolstoy in London*, p.96.
[44] Ibid.
[45] Ibid.

Excellency to the general tendency and spirit of the review, which very often attacks the fundamental rules of religion and morality ... The evil lies in the sophistry and eccentricity of his [Tolstoy] convictions which, being expounded with extraordinary eloquence, may carry away inexperienced teachers in this direction, and thus give a wrong turn to popular education.[46]

Tolstoy's "eccentric" journal embraces the richness of his liberating approach to pedagogy, a pedagogy that embraces experiential learning, individual freedom, and an authentic desire to learn. In his educational journal, Tolstoy speaks against coercion and authoritarianism in schools and promotes free inquiry and critical thinking.

It is tempting to compare Tolstoy's view of education with the view posited by libertarian and progressive educators. In many ways, they approach education in a similar fashion, but there are also some fundamental differences. For example, all of them reject authoritarian or disciplinarian approaches to schooling. They condemn the use of a traditional, prescriptive curriculum and the coercive forms of classroom discipline. In addition, they highlight the importance of student-based, experiential learning, and the promotion of critical inquiry. Also, they relate the curriculum to broader social and political issues in the lives of students. Nevertheless, Tolstoy rejects the quasi-scientific, rationalist approach to teaching and learning found commonly in progressive education, with its emphasis on inductive and deductive methods of inquiry. This is quite foreign to Tolstoy's ethico-religious approach with its emphasis on the primacy of the law of love proclaimed in the gospels.

In many respects, the success of Tolstoy's school is reflected in the way he leads a group of peasant children from an initial stage of complete illiteracy to a stage where they compose creative essays and plays. For instance, Tolstoy taught composition by involving himself in the creative process. He would write a few lines, and the children were invited to comment. They would edit his work, add to it, and insert metaphors and descriptive scenarios. Tolstoy, in turn, would offer comments and suggestions, and the dynamic, collaborative process would continue until the story was complete. Tolstoy and his students also wrote folk tales and fairy stories, exercises that encouraged students to think in a creative and imaginative fashion. Some of these stories and folk tales were eventually included in his educational journal. For example, Tolstoy and his children wrote the 'Tale of the Peasant and the Cucumbers':

---

[46] Bob Blaisdell (ed.), *Tolstoy as Teacher* (New York: Teachers and Writers Collaborative, 2000), pp.3-4.

A peasant once went to a vegetable garden to steal cucumbers. "I'll carry off this sack of cucumbers." he thought, "and with the money I get for them I'll buy a hen. The hen will lay eggs, she will sit on them and hatch a brood of chicks, and I'll feed the chicks till they grow, then I'll sell them and buy a suckling pig. I'll feed the suckling pig till it grows into a sow, I'll breed her, she'll have a litter of pigs, and I'll sell them. With the money I get for the pigs I'll buy a mare. She will foal. I'll feed the foals till they grow, then I'll sell them. With the money I get for the foals I'll buy a house with a garden. I'll plant cucumbers in the garden, and I won't let anyone steal them. I'll keep guard over them. I'll hire a strong watchman, and from time to time I'll go out to the garden and shout: 'Hey, you! Take care!' The peasant was so carried away by his thoughts that he completely forgot he was in someone else's garden, and he shouted at the top of his voice. The watchman heard him and came running out. He caught the peasant and gave him a good beating.[47]

It is easy to imagine Tolstoy sitting with his inquisitive and creative students and generating such a tale. It incorporates the experiences, dreams, and aspirations of young children and also the gentle guidance of a literary master. To take a ragged group of illiterate children and eventually produce such a tale is an enormous accomplishment and something that far exceeds the expectations of most contemporary teachers. By May 1862, Tolstoy was completely exhausted. He suffered from symptoms of consumption and was advised by his doctor to close the school permanently and seek recuperation in the Samara province.

I have considered ever so briefly a few details associated with Tolstoy's school. To do justice to the topic, I need to consider many other factors that play an indirect role in his overall approach to education, including the law of love, non-resistance to evil, patriotism, government, religion, work, property, war, and death. Tolstoy addresses virtually every aspect of human existence, and they play a role in the way he develops and implements his pedagogy. It is far beyond the scope of this manuscript to address thoroughly even a few of these topics, but I can, at least, portray a sense of his expansive vision as an educator.

The Laboratory School

In 1894, John Dewey, one of the pre-eminent philosophers of education in the twentieth century, and University of Chicago's President, William Harper,

---

[47] Ibid., pp.99-100.

founded the Laboratory School, later to be known simply as the Dewey School. One of the most distinguished progressive schools of the time, it was structured around Dewey's progressive ideas in education. The school opened in 1896 with 16 students and two teachers, and by 1902, the enrollment increased to 140 students, 23 teachers, and 10 graduate-student assistants.

The actual name of the school became somewhat problematic. In 1897, the school was officially called the University Elementary School, but in 1901, it was renamed the Laboratory School because, at that time, the University of Chicago maintained a recently incorporated private normal school (Chicago Institute), also referred to as the University Elementary School. Dewey appointed his wife as principal of the Laboratory School, a move that would prove fatal to Dewey in the near future. In 1902, Dewey was elected director of the University of Chicago's School of Education (formerly Chicago Institute), but with declining enrollment and financial difficulties, the two schools were eventually consolidated into one school, and Dewey's wife became its principal. By 1904, for various reasons, Dewey and his wife resigned their positions, and he accepted a professorship at Columbia University.

Fundamentally, the Laboratory School has two primary functions. First, it is designed to implement experiments and evaluate Dewey's progressive ideas in education. Second, these ideas are used to develop specific curricula and effective pedagogy that incorporate the results of earlier experiments. In essence, the Laboratory School is a truly experimental school. In fact, 'experimentalism' is a term used frequently by Dewey to designate his philosophy, that is, a philosophy based upon pragmatic, experimental, and scientific methods. There are some fundamental principles that provide Dewey's school with a solid foundation and clear direction. For instance, Dewey believes that learning should be associated with concrete forms of application. In other words, the curriculum must embody a practical element. In addition, education should promote freedom of individual inquiry and also highlight the importance of experimentation. It should favour cooperation in the classroom over individualism and competition, and foster an authentic sense of social sensitivity and moral conscience. Classroom discipline is not dictated by the sole interests of teachers; rather, it is formulated and implemented in a collaborative effort by both teachers and students. Also, Dewey supports the idea of self-directed learning, that is, students should be allowed to explore course content at their own pace and in their own way.

In Dewey's school, young children up to the age of eight are encouraged to relate school activities to issues of import in the family and local community. The learning process focuses primarily on 'learning as doing'. Creative play is an integral element at this stage, but unfortunately, at least in my opinion, Dewey does not emphasise the importance of teaching young children to read, write, and learn basic arithmetic skills. True, these skills are promoted with older children, but for some reason, Dewey does not believe that children between the ages of four and eight should be taught literacy and numeracy skills. In my opinion, this is a rather unfortunate mistake on Dewey's part because it is clearly obvious that children as young as two-years-of-age naturally master basic literacy and numeracy skills, and these acquired skills open up to them a completely new world of ideas found in books. In fact, it may be argued that this particular age is the prime window of opportunity for young children to master such skills. If the process is delayed, then these skills are only developed with tremendous effort. It may be argued that a combination of self-directed learning, especially for young children, and a neglect of basic literacy and numeracy skills is inefficacious for students who lack self-motivation and an overall love of learning. This sentiment is supported by a former student in Dewey's school, who states,

> I never learned to spell. I do not know how to spell now, I have no sense of spelling. Of my group some were spellers and some were not. I had two sisters and a brother in the school. My brother and one sister learned to spell; the other sister and I did not. My brother was of the book type and began to read early. I was of the shop type and was not interested in books. I did not feel the need of reading or writing and hence no desire to learn to spell. There would have come a time when I would have wanted to write up what I had found out and what I was doing in the shop. Then I would have learned to spell. But the school as an experiment stopped just before we non-book people came to the point where we wanted to write or read. This was bad for the experiment and very bad for us.[48]

For most of his career, Dewey was convinced that schools could be used as forums for the promotion of democracy and that, eventually, democratic sentiments would seek into society at large. Similar in fashion to other progressive and libertarian schools, Dewey promotes the idea that the natural interests of students can be used to direct the nature and content of the curriculum. Dewey's emphasis on the pragmatic nature of education suggests that learning should be directed towards the students' future participation in a democratic society.

---

[48] Katherine Camp Mayhew and Ann Camp Edwards, *The Dewey School: The Laboratory School of the University of Chicago 1896-1903* (New York: D. Appleton-Century Company, 1936), pp.404-405.

For Dewey, education incorporates a fostering, nurturing, and cultivating process. It embraces a "continuous process of growth, having as its aim at every stage an added capacity of growth."[49] Education can also be regarded as an "unfolding of latent powers"[50]or a "constant reorganizing or reconstructing of experience which adds to the meaning of experience, and which increases the ability to direct the course of subsequent experience."[51] It is clear that, at least for Dewey, education involves a strong nurturing element, similar to the way a gardener nurtures the growth of a plant. A gardener provides the plant with the required soil, nutrients, and support to ensure maximum growth. Similarly, teachers provide students with the proper environment, ideas, and motivation to ensure intellectual and moral growth. Most importantly, education begins with the experiences of students. Unlike more traditional forms of education, with their emphasis on the transmission of knowledge that is often foreign to the lives of students, Dewey claims the most effective pedagogy is rooted in the life experiences of learners themselves. Students are then able to relate the classroom content more effectively to the real world. In essence, says Dewey in 1897, "schools must represent present life - life as real and vital to the child as that which he (sic) carries on in the home, in the neighborhood, or on the playground."[52] In 1938, in his reflection on traditional and progressive education, and, in some ways, a summary of his approach to education, Dewey states,

> To imposition from above is opposed expression and cultivation of individuality; to external discipline is opposed free activity; to learning from texts and teachers, learning through experience; to acquisition of isolated skills and techniques by drill, is opposed acquisition of them as means of attaining ends which make direct vital appeal; to preparation for a more or less remote future is opposed making the most of the opportunities of present life; to static aims and materials is opposed acquaintance with a changing world.[53]

In addition to the key role played by experience in education, Dewey also highlights the importance of freedom. Even though Dewey does not suggest that students should have absolute freedom in the classroom, he nevertheless

---

[49] John Dewey, *Democracy and Education* (New York: The Free Press, 1966), p.54.
[50] Ibid., p.56.
[51] Ibid., p.76.
[52] John Dewey, *My Pedagogic Creed*. Originally published by E.L. Kellogg and Co., 1897. Reprinted in Reginald Archambault (ed.), *John Dewey on Education* (Chicago: The University of Chicago Press, 1974), p.430.
[53] John Dewey, *Experience and Education* (New York: Collier Books, 1963), pp.19-20.

claims that excessive discipline and control inhibit the natural process of learning and growth. He states,

> Enforced quiet and acquiescence prevent pupils from disclosing their real nature. They enforce artificial uniformity. They put seeming before being. They place a premium upon preserving the outward appearance of attention, decorum, and obedience.[54]

For Dewey, enforced acquiescence may generate a well-controlled classroom, but it is far from a space of freedom of expression and intellectual inquiry. At best, it is an illusion of freedom. Even so, any experienced teacher knows that there is a delicate balance between individual student freedom and effective classroom management. Dewey states, "freedom to express in action is a necessary condition of growth, but that guidance of such expression is an equally necessary condition, especially of childhood's freedom."[55] He extends this argument regarding the balance between individual freedom and classroom cohesion into the complexities of the social world. He states,

> The problem of the relation between individual freedom and collective well-being is today urgent and acute, perhaps more so than at any time in the past. The problem of achieving both of these values without the sacrifice of either one is likely to be the dominant problem of civilization for many years to come. The schools have their part to play in working out the solution, and their chief task is to create a form of community life and organization in which both of these values are conserved.[56]

In addition to his emphasis on experiential learning, for most of his career, Dewey supports the idea that "education is the fundamental method of social progress and reform."[57] Schools act as agents of social change and sites for the practice and perpetuation of democracy. In fact, Dewey regards schools as a microcosm of a larger democratic society. In 1916, Dewey states, "[a] democracy is more than a form of government; it is primarily a mode of associated living, of conjoint communicated experiences."[58] For Dewey, the ideal conditions of democracy and education include,

---

[54] Ibid., p.62.
[55] Mayhew and Edwards, *The Dewey School*, p.vi.
[56] Ibid., p.xv.
[57] Archambault (ed.), *John Dewey on Education*, p.437.
[58] Dewey, *Democracy and Education*, p.87.

A society which makes provisions for participation in its good for all its members on equal terms and which secure flexible readjustments of its institutions through interaction of the different forms of associated life is in so far democratic. Such a society must have a type of education which gives individuals a personal interest in social relationships and control, and the habits of mind which secure social changes without introducing disorder.[59]

This overview of Dewey's approach to education is far from complete. Even so, it is possible to detect, at a superficial level, the way he applies his progressive ideas about education to concrete classroom settings. Granted, the Laboratory School consisted of mostly privileged students, so his experiments do not incorporate a concern about troublesome behaviour in the classroom - a key concern for any practising pedagogue and often a demanding, time-consuming, and energy-depleting part of a teacher's day. Nevertheless, Dewey and his associates envision the classroom setting as a first line of defence against more tyrannical approaches to teaching and learning, and a foundation for the creation and preservation of a democratic society.

The Modern School

In 1901, Francisco Ferrer, a Spanish anarchist, founded La Escuela Moderna (The Modern School) to educate students in a rational, secular, and non-coercive environment. According to Judith Suissa, Ferrer's school was "[o]ne of the first systematic attempts to translate anarchist ideas into educational practice."[60] The school was co-educational, emphasised the absence of grades, and forbade corporal punishment. It promoted critical literacy skills, but also highlighted the practical side of learning. Also, the curriculum embraced an anti-dogmatic overtone and emphasised the importance of science and reasoning skills. In his prospectus, Ferrer states,

> I will teach them only the simple truth. I will not ram dogma into their heads. I will not conceal from them one iota of fact. I will teach them not what to think but how to think.[61]

By all accounts, Ferrer was a radical architect of anarchist thought. He did not shy away from violent action. In 1906, an employee of Ferrer's publishing firm threw a bomb at King Alphonso XIII's wedding party. Ferrer was arrested

---

[59] Ibid., p.99.
[60] Suissa, *Anarchism and Education.* p.78.
[61] Quoted in Suissa, *Anarchism and Education,* p.79.

because the police suspected he encouraged the bombing, but was released a year later due to insufficient evidence. As a result, wealthy parents became hesitant to send their children to a school directed by Ferrer, and shortly thereafter, the Modern School closed permanently. Ferrer rekindled his interest in anarcho-syndicalism and devoted his time to the Catalan labour movement. In 1909, political events took a turn for the worse, resulting in a massive general strike, leading eventually to the so-called "Tragic Week" five-day mob rule. Inevitably, martial law was declared in the country, followed by violent military suppression. Both the monarchy and the Catholic Church hierarchy wanted to rid themselves of Ferrer, and once again, he was arrested and accused of inciting the insurrection. A brief five-hour military trial took place where Ferrer was not permitted to call any witnesses or even choose his own lawyer, and four days later, on October 13, 1909, with the assistance of false evidence and forced confessions, Ferrer was executed by a military firing squad. Standing in front of a line of riflemen, Ferrer exclaimed, "Muchachos, aim well and fire without fear! I am innocent! *Viva la Escuela Moderna!*"[62] The man was killed, but the martyr was born.

In Spain, at the beginning of the twentieth century, illiteracy rates among adults were more than 50%. Even though elementary school was free and compulsory since 1857, almost 10,000 schools lacked the basic supplies necessary to operate properly. The *ayuntamiento*, or town council, controlled schools in villages and small towns, and its members, mostly illiterate themselves, cared little for education. Even though the wealthy sent their children to elite institutions founded by Jesuits and other religious orders, the general public was forced to resort to state-run schools. Even so, public schools were tightly monitored by Catholic priests and diocesan inspectors to ensure that faith took its dominant position in the school curriculum. According to testimony provided by William Archer, children "spend half of their school hours in prayers and recitations of the catechism and of 'sacred history.'"[63]

The dominant role played by the Catholic Church in public schools was one of the motivational factors that encouraged Ferrer to found the Modern School. For Ferrer, schools should not be places of faith-based indoctrination. Instead, schools should promote "modern and scientific methods of pedagogy … (and) the inculcation of definitely rationalistic, humanitarian, anti-military and anti-patriotic doctrine."[64] Similarly, Bakunin states education "must be

---

[62] Mark Bray and Robert H. Haworth (eds.), *Anarchist Education and the Modern School: A Francisco Ferrer Reader* (Oakland: PM Press, 2019), p.1.
[63] Willam Archer, *The Life, Trial, and Death of Francisco Ferrer* Honolulu: University Press of the Pacific Honolulu, 2001), p.31.
[64] Ibid., p.32.

founded wholly upon the scientific development of personal dignity and independence, not upon piety and obedience; upon the cult of truth and justice at any cost; and above all, upon respect for humanity, which must replace in everything the divine cult."[65]

Also, schools should promote creative and independent thought, autonomy, human dignity, and the rights of the individual. Ferrer's subversive approach to pedagogy is highlighted by Archer, who states,

> Having attained absolute clearness on all things mundane, and convinced himself that things extramundane either did not exist or did not matter, he felt that the first duty of the educator was to bring this gospel home to the infant mind, before any shades of the prison-house of supernaturalism had begun to gather around it. There is not the least doubt that his teaching was not merely anti-clerical but anti-religious. And even deeper than the rebellion against supernaturalism lay the rebellion against class domination and exploitation. State-education was in Ferrer's eyes at least as noxious as church-education.[66]

It was only natural that Ferrer's school would upset state officials and members of the Catholic Church hierarchy. They willingly travelled far and wide to ensure that the Modern School's doors were shut permanently and Ferrer's threat was extinguished. Nevertheless, Ferrer's early reputation as an educator spread quickly in Spain, and in a short time, he recruited enough teachers to instruct 126 students.

For Ferrer, governments want schools "not because they hope for the renovation of society through education, but because they need individuals, workmen (sic), perfected instruments of labor to make their industrial enterprises and the capital employed in them profitable."[67] The overall tone of the school's approach to organised religion is detected in one of Ferrer's school books and opens with an introduction by Mme. Jacquinet, the directress of the school. She states,

> Christianity has always, throughout history, placed obstacles in the path of progress ... the support of absolutism, and of the inequality of the social classes; the oppressor of the human conscience in the

---

[65] Paul Avrich, *The Modern School Movement: Anarchism and Education in the United States* (Princeton, New Jersey: Princeton University Press, 1980), p.8.
[66] Ibid., pp.32-33.
[67] Joel Spring, *A Primer of Libertarian Education* (Montreal: Black Rose Books, 1975), p.22.

clamps of its false morality; the odious standard in whose shadow all crimes have been committed."[68]

Ferrer also produced numerous monthly bulletins for parents in which he clearly articulated his view of education. He also translated works from key libertarian thinkers, including Paul Robin, Elisee Reclus, Peter Kropotkin, and Leo Tolstoy. In one of his bulletins, Ferrer discusses the role of state-sanctioned schools, and his insights reflect many of the sentiments discussed by Chomsky. He states,

> [State-sanctioned schools] have only one clear idea and one desire: that the children shall learn to obey, to believe, and to think according to social dogmas which rule us ... The object is always to impose on the child ready-made thoughts; to debar him from all thinking which does not tend to the conservation of existing institutions: to make of him (sic), in short, a personage strictly adapted to the social mechanism ... The educator as we know him (sic) always imposes, obliges, forces; whereas the true educator is he (sic) who can defend the child even against his (the educator's) own ideas and volitions, appealing in a higher degree to the energies of the child himself (sic). [69]

Even though Ferrer's life as an anarchist educator is certainly an interesting one, nevertheless, in many respects, it is quite difficult for one to actually come to know the real person. At times, he appears to be a revolutionary agitator and, in his school, a radical propagandist, but also, at times, embraces freethinking, pacifist, and scientific ideas. It is also worth noting that Ferrer did not contribute any new ideas or practices to libertarian pedagogy. Many of the ideas he proclaimed were already embraced by radical pedagogues. For example, his emphasis on coeducation, anti-authoritarianism, student autonomy, integral education, opposition to rewards and punishments, and an emphasis on science were ideas current in established libertarian schools. It is also important to recognise that Ferrer's approach to pedagogy embodied a degree of inconsistency. He inherited a fortune and embraced a lifestyle inconsistent with his working-class ideology; he founded a libertarian school but contributed no original ideas to a libertarian theory of education; and he envisioned a new way of life defined by fraternity and cooperation, but it would only become a reality through a bloody revolution.

---

[68] Archer, *Life, Trial, and Death.*, p.50.
[69] Ibid., p.53.

It is no wonder that the governing state authorities and the Catholic Church hierarchy regarded Ferrer and the Modern School as a threat to the established order. Ironically, rather than extinguish the rebellious flame, Ferrer's execution initiated a wave of protest throughout Europe, Latin America, and the U.S. The event also acted as a catalyst for the founding of numerous libertarian schools based on Ferrer's ideas, including the Modern School in New York, the Walden Center and School in Berkeley, and numerous alternative schools in Britain.[70]As Emma Goldman suggests, "Never before has one man's death called forth such a universal cry of indignation."[71] Over the next 50 years in the U.S., anarchists, inspired by the execution of Ferrer and rooted in the anarchist tradition of Bakunin, Kropotkin, Tolstoy, and other libertarian thinkers, established more than 20 schools. These schools promoted the fundamental ideas inherent in Ferrer's school, especially his attempts to abolish all forms of authority in education and his emphasis on the school's role in establishing a society based on the voluntary cooperation of free individuals.

Beacon Hill School

In 1927, Bertrand Russell and his then-wife, Dora, founded Beacon Hill School in order to educate their own children in what they thought would be the best fashion. At that time, Russell was not impressed with the quality of education in existing British schools. He wanted to create a school that kept a safe distance from "religious instruction and a great many restraints on freedom … on the other hand, we could not agree with most 'modern' educationists on thinking scholastic instruction unimportant, or in advocating a *complete* absence of discipline."[72] Russell rented a house on the South Downs, surrounded by 230 acres of forests, wild life, and an array of gorgeous plants. Freedom was taken for granted in the school, but there were strict conditions attached to it. For example, when children played outside, bullying was not allowed, and they were supervised by an adult at all times. As Russell states, "young children in a group cannot be happy without a certain amount of order and routine. Left to amuse themselves, they are bored, and turn to bullying or destruction."[73] Contrary to what was often reported in the media, the children in Russell's school were not free to do as they will. He states,

---

[70] See Ibid., pp.82-97 for further details. Also see John Shotton, *No Master High or Low: Libertarian Education and Schooling 1890-1990* (Bristol: Libertarian Education, 1993).
[71] Bray and Haworth (eds.), *Anarchist Education*, p.259.
[72] Bertrand Russell, *Autobiography* (London: Unwin, 1978), p.387.
[73] Ibid., p.390.

There was very little freedom where health and cleanliness were concerned. The children had to wash, to clean their teeth, and to go to bed at the right time ... foolish people, and especially journalists in search of a sensation, had said or believed that we advocated a complete absence of all restraints and compulsions.[74]

Similarly, in a letter dated June 27, 1931, Russell addresses the issue of freedom and creativity in his school. On freedom, he states,

We see to it that children are clean twice a day, and that they get a sufficient length of time in bed. Neither of these things would happen if the children were left completely free, but neither entails any curtailment of free speech, and we find both easy to carry out without resort to punishment.[75]

Russell also promoted various forms of creative thinking, especially what he called "co-operative poetry." He encouraged students to form into groups and, with "a kind of instinctive co-operation among them," write poems of all sorts. For example, after a visit to a local cemetery, students reflect in verse on their experience. In the same letter, Russell states,

Having just seen a graveyard, the five concerned spontaneously decided they would like to write a poem on the subject. One of them contributed the idea of an old crowe; another the idea of the love-bird. Even the tone of the poem is, I think, generally co-operative; certainly the detail was so. For the end of the third verse, for example, one child suggested: "One was her love bird wild", a second said, "That is too short"; third said, "yes, we must have another word with a 'w'"; and the fourth suggested, "Once was her love-bird weird and wild," which was adopted.[76]

Russell closes the letter with an emphasis on the importance of collaborative learning. He reminds his readers that "Homer and the Authorised Version were not the products of individual genius and that the individualism of the artist is perhaps over-emphasised in modern times."[77]

---

[74] Ibid.
[75] Ray Perkins (ed.), *Yours Faithfully, Bertrand Russell: A Lifelong Fight for Peace, Justice, and Truth in Letters to the Editor* (Peru, Illinois: Open Court Publishing, 2002), p.148.
[76] Ibid., p.149.
[77] Ibid.

According to Russell's daughter, Katharine Tait, who attended Beacon Hill School, absolute freedom was granted in pursuit of natural inquiry, curiosity, and truth. There were no restrictions imposed upon learning. She states,

> It was hoped that, in this way, we would acquire an interest in learning and a habit of seeking after truth. The teaching was to be based on our appetite for knowledge, rather than on a preconceived program of basic skills and facts to be fed into the living computer of each child's mind.[78]

However, freedom was severely restricted when the powerful tried to dominate the weak. For Russell, "many of the children were cruel and destructive. To let the children go free was to establish a reign of terror in which the strong kept the weak trembling and miserable."[79]

Science, French, German, mathematics, history, literature, and music were elements of the set curriculum. In addition, Russell often escorted students outdoors to explore the local geography, geology, and biology of the surrounding area and encouraged them to write and perform plays. Unlike in anarchist alternative schools, where one would often sense a degree of propaganda in the overall philosophy of the school, Russell always promoted critical inquiry and honest consideration of all sides of an argument.

In order to obtain a clear understanding of Russell's view on education, it is necessary to move beyond the dynamics of Beacon Hill School. I sense that Russell was unable to implement, in a dynamic and effective fashion, his ideas on education. In part, this is because he accepted many troublesome students, and they disrupted the overall success of the school, and in part because Russell often had obligations with publishers or commitments to speak elsewhere and, as a result, was frequently absent from the school. As a result, my impression is that Beacon Hill School was not what Russell had expected it to be. Therefore, in order to obtain a more accurate understanding of Russell's views on education, we need to consider some of his key works on the subject.

In 1916, Russell wrote a set of essays on his political philosophy and included an essay on education. He states,

---

[78] Katharine Tait, *My Father Bertrand Russell* (New York: Harcourt, Brace, Jovanovich, 1975), p.73.
[79] Ibid., p.77.

Most impulses may be divided into two groups, the possessive and the creative ... I consider the best life that which is most built on creative impulses, and the worst that which is most inspired by love of possession ... education ... ought to embody the creative impulses, though at present [it does not] do so very adequately. [80]

In this early essay, Russell highlights the importance of creativity but also considers the issue of freedom in education. He realises that children's absolute freedom will lead to complete chaos in the classroom. To a degree, liberty is permitted in the classroom, but it must not impinge upon the learning environment. The authority of a teacher is necessary for a properly functioning classroom, but it must be exercised "in accordance with the *spirit of liberty.*[81] Interestingly, Russell also emphasises the important role played by reverence in the teaching and learning process. He states,

A man (sic) who is to educate really well, and is to make the young grow and develop into their full stature, must be filled through and through with the spirit of reverence. It is reverence towards others that is lacking in those who advocate machine-made cast-iron systems: militarism, capitalism, Fabian scientific organisation, and all the other prisons into which reformers and reactionaries try to force the human spirit. In education ... the lack of reverence for the child is all but universal.[82]

In many respects, reverence is a forgotten virtue. Teachers often talk about the importance of mutual respect in the classroom, but they do not mention reverence. As I will discuss in the next chapter, revering students is an essential quality of an effective teacher. A teacher without reverence lacks authentic compassion for students and will easily fall prey to sentiments of superiority and meanness. A reverent teacher, on the other hand, "feels in all that lives, but especially in human beings, and most of all in children, something sacred, indefinable, unlimited, something individual and strangely precious, the growing principle of life."[83] Russell acknowledges that education conducted by the state, Church, or institutions subservient to them often lacks the spirit of reverence. Rather than focusing on the sacredness of children, this type of education is directed toward the maintenance of the

---

[80] Bertrand Russell, *Principles of Social Reconstruction* (London: Routledge, 1997). Preface.
[81] Ibid., p.102.
[82] Ibid., p.102.
[83] Ibid.

existing social order. In this case, the child becomes an insignificant cog in a gigantic wheel of production and consumerism.

Even though Russell's emphasis on reverence embodies a slightly religious overtone, especially when he talks about a feeling of awe and the sacredness of life, one should keep in mind that his understanding of reverence in no way reflects a formally religious understanding of the word. As an agnostic, when Russell talks about awe, it is not a sentiment in the presence of God; rather, it is an awareness of one's minuteness in the presence of a vast universe. Formal religions, for Russell, are bound by dogmatism and prevent free inquiry. He states,

> The prevention of free inquiry is unavoidable so long as the purpose of education is to produce belief rather than thought, to compel the young to hold positive opinions on doubtful matters rather than to let them see the doubtfulness and be encouraged to independence of mind. Education ought to foster the wish for truth, not the conviction that some particular creed is the truth.[84]

Credulity in education inevitably leads to mental decay. Irreverent teachers promote certain mental habits in the classroom that prevent free inquiry. For Russell, these habits include "obedience and discipline, ruthlessness in the struggle for worldly success, contempt toward opposing groups ... (and) a passive acceptance of the teacher's wisdom. All these habits are against life."[85] They act against free inquiry, independence of thought, justice, reverence, creativity, constructive doubt, and the nourishment of mental growth. Russell reflects on the power of thought, and states,

> Men (sic) fear thought as they fear nothing else on earth - more than ruin, more even than death. Thought is subversive and revolutionary, destructive and terrible; thought is merciless to privilege, established institutions, and comfortable habits; thought is anarchic and lawless, indifferent to authority, careless of the well-tried wisdom of the ages. Thought looks into the pit of hell and is not afraid. It sees man, a feeble speck, surrounded by unfathomable depths of silence; yet it bears itself proudly, as unmoved as if it were lord of the universe. Thought is great and swift and free, the light of the world, and the chief glory of man.[86]

---

[84] Ibid., p.107.
[85] Ibid., p.108.
[86] Ibid., p.115.

In 1926, Russell wrote a book devoted entirely to education. In part, this book is the product of his concern, as a parent, about how to educate his children properly, but reluctant to expose them "to the evils of most existing institutions."[87] The entire book acts as a preface to his efforts as an educator at Beacon Hill School. The overall aims he posits in the book reflect, in many ways, what he tries to accomplish in his school. Even Russell's ideas on school curriculum in elementary school reflect the curriculum he introduces in his school. He addresses many common concerns of parents with young children, including issues regarding the first year of child development, play, fear, punishment, affection, and the development of other elements of a young child's character. Eventually, Russell moves away from a discussion about improvements in character and discusses matters relevant to classroom learning. Once again, he emphasises intellectual virtues, a scientific attitude, "a sense of an intellectual adventure,"[88] and highlights the importance of free inquiry, open-mindedness, concentration, patience, exactness, and curiosity that is "fundamental; where it is strong and directed to the right objects, all the rest will follow."[89]

In 1932, Russell once again addressed the issue of education, but this time, rather than focussing on individual character and development, he raises for consideration the question of whether education should train good individuals or good citizens.[90] He asks, "Can the fullest individual development be combined with the necessary minimum of social coherence?"[91] It is an important question to ask because, even though education appears on the surface to meet the needs of individual learners; nevertheless, schools are funded by governments, and governments want productive workers to maintain the economic engines. Russell states,

> [E]ducation has become part of the struggle for power between religions, classes, and nations. The pupil is not considered for his (sic) own sake, but as a recruit: the educational machine is not concerned with his welfare, but with ulterior political purposes. There is no reason to suppose that the State will ever place the interests of the child before its own interests.[92]

---

[87] Bertrand Russell, *On Education: Especially in Early Childhood* (London: Unwin Paperbacks, 1976), p.9.
[88] Ibid., p.187.
[89] Ibid., p.158.
[90] Bertrand Russell, *Education and the Social Order* (London: Unwin Paperbacks, 1977).
[91] Ibid., p.144.
[92] Ibid., p.145.

Russell claims, "our world is a mad world."[93] Rather than being constructive, one tends to be destructive, and rather than using one's intelligence for self-preservation, one uses it for violence, war, and self-destruction. These sentiments are cultivated at a young age, but Russell maintains a degree of hope, and it is grounded in a vision of education that returns the world to a degree of sanity. He states,

> The cure to our problem is to make men (sic) sane, and to make men (sic) sane they must be educated sanely. At present the various factors ... all tend towards social disaster. Religion encourages stupidity, and an insufficient sense of reality ... nationalism as taught in schools implies that the most important duty of young men (sic) is homicide; class feeling promotes acquiescence in economic injustice; and competition promotes ruthlessness in the social struggle.[94]

Russell is correct - it is a mad world, but he is also correct to suggest that education has a key role to play in promoting a saner world.

Additional Libertarian Schools: Past and Present

One may assume, in light of this overview of individuals who founded libertarian schools, that perhaps these schools were part of an alternative education experiment that faded away in the early twentieth-century. In fact, various types of libertarian schools that were founded a century ago continued their existence for many years. Granted, some schools operated for only a short time and were closed by the state authorities. Other schools existed for decades and eventually closed due to lack of funds. However, a few schools that were founded during the early part of the twentieth-century continue to operate in recent times.

Libertarian schools are founded upon numerous key thinkers in the libertarian movement. Many of the earlier schools were influenced significantly by Francisco Ferrer, Paul Robin, Leo Tolstoy, and Sebastian Faure. More recently, A.S. Neill, Paul Goodman, Ivan Illich, and other leading theorists tend to influence the policies and procedures of contemporary libertarian schools. These schools are found in various parts of the world, including the U.S., Canada, England, France, Mexico, and Russia.

There are a few key works that highlight the historical development of libertarian schools in various parts of the world. For instance, John Shotton

---

[93] Ibid., p.152.
[94] Ibid., p.153.

offers a comprehensive overview of libertarian schools in Britain.[95] Joel Spring provides a philosophical overview of libertarian education and makes reference to various libertarian schools.[96] William Edgerton provides memoirs by early Tolstoyans in Russia and their efforts to establish communes and alternative schools based on the anarchist and pacifist philosophy of Leo Tolstoy.[97] Also, Charlotte Alston presents a comprehensive history of the international Tolstoyan movement.[98]

According to Shotton, there are a few precursors to contemporary libertarian education in Britain. In 1890, for example, the International School was founded by Louise Michel. A revolutionary of the Paris Commune, a trained school teacher, and strongly influenced by the philosophy of Michael Bakunin, Michel immigrated to England and established what is considered to be the first libertarian school in Britain, a school for children of political refugees. Michel acknowledges a debt to the thought Bakunin, who states,

> The whole education of children and their instruction must be founded on the scientific development of reason, not on that of faith; on the development of personal dignity and independence, not on that of piety and obedience; on the worship of truth and justice at any cost, and above all on respect for humanity, which must replace always and everywhere the worship of divinity.[99]

The International School was operated by a committee, a secretary, and eight teachers. Teaching was an entirely voluntary activity. The school was maintained financially through private donations and parental contributions. It offered students a broad curriculum, including science, music, English literature, physical education, and technical studies. A particularly unique attribute of the International School is its focus on the study of foreign languages. The school's prospectus states, "He (sic) who has acquired one or more foreign languages commands a capital of which no one can deprive him, and which will at all times assure him a safer and more abundant return than any investment."[100] The school was closed by state authorities in the

---

[95] John Shotton, *No Master High or Low: Libertarian Education and Schooling 1890-1990* (Bristol: Libertarian Education, 1993).

[96] Joel Spring, *A Primer of Libertarian Education* (Montreal: Black Rose Books, 1975).

[97] William Edgerton, *Memoirs of Peasant Tolstoyans in Soviet Russia* (Bloomington: Indian University Press, 1993).

[98] Charlotte Alston, *Tolstoy and His Disciples: The History of a Radical International Movement* (London: I.B. Tauris, 2014).

[99] Shotton, *No Master High or Low*, p.34.

[100] Ibid.

early 1890s. Apparently, police found bombs and bomb-making equipment in the school's basement, and eventually, three anarchists were sentenced in the famous Walsall anarchist show trial to ten years of hard labour.

At this time, the International Modern School was founded by a small group of Jewish anarchists associated with Michel's school. The aim of the school is to "combat the anti-social environment of capitalist education as operating through the state schools and the religious institutions, and to bring up the child in the spirit of freedom."[101]The curriculum embraced the rational approach to pedagogy developed in Ferrer's school, and exposed students to a variety of subjects, including astronomy, the natural sciences, art, literature, and foreign languages. The International Modern School closed in 1928 due to insufficient funds and a shortage of teachers.

Other precursors to contemporary libertarian education include anarchist Sunday schools, libertarian adult education centres, and the free playground movement. In this particular movement, children play in areas without the use of manufactured equipment. Rather, children are given tools, nails, shovels, and other building supplies and encouraged to build, destroy, and rebuild their own playgrounds. The founders of free playgrounds argue that manufactured equipment automatically structures play itself and leaves virtually no opportunity for creativity and experimentation.

Arguably, the most significant precursor to contemporary libertarian education is A.S. Neill's Summerhill School, and, according to Shotton, "undoubtedly the most famous libertarian school in the world."[102] Founded by Neill in 1921 in Suffolk, the school promotes informal teaching, rejects teacher authority, encourages freedom of the individual child, and abides by democratic principles. For instance, children are free to come and go as they like, attend classes of their own preference, and even participate in the decision-making processes regarding school policy and procedure. Summerhill School continues to operate, and in the 1960s, numerous schools in the U.S. were established based on Neill's approach to schooling.

A particularly interesting precursor to contemporary libertarian education that is often neglected in historical literature is the development of Tolstoyan communities in Russia and eventually throughout the world. During the last three decades of his life, Tolstoy published a vast array of short stories, children's fables, religious tracts, philosophical essays, and political texts that reflect his particular philosophy of life. As I noted earlier, Tolstoy developed a Christian-anarchist perspective, and its influence on the peasant population

---

[101] Ibid., p.57.
[102] Ibid., p.77.

agitated both the State and the Church. Tolstoy's philosophy of life is based upon a primitive form of Christianity, which is an interpretation of the gospels free of any sense of superstition or irrational belief. It also promotes nonviolence, non-resistance to evil by violence, and the rejection of institutions of power and corruption that resort to physical force - government, Church, police, law courts, and the army. Tolstoy condemned private property and advocated a simple life dictated by one's own physical labour. He even expanded his philosophy to include strict vegetarianism, chastity, and abstinence from alcohol and tobacco.[103]

Tolstoy's philosophy of life influenced large groups of peasants who felt alienated and oppressed by the policies and procedures of Church and State. They formed groups and social networks, met with Tolstoy at Yasnaya Polyana, produced newspapers, founded publishing houses, and formed agricultural colonies based on Tolstoyan principles. Eventually, similar communes were established in Britain, the U.S., Finland, Japan, South Africa, Chile, and the Netherlands. These early followers became what is referred to as 'Tolstoyans'.

In his collection of memoirs of Tolstoyans in Soviet Russia, Edgerton highlights in detail how the State continually harassed, humiliated, persecuted, arrested, and tortured Tolstoyans and eventually closed their communes and sent them to years of confinement in labour camps. But, even amidst their grim reality, many Tolstoyans persisted with optimism and determination. Their memoirs are full of authentic love, joy, and hope. A key component of a Tolstoyan commune is the school. The curriculum offered students lessons on reading, writing, mathematics, history, and science but also included the teaching of moral principles and the development of character. Tolstoy's fables and short stories were often used as pedagogical tools in the classroom.

Mitya Pashchenko, an early Tolstoyan in Russia, wrote a brief historical account of schools in Tolstoyan communes. In the school's second year of operation in 1932-1933, state officials of the Department of People's Education inspected the school and insisted that the curriculum coincide with government policy. Teachers reviewed the four-year program of the People's Commissariat of Education and implemented it in a particularly creative fashion. For example, teachers agreed that the state-proposed social studies curriculum would be used in the commune "only to the extent that it

---

[103] The cover of Edgerton's book of memoirs reflects wholeheartedly the authenticity and sincerity of early Tolstoyans in Russia. It portrays a group of peasant men and women pulling a plough through a field without the use of livestock. Early Tolstoyans extended their firm belief in nonviolence to all sentient beings.

does not contradict the principles of Leo Tolstoy's teaching."[104] Similarly, states Pashchenko,

> The material for the study of animal husbandry, hunting, and the fishing industry, studied according to the program with a view to slaughtering animals for food and for technical and scientific purposes, can be studied in the Leo Tolstoy School not for its practical application but only for informational purposes, with a view to developing altruistic feelings toward animals.[105]

Religion was also taught in the school (forbidden by Soviet authorities) but presented in a way that highlighted the importance of moral virtues and liberation from superstitious beliefs. Other state-defined subject matter was used tactfully to enhance a sense of community, compassion, equality, justice, industriousness, mutual aid, peace, and humility. During its third year, students were involved in various clubs, including stenography, art, and singing. Additional reading sessions were offered in the evenings. Students would recite poetry and give speeches on Tolstoy, Pushkin, Turgenev, and other leading Russian writers and poets. Students also participated in excursions to local museums and theatres. Inevitably, the school was eventually closed by government authorities. Even so, a profound Tolstoyan sentiment spread throughout the world, and communes and schools eventually appeared in Britain, the U.S., Finland, Japan, South Africa, and Chile. Libertarian educators attracted to the works of Leo Tolstoy continue to promote his Christian-anarchist philosophy of life.

Contemporary libertarian education is influenced significantly by the ideas of Leo Tolstoy and A.S. Neill but also by the ideas posited by thinkers like Paul Goodman and Ivan Illich. Goodman is a major spokesperson for the free-school movement and the decentralisation of the urban and technological society. For Goodman, state schooling envelops a process by which students are programmed and then returned to society for the benefit of the industrial ruling elite. In his *Compulsory Miseducation* (1966), Goodman states, "a few corporations are getting the benefit of an enormous weeding out and selective process - all children are fed into the mill and everybody pays for it."[106] Goodman argues that what is needed is a movement to decentralise large, inefficient, bureaucratic school systems and replace them with small-scale

---

[104] Quoted in Edgerton, *Memoirs of Peasant Tolstoyans*, p.89.
[105] Ibid.
[106] Paul Goodman, *Compulsory Miseducation and the Community of Scholars* (New York: Vintage Books, 1966), p.57.

schools that serve the interests of individual learners. Ivan Illich's *Deschooling Society* (1971) and other works also play a significant role in contemporary libertarian education. Illich argues that large bureaucratic schools often promote a teacher-student relationship that encourages obedience, domination, passivity, and trust in the judgement of authority figures and prepare students to be effective consumers in a technologically-driven consumer society. Illich argues that the only way to combat such a powerful trend in education is to 'deschool' society by promoting institutions and forms of technology that serve the interests of the individual learner. He favours a network of what he calls 'learning webs' that would be used by students for their own interests. A learning web would be like a distinct information centre focussed on a particular body of knowledge or group of skills. If, for instance, students would like to learn about plumbing or architecture, then they would attend free public learning webs that offer knowledge and training in these particular fields. In this case, students take responsibility for their learning and are guided by trained individuals in a cooperative and creative fashion.

Neill, Goodman, Illich, and others continue to influence alternative schooling projects. For example, the Walden Center and School (1956-present) is self-identified as an arts-based, progressive, teacher-run elementary school in Berkeley. Its program is coeducational and focussed on experiential learning. Grading and standardised testing are not permitted, and the school embraces an anarchist-pacifist philosophy. Also, the 1960s witnessed the development of the free school movement, an attempt to establish alternative schools beyond the immediate influence of state and church authorities. According to Shotton, free schools "were mostly found in working class communities, and were short of money, resources, and often help. They shared, though, a common ideal, the liberation of learning."[107] Free schools reflect Illich's idea of public utilities, that is, self-contained and specialised centres of learning. Parents, students, and teachers act together in a communal fashion to promote a truly effective learning environment. The essential concept of free schools is freedom. For instance, the aim of the Liverpool Free School is,

> ... for our kids to become free people - instead of dependable consumers – aware of our environment and capable of working together to shape (or preserve) it. Our education must be a way of life instead of a training for subsequent living ... It must enable us to create community consciousness and control, and consequently a capacity for active social change.[108]

---

[107] Shotton, *No Master High or Low*, p.202.
[108] Quoted in Shotton, *No Master High or Low*, p.203.

Students are free to direct their own learning. This concept is not unique to free schools. It is a key element in most alternative forms of schooling and plays a key role in the works of the libertarian thinkers discussed above.

A Brief Note on Chomsky and Critical Pedagogy

At this point, one may wonder why I have not included a detailed discussion about the relationship between Chomsky's views on education and critical pedagogy. It would be a valid point of criticism and deserves at least a brief explanation on my part. First, I feel a detailed presentation of key ideas in critical pedagogy lies far beyond the overall scope of this manuscript. It would include a critical analysis of foundational works by Paulo Freire, Stanley Aronowitz, Ira Shor, Peter McLaren, Henry Giroux, and other thinkers, in addition to an extensive overview of recent developments related to critical pedagogy, including Marxist, postmodern, feminist, anti-racist, and environmental theories. Critical pedagogy is a continuously evolving approach to schooling and socio-political analysis, and an attempt to summarise and evaluate its various expressions would make for a manuscript in itself. Second, even though Chomsky and critical pedagogues share an array of common interests, including social class analysis, racism, ethnocentrism, imperialism, corporate hegemony, and neoliberalism; nevertheless, I argue that Chomsky's approach to schooling, especially in light of the historical figures who continue to influence his thought, is fundamentally different than the approach developed by critical pedagogues. Chomsky's political discourse is based upon Enlightenment, classical liberal, and anarchist social thought, but critical pedagogy is, to a significant degree, firmly rooted in Marxist class analysis.

Some contemporary critical pedagogues have tried to bridge the gap between Chomsky and themselves. For instance, Donaldo Macedo's *Chomsky on Miseducation* (2000) offers an analysis of schooling, similar in nature to the ideas expressed in the works of Freire and Giroux, that attempts to align itself with Chomsky's libertarian views. There are many common threads that bind Macedo and Chomsky. Macedo is an academic and has published extensively in the areas of education and linguistics, including critical pedagogy, the Creole languages, critical literacy, bilingualism, and multilingualism. Even so, Macedo's approach to schooling embraces a strong Marxist/postmodern critique that is foreign to Chomsky's approach to schooling. Clearly, Chomsky and Macedo are fellow-travellers, at least for a reasonable distance, on the road to democracy and social justice. Inevitably, Chomsky's reliance on Enlightenment, classical liberal, and anarchist thought parts company with Macedo and other critical pedagogues. A second work worth noting here is

Pierre Orelus's *On Language, Democracy, and Social Justice* (2014).[109] The work includes dialogues between the author and Chomsky over a nine-year period. In it, they discuss various socio-political issues, including democracy, authoritarianism, U.S. foreign policy, critical education, language-based discrimination, and the role of organised resistance, and relate many of the issues to the current crisis in Haiti. A particularly interesting chapter addresses the issue of linguicism, that is, the use of a dominant language as a form of discrimination against speakers of subjugated languages. Clearly, Orelus's work relates well to Chomsky's overall political analysis of U.S. domestic and foreign policy, and his reflections as an applied linguist are especially enlightening. Nevertheless, when I read the dialogues, I feel that Chomsky's responses to Orelus's questions are, in many respects, a reiteration of ideas included in Otero's work mentioned above. Chomsky's fundamental political view has remained consistent throughout most of his life, and any recent discussion about political issues, such as those in Orelus's work, is merely a reiteration of earlier views and its applicability to recent socio-political events. Therefore, a detailed analysis of Orelus's work would merely reflect what I have already discussed in earlier chapters. A third interesting connection between Chomsky and critical pedagogy is James Kirylo's *A Critical Pedagogy of Resistance* (2013).[110] In this work, Kirylo presents a fine overview of key thinkers in what he believes to be the critical pedagogy tradition, including Paulo Freire, Michael Apple, Henry Giroux, Stanley Aronowitz, bell hooks, Donaldo Macedo, Ira Shor, and Peter McLaren. Interestingly, included in his list are thinkers who are not often associated with critical pedagogy but are more frequently mentioned in libertarian and alternative schooling literature. Chomsky is included here, along with philosopher John Dewey, Catholic theologian Ignacio Ellacuria, de-schooler Ivan Illich, and proponents of alternative schools, such as Jonathan Kozol and Maria Montessori. Needless to say, even though the latter group of thinkers supports a critical approach to schooling; nevertheless, it is inaccurate to represent them as part of the critical pedagogy tradition. They rarely, if ever, rely on a strictly Marxist social class analysis, and anything like a postmodern critique of society would be completely foreign to their overall socio-political analysis. A fourth effort to unite Chomsky and critical pedagogy is found in an online presentation entitled "Pedagogy of the Oppressed: Noam Chomsky, Howard Gardner, and Bruno della Chiesa". In this presentation, Chomsky highlights the importance of Freire's contribution to schooling, especially his

---

[109] Pierre W. Orelus, *On Language, Democracy, and Social Justice: Noam Chomsky's Critical Intervention* (New York: Peter Lang Publishing, Inc., 2014).
[110] James Kirylo, *A Critical Pedagogy of Resistance: 34 Pedagogues We Need to Know* (Boston: Brill Publishers, 2013).

emphasis on the concept of conscientization, and also the contrast between banking education and problem-posing education. Chomsky relates the Brazilian pedagogue's ideas to earlier expressions of thought found in the Enlightenment, classical liberalism, and libertarianism/anarchism.[111] Once again, Chomsky moves beyond the boundaries traditionally defined by Freire and other critical pedagogues and embraces thinkers not normally associated with this particular tradition.

It is fair to say that Chomsky has a lot in common with critical pedagogy, but this, in itself, does not justify identifying him as a representative of the critical pedagogical tradition. It is interesting to note that when I randomly selected 10 works that I felt represented the critical pedagogical tradition and analysed their notes and bibliographies, Macedo alone made extensive references in his work to Chomsky's ideas.[112] All but two of the remaining nine key works made no reference at all to Chomsky's ideas, and the other two works each made one reference. Interestingly, only one work made a reference to Bakunin or the anarchist tradition, a tradition found throughout Chomsky's political discourse. Clearly, Chomsky is not a representative figure of critical pedagogy.

I identify Chomsky as a critical educator in the sense that he encourages critical thought and freedom of expression in the classroom, but he is not a critical pedagogue. It's important to recall that Chomsky's approach to effective teaching and learning is rooted in a tradition that extends far beyond the boundaries defined historically by critical pedagogy.

The understanding of education expressed by Chomsky and other libertarian, progressive, and anarchist educators mentioned above is shared by other educators in the strictly libertarian tradition. This tradition, rooted in

---

[111] It is worth noting here that Freire's work is also heavily dependent on Marxist discourse and Catholic social teachings.

[112] Samuel Bowles and Herbert Gintis, *Democracy & Capitalism: Property, Community, and the Contradictions of Modern Social Thought* (New York: Basic Books, 1986); *Schooling in Capitalist America: Educational Reform and the Contradictions of Economic Life* (New York: Basic Books, 1987); Stanley Aronowitz and Henry Giroux, *Education Under Siege: The Conservative, Liberal, and Radical Debate Over Schooling* (Bergin & Garvey Publishers, 1985); Ira Shor, *Critical Teaching and Everyday Life* (Boston: South End Press, 1980); Shor (ed), *Freire for the Classroom: A Sourcebook for Liberatory Teaching* (Boynton/Cook Publishers, 1987); Michael Apple, *Ideology and Curriculum* (New York: Routledge, 1979); Donaldo Macedo, *Literacies of Power: What Americans Are Not Allowed to Know* (Boulder: Westview Press, 1994); Peter McLaren and Peter Leonard, *Paulo Freire: A Critical Encounter* (New York: Routledge, 1993); Marc Pruyn and Luis Huerta-Charles (eds.), *Teaching Peter McLaren: Paths of Dissent* (New York: Peter Lang Publishing, 2005); Peter McLaren, *Pedagogia, Identidad y Poder: Los Educadores Frente al Multiculturalismo* (Santa Fe: Homo Sapiens Ediciones, 2003).

eighteenth-century rationalism, nineteenth-century romanticism, classical liberalism, non-authoritarian Marxism, and classical anarchism, professes a common set of beliefs and practices. Freedom of expression and creative thought are the cornerstones of libertarian education. It is accepted unconditionally within this particular educational tradition and challenges current educational practices that promote a rigid hierarchy of power, teacher authority figures, formal discipline, and strict regulations. Students are invited to freely explore ideas and concepts without the fear of punishment, and develop their sense of authenticity and spontaneity. In addition, contemporary schooling tends to treat education as a preparation for life, but libertarian educators regard education as life itself. Education, in this sense, is not a means to an end (say, employment), but is an end in itself. Most importantly, libertarian educators treat students with decency and respect, and their rights as human beings are protected at all costs. Paul Avrich suggests, "Libertarians were perhaps the first educational theorists to defend the rights of children, whom they regarded as fundamentally equal to adults, with the same need for freedom and dignity."[113] The rights of children include the right to a proper education, one that, according to William Godwin, stimulates creative thought and a critical attitude towards authority. According to Avrich, Godwin "emancipated the child from the shackles of authority and placed him at the center of the learning process."[114] Godwin, like many anarchists after him, values the relationship between learning and action. Words alone can easily become meaningless empty rhetoric, but if they are applied in a concrete setting, then they become useful. John Dewey, as I noted earlier, adopts a similar position, and it is also a staple in Kropotkin's approach to education. In his *Fields, Factories and Workshops* (1898), Kropotkin proposes what he calls "integral education," that is, a system of education that combines intellectual and manual work. Schools of this nature provide students with "a thorough knowledge of science - such a knowledge as might enable them to be useful workers in science - and, at the same time, to give them a general knowledge of what constitutes the basis of technical training, and such a skill in some special trade as would enable each of them to take his or her place in the grand world of the manual production of wealth."[115] The concept of integral education is rooted in a long tradition of libertarian socialist pedagogical theory. Its original idea was formulated by the French socialist Charles Fourier and subsequently adopted by Pierre-Joseph Proudhon, Bakunin, Kropotkin, and other anarchist theorists. Its essence, argues Kropotkin, is to

---

[113] Avrich, *Modern School Movement*, p.12.
[114] Ibid., p.10.
[115] Peter Kropotkin, *Fields, Factories and Workshops* (Montreal: Black Rose Books, 1994), p.168.

encourage students to pursue a "sincere longing for truth, to like what is beautiful, both as to form and contents, ... and thus to feel ... at unison with the rest of humanity.[116]

Clearly, the views of Kropotkin, Godwin, and other libertarian and anarchist thinkers reflect, at least to a degree, the sentiments expressed earlier by Chomsky and the founders of alternative schools. Essentially, they are rooted in the same soil, and their criticisms and visions of education are quite similar. The common thread which unites them is the emphasis placed on freedom of expression and creative thought in education. Chomsky, for instance, argues that a creative impulse and individual freedom of expression are essential in order to challenge a prevalent, corporate-defined social order. In this sense, freedom and creativity are the twin pillars of a subversive approach to education. For Thoreau, in his Concord Academy, the primary purpose of education is the development of inner freedom, and this is accomplished, in part, by promoting a harmonious balance between experiential learning and the study of a classical curriculum. Dewey, in his Laboratory School, emphasises the importance of freedom in education, the essential role played by experiential learning in an effective pedagogy, and the role played by schools in a democratic society. In Tolstoy's Yasnaya Polyana school, he regards individual freedom as an important element in education, supports a student-based learning which embraces creativity and critical inquiry, and promotes a pedagogy based upon the gospel teachings of love for one's neighbour and non-violence forms of social change. In Russell's Beacon Hill School, he promotes freedom and creative impulses, open-mindedness, and a sense of intellectual adventure. He recognises the role played by reverence in a school setting, and in order to prevent absolute chaos in the classroom and bullying in the playground, he promotes freedom with restrictions. In Ferrer's anarchist Escuela Moderna, there appears to be, at least to a modest degree, an element of propaganda in his overall approach to education. Even though he promotes the importance of individual freedom, creative thinking, and a modern scientific approach to learning; nevertheless, as a result of the prevalent authoritarian influence of both the State and the Roman Catholic Church in Spain at that time, one gets the sense that he uses his school curriculum to propagate his personal anti-State, anti-religious, and anti-dogmatic sentiments. As Suissa states, "In short, Ferrer saw his school as an embryo of the future, anarchist society."[117] Even so, he is reacting to the signs of the times, commits himself wholeheartedly to his vision of education, and pays the ultimate price for it.

---

[116] Ibid., p.173.
[117] Suissa, *Anarchism and Education*, p.81.

Clearly, individual freedom of expression and creativity, as two elements of human nature, play a significant role in earlier attempts to establish and operate libertarian and progressive schools. Inevitably, schools of this sort become the target of assault by powerful forces in society because, in the long run, they are a direct threat to wealth and power.

Critics regard libertarian approaches to education with a high degree of scepticism. They argue that schools that promote freedom inevitably lead to chaos. Chomsky would agree that, in part, the critics are correct. An experienced classroom teacher knows that students often take advantage of inexperienced teachers who lack classroom management skills. It is imperative that teachers maintain control in the classroom. Russell learned firsthand that absolute freedom in the classroom leads to tyranny of the strong over the weak. For Russell, a degree of freedom is permissible, but absolute freedom leads to disaster. The freedom promoted by Chomsky and other libertarian thinkers is, in most cases, related to intellectual freedom. Students should be granted the absolute freedom to explore ideas in a creative fashion. Even so, as I will highlight shortly, there are times when students should also be granted the freedom to move beyond ideas to forms of action for social change. Clearly, critics are vehemently against this sort of freedom because it undermines their vision of schools as institutions that promote authoritarian control, manipulation, and power, characteristics which are easily adaptable to an obedient work environment.

In the next chapter, I use the findings discussed above and relevant ideas in earlier chapters to develop a Chomskyan approach to pedagogy. It is based upon Chomsky's understanding of human nature and also his liberatory approach to education. It is fair to say that the following chapter moves from an emphasis on theory to a concentration on practical forms of teaching and learning. Nevertheless, the practical elements in the pedagogy to follow are a product of the theoretical elements discussed earlier in the manuscript.

Chapter 6

A Chomskyan Approach to Pedagogy

What is a student but a lover courting a fickle mistress
who ever eludes his grasp?

Sir William Osler, The Student Life

In this chapter, I present four moments of a Chomskyan approach to pedagogy and show how they can be applied in a concrete classroom setting. The pedagogy itself is motivated by Chomsky's understanding of human nature and education, but before I consider it in detail, it is important to review some of the key ideas cited in earlier chapters. This will provide me with a solid foundation upon which to build a dynamic pedagogy. In light of what has been discussed earlier, one can safely assume that any approach to teaching and learning is based upon a concept of what it means to be human. In addition, if one embraces Chomsky's approach to the study of human nature, then one can conclude that the promotion of freedom and creativity in the classroom is an absolutely essential component of an effective pedagogy. How does one promote freedom and creativity? What are the key components of an overall learning environment that promote a free and creative classroom environment? The following list identifies some of the important components, and its extensive nature suggests that a dynamic classroom embodies many variables interacting in a dynamic fashion. It is the responsibility of the classroom teacher to encourage, at all times, the following components:

- Free inquiry and independent thought

- Resist conformity and acquiescence

- Non-hierarchical, non-competitive, anti-authoritarian learning environment

- Reasoning and problem-solving skills

- Freedom of thought and expression

- Open-mindedness

- Socio-political awareness

- Cooperation and solidarity

- Experiential learning

- Reverence

- Self-worth

- Scientific method

- Self-directed and collaborative learning

- Intellectual and moral growth

- Creative impulses

- Curiosity

- Tolerance for ambiguity

A teaching and learning environment that incorporates these components is strictly against conformity and acquiescence. It is also important to recognise that students are not empty vessels to be filled with knowledge; rather, they are to be treated with reverence and encouraged to unfold their latent intellectual and moral powers. They should be invited to critically engage in their socio-political reality and seek means to create a better world. Students are not blank slates but inquiring subjects who enter the classroom with thoughts and emotions that are a product of their genetic inheritance and immediate environment. Language is innate and a uniquely human trait, and it implies that students are, by their very nature, creative beings. It is not quite so simple for a teacher to establish a teaching and learning environment that promotes freedom and creativity in the classroom. It involves the promotion and intricate monitoring of a dynamic relationship between various key components.

It is necessary at the outset to raise for consideration a few preliminary comments on the role of the teacher. Granted, teachers are expected to follow a standard curriculum, and I noted earlier that alternative education is often a reaction against government-defined curriculum and its infringement on personal freedom, but, in some respects, the curriculum is merely a guide to the bare minimum knowledge to be taught in the classroom. In many cases, there is nothing to prevent a teacher from encouraging students to transcend the boundaries set by curriculum guidelines and explore in a creative fashion more advanced concepts and ideas. Fundamentally, when the door is closed, what happens in the classroom is determined almost entirely by the teacher. The teacher sets the tone and overall dynamics in the classroom, and everything else becomes secondary. In essence, unless teachers go beyond the boundaries of teacher professionalism, there is nothing to prevent them from moving far beyond the set curriculum with their students, engaging them in creative and critical thought, and expanding their intellectual horizons. Therefore, before I develop a pedagogy that fosters freedom and creativity, it is important to take a closer look at the qualities of an effective teacher.

Qualities of an Effective Teacher

It may sound strange to say, but a teacher is an artist. Granted, effective teaching often relies on findings in science, especially in psychology and biology, but, in itself, teaching is an art. Gilbert Highet, a twentieth-century classicist at Columbia University and a well-respected and popular teacher in his own right, wrote an entire book on teaching as an art. He states,

> I believe that teaching is an art, not a science. It seems to me very dangerous to apply the aims and methods of science to human beings as individuals ... a "scientific" relationship between human beings is bound to be inadequate and perhaps distorted ... Teaching involves emotions, which cannot be systematically appraised and employed, and human values, which are quite outside the grasp of science. A "scientifically" brought-up child would be a pitiable monster ... "Scientific" teaching, even of scientific subjects, will be inadequate as long as both teachers and pupils are human beings. Teaching ... is like painting a picture or making a piece of music.[1]

At a minimum level, teachers should respect students and appreciate their attempts to master the curriculum. If the respect is not there, then the teacher should be elsewhere. Respect underlies the classroom dynamics, establishes a positive tone, and often prevents student misbehaviour or resistance to learning. Students are quick to detect a teacher who does not want to be with them or does not value the material being taught, and they can be merciless in the ways they express their disapproval. Students can tolerate authority figures, and can even tolerate closed-mindedness on the part of a teacher, but they cannot tolerate insincerity and hypocrisy. They rebel against an adult who portrays "ingrained conceit, calculated cruelty, deep-rooted cowardice, slobbering greed, vulgar self-satisfaction, [and] puffy laziness of mind and body."[2] Besides, teaching is challenging enough on a good day, but if a teacher actually dislikes the company of students, then, as Highet notes, "she (sic) will become like the horse harnessed to the millstone, plodding round and round

---

[1] Gilbert Highet, *The Art of Teaching* (New York: Vintage Books, 1977), pp.vii-viii.
[2] Ibid., p.25.

the same circle, without hope, day after day."[3] Teaching does not come with a magic wand - there is no royal road to success in the classroom. Teachers cannot assume that, with a predefined model of teaching in their pocket, they will automatically succeed in the classroom. Put the model away, at least for a while, and get to know the students. Try to understand the way they see the world, appreciate their dreams, and be sensitive to their needs. This may take some time to establish, but once it takes root, the sky's the limit. Students travel far and wide with a well-respected teacher; they are eager to explore ideas, often far beyond the set curriculum, in a creative and enthusiastic fashion and embrace an authentic love of learning.

Therefore, it is important that I revisit Highet's work and highlight some of the qualities of a truly effective teacher. He highlights qualities of effective teaching that are often neglected in critical pedagogical discourse. In part, critical pedagogues do not discuss these essential qualities because the qualities themselves lack a strictly political overtone, and in part because they focus primarily on the individual teacher rather than on the overall political structure of the teaching profession. Nevertheless, the elements raised by Highet determine, to a significant degree, the overall efficacy of the teaching and learning process. I should clarify, at this point, what I mean by the expressions 'effective teacher' and 'ineffective teacher'. They are often used ambiguously in educational discourse. When I refer to effective teachers, I mean teachers who contribute in a positive fashion to the liberatory and creative aspects of human nature. Contrarily, ineffective teachers stifle creative thinking, restrict individual freedom of expression, and often treat students in a dehumanising way.

In some respects, it's easier to identify the qualities of an ineffective teacher than those of an effective teacher. Teachers generally know what they should not do in the classroom because, inevitably, strident and disgruntled students tend to respond in creative ways. But, it is sometimes difficult to identify what actually happens in a classroom that results in a creative and highly dynamic learning experience. In part, this is because, fundamentally, teaching is an art of human interaction. It is like trying to identify what makes a good parent, friend, or spouse. Human interactions can be complicated and often involve a dynamic relationship between numerous social, political, economic, and psychological factors. These factors impact the lives of students and influence the way they respond in a classroom setting. The outcome is rarely predictable but often extremely rewarding. Even so, there are a few qualities that common sense dictates should be part and parcel of an effective teacher.

---

[3] Ibid., p.19.

Highet was a highly gifted classroom teacher, and his gifts are evident in his contemporary classic, *The Art of Teaching* (1950). He considers various facets of teaching, but the value of Highet's work lies in his discussion about the important qualities of an effective teacher.[4] This is where Highet shines. Only a truly great teacher with a vast amount of teaching experience could write about teachers in such an insightful manner.

The first quality of an effective teacher is the possession of a sound knowledge of the subject matter. This may sound like an obvious fact, but in reality, teachers tend to master, at best, the set curriculum but lack an understanding of the broader nature of the subject - its history, recent developments and current applications. In 1931, Bertrand Russell stated in a rather ironic fashion, "there is much to be said for the view that those concerned in education should be competent to teach it."[5] Teachers should be continual learners in their particular field of study and share with students an authentic love of the subject. They are expected to keep abreast of recent developments, at least at a rudimentary level, and be prepared to encourage students to expand their intellectual and moral horizons. Highest states,

> A limited field of material stirs very few imaginations. It can be learnt off by heart but seldom creatively understood and never loved. A subject that carries the mind out in limitless journeys will, if it is well taught, make the learner eager to master all the preliminary essentials and press on.[6]

Students can detect a teacher who lacks an authentic interest in or knowledge of the subject matter and also someone who embraces an authentic love of learning and an inquisitive embrace of the subject matter. An effective teacher can move students beyond the boundaries set by the curriculum, encourage them to think creatively and inspire them to reach their full potential as learners. For Highet, ineffective teachers disregard these goals and often incite within students a dislike of the subject matter. Teachers of this sort are common in schools. Frequently, teachers show up to work, punch in like factory workers, and go through the motions. Over the years, they have done nothing more than the bare minimum required to justify a salary and a pension. Highet states,

---

[4] It should be noted that in Highet's *The Art of Teaching*, he uses the expressions "good teachers" and "bad teachers." I prefer to distance myself from the clear moral implications of such expressions, and replace them with "effective teachers" and "ineffective teachers."
[5] Bertrand Russell, *Mortals and Others: American Essays 1931-1935* (London: Routledge, 2009), p.24.
[6] Highet, *Art of Teaching*, p.14.

Sounds ridiculous, doesn't it? But there are millions of people doing the same thing every day all over the world. They have a job they hate, they perform it grudgingly and inefficiently, they make it more difficult for themselves and for everybody associated with them ... it is terribly important when a teacher, whose job is to awaken young minds to a valuable subject, shows his (sic) pupils by every gesture, by every intonation of his voice (and remember, young people notice such things very quickly and sensitively), that he thinks the subject is not worthwhile learning; and that learning anything whatever is a waste of time.[7]

The second quality of an effective teacher is an authentic love of the subject. It is virtually impossible for teachers to continuously learn about new developments in a subject area if they lack a passion for the subject itself. Teaching, in this case, becomes routine, a drudgery, a penance, a Sisyphus in disguise. Passion is the fuel that ignites within students a true love of learning. It motivates them to want to know, to expand their intellectual and moral horizons, and to become authentic human beings. Highet states,

> Think how astonished you would be if your doctor told you that personally he (sic) really cared nothing about the art of healing, that he never read the medical journals and paid no attention to new treatments for common complaints, that apart from making a living he thought it completely unimportant whether his patients were sick or sound, and that his real interest was mountain-climbing. You would change your doctor. But the young cannot change their teachers ... They have sometimes to submit to being treated by doctors of the mind, who seem to believe the treatment useless and the patient worthless. No wonder they often distrust education.[8]

Teachers who actually enjoy the subject matter project that sense of enthusiasm in the classroom. Students become motivated to learn. Classroom misbehaviour is virtually nonexistent in a classroom full of inquiring minds. An authentic love of learning directs the overall dynamics in the classroom. Students easily detect an authentic teacher and are willing to travel far and wide to meet the teacher's expectations. But, a teacher who lacks a love of the subject but expects it from students is intolerable. As Highet states, "For the

---

[7] Ibid., pp.17-18.
[8] Ibid., p.19.

young do not demand omniscience. They know it is unattainable. They do demand sincerity."[9]

The third quality of an effective teacher is to actually like being with students. Students can easily detect if their presence is not appreciated by the teacher, and they have highly creative ways to display their discontent. We can extend Highet's position and argue that it's imperative that teachers spend as much time as possible with groups of students outside the classroom. This might include spending free time walking through the hallways and meeting casually with students, sitting with them in the school's cafeteria, chatting with them in the school parking lot, or spending time with them at a school sports event - any place where students feel comfortable, where their guards are down, formalities are put to rest, and it's possible for a teacher to appreciate students' rich and diverse characters. The trusting and respectful relationship developed outside the classroom is easily transferred into a dynamic teaching and learning environment in a classroom setting. As Highet states, "If you do not enjoy the prospect of facing the young in large groups, if you would always prefer working in a laboratory or reading in a library, you will never be a good teacher."[10]

The fourth quality of an effective teacher is to spend time getting to know the students. In part, this can be accomplished through the third quality, by spending time with groups of students in alternative settings, but it can also be done in a formal classroom setting. In either case, teachers must realise that students are unlike adults. They portray rather unique and somewhat peculiar patterns of thought and behaviour, but good teachers know that this is merely a phase of human development. To know students means to know their inner being - their wants, desires, future dreams, and present concerns. It means to be comfortable walking in their shoes, to re-awaken youthful dreams and aspirations, and to treat students with a degree of reverence.

These four qualities of an effective teacher play an absolutely crucial role in the overall efficacy of a classroom dynamic. A teacher's knowledge and love of the subject matter are highly contagious in the classroom. Students sense it and are motivated to explore the various facets of the subject in a creative manner. In addition, students can detect if they are respected and appreciated by the teacher. If a teacher truly respects students and enjoys spending time with them, then students will, as a response, travel far beyond the norm and exceed standard curriculum expectations. It is quite possible for one to supplement Highet's qualities with a consideration of other factors, but in either case, it is apparent that his insights are the product of a rich and

---

[9] Ibid., p.20.
[10] Ibid., p.27.

successful teaching career. One does not learn about such qualities in either teacher education programmes or standard pedagogical textbooks; rather, they are the product of years of successful teaching experiences. Even so, there is one additional quality of an effective teacher that Highet does not mention, a quality that, in many respects, determines the overall effectiveness and dynamics of a teaching and learning environment. Its importance is rarely mentioned in educational discourse, so it is worth spending some time here exploring it in detail.

Earlier, it was noted that reverence is a forgotten virtue, especially in education. Russell highlights the important role played by reverence in schools, and, in fact, one may argue that, in many ways, reverence for the learner is the cornerstone of effective teaching. It is true that teachers often refer to the importance in effective pedagogy of actually liking students and having a cordial relationship with them. In itself, cordiality is an important quality, and Highet makes reference to it in his comments regarding an effective teacher. But, reverence is far more profound than cordiality because, even though a cordial teacher treats students with a degree of affection, kindness, and respect, a reverential teacher regards students with absolute awe. That is, students envelop a degree of sacredness in their inner being, in their soul, if I may use that word - even though reverence is not necessarily overtly religious in its sentiment. It is true that religions often acknowledge the importance of a reverential attitude toward the divine, but reverence can also adopt a purely secular interpretation.

Reverence is a fundamental sense that there is more to life than the merely tangible and quantifiable, that there is a mysterious element to reality that cannot be explained through empiricism or reason. Awe is what is left over after one has addressed all the questions; it is a sense that there is something more to the question, that one somehow missed something that is beyond one's grasp. It is what Rudolf Otto calls the 'numinous', that is, the fascinating and awesome mystery of life itself.[11] The word 'numinous' is based on the Latin word *numen,* or divine power. For Otto, numinosity leads naturally to a belief in God, but one can also interpret it to mean that there is a mysterious dimension to human existence.

There is a profound difference between respect and reverence. Teachers highlight the importance of respect and often use it as a cheap and easy solution to classroom management, but reverence is nowhere to be found. Respect follows automatically from reverence, but respect itself by no means

---

[11] Rudolf Otto, *The Idea of the Holy: An Inquiry into the Non-Rational Factor in the Idea of the Divine and Its Relation to the Rational* (London: Oxford University Press, 1950). Originally published in German in 1917 and first published by OUP in 1923.

assures a reverential approach to life. Reverence embraces a continuous state of awe that there is something larger than life and that, fundamentally, life is full of mystery. A reverent teacher realises that the life of a student is precious and should not be taken for granted. Albert Schweitzer broadens the understanding of reverence in his expression 'reverence for life', and states,

> A man (sic) is truly ethical only when he obeys the compulsion to help all life which he is able to assist, and shrinks from injuring anything that lives. He does not ask how far this or that life deserves one's sympathy as being valuable, nor, beyond that, whether and to what degree it is capable of feeling. Life as such is sacred to him.[12]

A reverent teacher does not act like an omniscient and omnipotent God. As Paul Woodruff states,

> Reverence in the classroom calls for a sense of awe in the face of the truth and a recognition by teachers and students of their places in the order of learning ... Teachers must not pretend to omniscience, and from this it follows that they must be open to the possibility of learning something from their students.[13]

The importance of reciprocal learning between teacher and students is discussed at length by Paulo Freire and other critical pedagogues. It suggests that teachers and students can learn from each other and that no one person holds a monopoly on human knowledge. Reverence teaches us that life is finite and precious and that we should cherish it, even with all its blemishes. It highlights one's fallibility and the importance of regarding others as fellow-travellers in life, as minute but significant equals in a vast universe. As Woodruff states,

> Every honest scholar knows that he (sic) too will die, that future generations will know more than he, and that someone will sooner or later refute him on some point or another. Knowing this - really knowing it in a way that enables you to feel respect for the faltering efforts of beginners in the field - is reverence.[14]

---

[12] Albert Schweitzer, *The Philosophy of Civilization* (New York: Prometheus Books, 1987), p.310.

[13] Paul Woodruff, *Reverence: Renewing a Forgotten Virtue* (New York: Oxford University Press, 2001), p.191.

[14] Ibid., p.195.

It is true that, in many respects, reverence is a forgotten virtue, but it is not dead. In a speech to the leaders of the Greeks, Heracles stated, "Reverence is not subject to the death of men; they live, they die, but reverence shall not perish." In the pedagogy to follow, reverence, in many respects, acts like a rudder on a boat. It provides overall direction to the teaching and learning environment.

Traditional and Modern Approaches to Education

Speaking very broadly, one commonly finds in schools two general approaches to education: traditional and modern. By no means are these two approaches mutually exclusive. In fact, teachers often rely on elements of the two approaches, but for simplicity's sake, I consider each approach to education as a distinct approach. I need to be careful when I use the terms 'tradition' and 'traditional' *approaches*. A tradition involves the transmission of customs, beliefs, practices, and general worldviews from generation to generation. Tradition is an important part of how people see themselves and relate to others. It is rich and diverse and, as I will highlight later, plays a key role in a Chomskyan approach to pedagogy. A traditional approach to education is quite different. Even though it relies upon a traditional body of knowledge, a traditional approach is a process, or a way of delivering knowledge, that often incorporates assumptions and practices that contradict the essence of what it means to be human. A traditional approach to education treats knowledge as static and never-changing. Knowledge, from this perspective, is something that was established in the past and is passed on from one generation to another. The primary purpose of teaching, in this case, is to pour knowledge into the empty minds of students. Thus, teaching is a process similar to filling a vessel, or what Freire calls 'banking education'. Its primary focus is on the dispersion of unchanging and universal knowledge. Content is often presented in a monotonous, authoritarian, and didactic fashion. There is little room for creative thinking or critical dialogue; the teacher merely delivers knowledge, and students receive it in an acquiescent fashion. Frederick Crowe asks a pertinent question.

> Should education be a kind of banking procedure in which the teacher hands over parcels of information that the pupil duly stores in the safety-deposit box of the mind, and draws out as occasion demands, especially the occasion of examinations? Or should education be a freely developing evolution of inner resources, where the pupil is put in a sandbox and left to grow in self-realization with the expectation that

he or she will advance steadily from a sandbox to, say, a laboratory for nuclear physics?[15]

Interestingly, for better or for worse, teachers often resort to a traditional approach because of its controlling effect on classroom behaviour. Over-emphasis on rote memory promotes an artificial sense of achievement and productivity in the classroom. Students, cooperative and disruptive alike, are so occupied with copying notes that they have few opportunities to express their sense of boredom, restlessness, and frustration.

Even so, a traditional approach to education is problematic in a few ways. First, it promotes passivity in the classroom - an unquestioning acceptance of the status quo. This approach discourages students from asking critical questions and exploring new ideas. Second, underlying the traditional approach is a strong undercurrent of indoctrination. It often embodies a vision of the world that promotes the interests of powerful groups in society. Third, for both teachers and students alike, a traditional approach is terribly boring to endure. Eyes wander from the board to the clock, anxiously anticipating the end of such drudgery. And when the bell rings, both teacher and students are like horses who can smell the barn. They bolt from their seats, not to be seen again until the next day of drudgery.

In contrast to indoctrination, rote memory, and boredom, a modern approach focuses on the relationship between course content and the life experiences of students. Their questions and concerns, hopes and aspirations, act as a base upon which they explore reality. Teachers are not authoritarian master figures; rather, they lead or guide the teaching and learning process. As the term *educere* suggests, education involves a process of leading forth, bringing out, and eliciting. Its focus is on the development of what Russell refers to as "the inner creative impulse" of students.[16]

It is worth noting here that Canadian theologian Bernard Lonergan argues that experience is an absolutely essential component in the process of knowing. Without experience, students are unable to acquire higher levels of thinking, including understanding and judgement. The modern approach relates course material to concrete life experiences. It permits students to become critically engaged in their own socio-political reality rather than being part of a predetermined, carefully selected reality that is often unrelated to their particular life experiences. Also, this approach to teaching encourages classroom participation. It uses group work, presentations, debates, plays,

---

[15] Frederick Crowe, *Old Things and New: A Strategy for Education* (Atlanta: Scholars Press, 1985), pp.ix-x.
[16] Bertrand Russell, *Unpopular Essays* (New York: Routledge, 2009), p.119.

and other dynamic and creative forms of classroom interaction to encourage students to participate actively in the learning process.

Nevertheless, even though specific features of modern education are commonly embraced by both libertarian and progressive educators, there are a few drawbacks to this particular approach to teaching and learning. First, the very nature of experiential learning implies an emphasis on classroom dialogue, and its control can be rather challenging for a teacher. Noise levels often far exceed the norm, and group discussions can sometimes take radical contextual turns. Increased noise levels are often regarded by neighbouring colleagues as being disruptive. Also, classroom dialogue can lead to some interesting discussions, but it can often be a challenge for teachers to keep the dialogue focused and moving in the right direction. Second, for teachers, this approach requires a high level of energy and effective classroom management skills. To lead group discussions with many enthusiastic, energetic, and highly vocal students is often tiring work. Third, amidst all the dialogue in the classroom, students sometimes express difficulty identifying the relevance of the discussion at hand to the overall focus of the lesson. It requires a skilful teacher to constantly relate classroom discussion to the content of the lesson. Fourth, a dialogical approach is not for everyone. The discussions can often be dominated by a few loud and opinionated students. The more reserved students may, at least initially, feel rather intimidated by the overall classroom dynamic. Fifth, there is a more practical concern associated with classroom discussion, especially if a teacher is sharing a classroom with other teachers during the school day. Normally, a dialogical approach requires a reconfiguration of the classroom chairs and desks into a semi-circular or circular formation. If other teachers who share the classroom during the day resort to more traditional approaches to teaching, then it's most likely they will want the desks in rows. Therefore, out of professional courtesy, it is expected that chairs and desks are rearranged, once again, at the end of the period. This often involves additional noise that is not received well by colleagues in nearby classrooms.

Four Moments of a Pedagogy

With these preparatory comments in mind, I will begin to develop a Chomskyan approach to pedagogy. It is important to clarify what exactly is meant by the word 'pedagogy'. Historically, the word has its roots in the Greek word *paidagogos*, meaning a slave who escorts boys to school, but by the fourteenth century, the word was used to mean a schoolmaster or teacher of children. At this time, pedagogy adopted a meaning that is used commonly today, that is, the profession (or art) of teaching and learning.

The primary aim of a Chomskyan approach to pedagogy is to foster a greater sense of freedom and creativity in the classroom. I use the term 'freedom' to mean both freedom to do something and freedom from something. That is, students are granted the freedom to express themselves in an articulate and respectful manner in the classroom and also encouraged to freely explore ideas that may extend far beyond the boundaries set by the standard curriculum - to run with ideas, so to speak. But, freedom is also freedom from something. An effective and dynamic teaching and learning environment should emancipate students from authoritarian forms of classroom management, domination, and marginalisation, and enable them to become truly human. As I noted earlier, the term 'creativity' means bringing new ideas into being, merging apparently conflicting and often ambiguous ideas and concepts, challenging presuppositions, and being receptive to new concepts and experiences. The enhancement of creative thought in the classroom also includes independent learning, self-evaluation, a rich and varied learning environment, openness to new and challenging ideas, tolerance for ambiguity, curiosity, persistence, and determination. A pedagogy that promotes freedom and creativity is firmly rooted in Chomsky's understanding of what it means to be human.

The pedagogy to follow is the product of three decades of personal teaching experience. It is designed for implementation in a high school setting, but its inherent flexibility suggests that it is easily adaptable to and effective in other teaching environments. The four pedagogical moments are interrelated and dependent upon one another. Each moment is connected to or flows into every other moment. They are not static parts of a whole, such that teaching moves systematically from one part to another, and when the last part has been addressed, the work is complete. Effective teaching does not work that way. The moments are dynamic, that is, they are interdependent and ever-changing within a particular context of teaching and learning. For Lonergan, dynamism between moments occurs "where each operation is related to the others, where the set of relations forms a pattern, where the pattern is described as the right way of doing the job, where operations in accord with the pattern may be repeated indefinitely, and where the fruits of such repetition are not repetition, but cumulative and progressive."[17]

The term 'moment' is used, rather than 'component', 'step', or 'element', because the latter three commonly used terms suggest a static quality that works against the overall nature of effective pedagogy. A moment reflects a period of time that is related dynamically to what came before and what lies ahead. Each moment of the pedagogy to follow has its own particular features,

---

[17] Bernard Lonergan, *Method in Theology* (Minnesota: Seabury Press, 1979), p.4.

embraces certain ideas, and proposes unique activities, but the features, ideas, and activities are designed with the sole purpose of promoting freedom of thought and expression and enhancing the creative impulses of learners.

1. Thematic Dialogue

The first moment of a Chomskyan approach to pedagogy is thematic dialogue. Through this moment students are introduced to a process of communal critiquing of and grappling with life experiences, social reality, traditions, customs, and values. Its purpose is to foster a passion to explore rationally and question critically their lives and the parameters and social structures that define them. It is rooted in the life experiences of the students themselves.

Dialogue is much more than daily discourse. It is not simply talking back and forth *at* each other; rather, it involves a dynamic interplay of numerous cognitive traits in communion with others: sharing and listening, agreeing and disagreeing, affirming and confronting, understanding, and judging. Freire explains what dialogue does not imply.

> dialogue cannot be reduced to the act of one person's "depositing" ideas into another, nor can it become a simple exchange of ideas to be "consumed" by the discussants. Nor yet is it a holistic, polemical argument between men (sic) who are committed neither to the naming of the world, nor to the search for truth ... It is an act of creation; it must not serve as a crafty instrument for the domination of one man (sic) by another.[18]

Dialogue permits students to express their sentiments, attitudes, intuitions, perceptions, understandings, and assessments about a particular theme. They learn to perceive themselves as part of a complex socio-political process and, at times, recognise their capacities as agents of social change. Students identify contradictions between the way life is and the way life should be and develop what Edmund Sullivan calls a "reciprocity of perspectives", that is, an "emphatic seeing from the stance of the other."[19]According to Aronowitz and Giroux, students in thematic dialogue develop "voices forged in opposition" to the exploitative institutions in society. They seek ways to "reclaim their own memories, stories, and histories."[20]

---

[18] Freire, *Pedagogy of the Oppressed,* p.77.

[19] Edmund Sullivan, *Critical Psychology and Pedagogy: Interpretation of the Personal World* (Toronto: OISE Press, 1990), pp.57-58.

[20] Stanley Aronowitz and Henry Giroux, *Postmodern Education: Politics, Culture, and Social Criticism* (Minneapolis: University of Minnesota Press, 1991), 101.

The process of thematic dialogue begins with some general questions related to the subject matter. The questions are always contextual; that is, they are rooted in the living contexts of students. In this way, prior to any formal investigation of the curriculum, students have an avenue in which to explore the overall nature of the subject matter. Contextuality implies, for instance, that an acceptable question or response in one situation may be considered unacceptable in another place or at a different time. The questions and concerns, the ways in which social, political, and economic problems are analysed, the appropriation of structural causes of oppression, and the derivation of feasible solutions are influenced significantly by the context of the lives of students. For Baum, all contextual theologies, and here I may include contextually-oriented pedagogies, assume that "the human predicament is not universal. That is, the predicament of the poor is not the same as the predicament of the non-poor, and the predicament of women is not the same as the predicament of men, and so on."[21] A contextual approach to pedagogy does not suggest a universally applicable way of effective teaching because it is sensitive to social, political, and economic differences in time and space. A so-called universally applicable pedagogy would be an artificial, highly static, and extremely ineffective form of teaching. Alfred North Whitehead suggests that "education is a difficult problem, to be solved by no one simple formula."[22] Pedagogies claiming to be *the* method would be deserving of scepticism. What is needed is a pedagogy that is flexible and responsive to the contexts, experiences, traditions, and transformative visions of students.

It is often useful to structure a unit or lesson around a particular theme, because it is an effective way to keep classroom dialogue and course content within specific boundaries. A theme is a topic that tends to pervade the entire unit of study, that is, an underlying message that unites the different strands of the lesson. For example, justice, perseverance, honesty, corruption, and greed are themes commonly found in the social science curriculum and can be related relatively easily to the existential realities of students. Shor differentiates between three effective types of themes used in classroom discussion: generative, topical, and academic.[23] These types of themes embrace Dewey's emphasis on experiential learning and are useful in a classroom setting. Generative themes emerge from the life experiences and cultural history of students. According to Freire, themes are normally

---

[21] Gregory Baum, *Theology and Society* (New York: Paulist Press, 1987), p.25.

[22] Alfred North Whitehead, *The Aims of Education and Other Essays* (New York: The Free Press, 1929), p.36.

[23] Ira Shor, *Empowering Education: Critical Teaching for Social Change* (Chicago: University of Chicago Press, 1992), pp.55-111.

"weighted with emotions and meaning, expressing the anxieties, fears, demands, and dreams of the group.[24] Generative themes are normally structured around issues of importance to students, including work, school, music, friendship, and family life. Topical themes reflect social questions of local, national, or global importance that do not emerge directly from the life experiences of students. These themes may include, for example, the role of the mass media in society or a nation's response to an uprising in another part of the world. The primary purpose of a topical theme is to expand the intellectual and moral horizons of students. It incites critical thought in areas of study that, at first glance, appear unrelated to the lives of students, but after analysis, offers them a broader and more profound understanding of reality. Academic themes are rooted in scholastic, professional, or technical bodies of knowledge. Shor argues that topical and academic themes may begin with knowledge beyond the existential reality of students but can be equally effective in the overall learning process. Themes can be presented in various ways, including the use of movies, photographs, stories, books, newspapers, and an endless array of internet sources.

Thematic dialogue is used to create an initial sense of community and mutual trust in the classroom. It promotes free inquiry and encourages students to pursue ideas in a creative fashion. It also enhances the application of higher-level cognitive skills to concrete reality. Classroom dialogue relies on both freedom of expression and creative thought for its overall success. Students must feel comfortable enough to freely explore new leads and express ideas and opinions in a non-threatening environment. Their thoughts should not be bound by authoritarian rules and expectations; rather, students should be granted free reign to pursue ideas and express themselves in a respectful classroom setting. Also, dialogue embraces creative thinking and critical analysis. Through the use of creative impulses, students raise critical discourse in alternative ways of seeing the world. This requires, on the part of students, a level of creative thought and critical analysis rarely promoted in contemporary high school settings. For Freire, this dialogical process encourages students to strive "towards awareness of reality and towards self-awareness"[25] and reflect on "the very condition of existence" itself.[26]

Even so, one should keep in mind the comments mentioned earlier regarding classroom dialogue. For the majority of students, especially in a high school setting, open and critical discussions do not come naturally. Students are a product of the schooling process, one that often embraces a

---

[24] Ibid., p.55.
[25] Freire, *Pedagogy of the Oppressed*, p.98.
[26] Ibid., p.100.

traditional approach to teaching and learning. Classroom discussion is often forbidden, and even raising a question about the content being delivered is often viewed by the teacher in a disdainful fashion as interrupting the delivery of course material. Granted, in elementary school, dialogue is encouraged, but as soon as students enter high school, for whatever reason, they are often exposed to an ineffective form of teaching and learning. As a result, at least initially, students resist the efforts of teachers to encourage dialogue, but over time the majority of students feel comfortable participating in classroom discussions.

2. Tradition

Through the initial moment of the pedagogy, students explore critically and dialogically specific themes and begin the process of discerning and balancing their own worldviews with the positive aspects of those held by others. The second moment is tradition and involves a process of re-awakening historical consciousness. The primary purpose of this moment is to ground the life experiences of students in history. Otherwise, thematic dialogue turns out to be a battle of individual opinions and lacks an overall historical context. Tradition makes reference to a variety of sources, including historical facts, fiction, biography, philosophy, theology, poetry, myths, and music. For Crowe, tradition includes "the accumulated patrimony of the community or nation or race. Although it is received as [a] gift, it is not to be conceived as a merely passive way, for it is not appropriated without struggle."[27] Tradition teaches people specific values and meaning in life. They learn from their parents and others how to live in the world, and their appropriation of life is embedded in a deep tradition of cherished values. The lessons people learn from tradition become a key part of who they are and are referred to in their quest to understand their role in life. If a teacher over-emphasises experiential learning at the cost of tradition, then tradition suffers, and students "will be deprived of a great deal of their rightful inheritance ... they will reach the adult stage ... with sharply trained minds that can go for the jugular in debates, but with impoverished and underdeveloped views and values."[28]

During this moment, students learn that knowledge passed down through tradition does not represent *the* truth but is an expression of reality at a specific time and place in history. Tradition is regarded as a social construct, something that accumulates over time and can change through the interaction of human agency and the structures of society. In this sense,

[27] Frederick Crowe, *Old Things and New*, p.1.
[28] Ibid., p.27.

tradition is no longer treated as a message in its final form but one in a continual process of growth and change. It is not something from the past that has been ossified; rather, as Jaroslav Pelikan suggests, it represents the "living faith of the dead,"[29] or what Mary Boys calls "the very 'stuff' out of which new was drawn from old."[30] Tradition gives the past a voice in the present for the sake of the future. Therefore, even though the use of tradition in the classroom involves a process of handing over or passing on historical facts to students; nevertheless, it is treated as something alive and forever evolving, influencing our present and shaping our future.

The primary responsibility of the teacher during this moment is to make accessible to students their rich and living traditions. A traditionalist approach merely deposits dead facts into empty vessels, but the dynamic element of this moment implies that the teacher brings tradition to the forefront of a discussion so it may be appropriated critically by students. The process of interpreting tradition involves affirming, cherishing, and making accessible the valuable messages of tradition and also identifying and discerning distortions and aberrations of goodness. The intent here is to encourage students to identify both the richness of tradition and the subjugated or forgotten memories from the past that may offer new life. Through a critical analysis of tradition, students rediscover those voices in history that have been distorted or silenced over time.

Freedom and creativity play an integral role in the second moment of a Chomskyan approach to pedagogy. Students conduct thorough historical research, revisit old historical documents, visit library archives, search internet sources, and even interview older members of the community. They are granted the freedom required to explore the many dark sides of history and generate some highly creative responses. They enhance their research skills, refine their ability to work collaboratively with others, formulate highly creative and well-written testimonies, and even develop their overall sense of self-confidence through classroom presentations. They are encouraged to interpret the historical record in a new light. Rather than conforming to the way things have always been and accepting facts in an acquiescent manner, students are invited to challenge the status quo and envision reality in a new light.

---

[29] Jaroslav Pelikan, *The Vindication of Tradition* (New Haven, CT: Yale University Press, 1984), p.65.
[30] Padraic O'Hare (ed.), *Tradition and Transformation in Religious Education* (Birmingham, Alabama: Religious Education Press, 1979), p.19.

3. Synthesis

During the third moment of the pedagogy, synthesis, things get rather tricky! Thematic dialogue is rooted in the experiences of students, and tradition makes reference to historical facts, but during the third moment, the two earlier moments of the pedagogy are held in a state of dialectical tension. Somehow, the tension that often develops between thematic dialogue and tradition needs to be resolved in order for the pedagogy to fully develop, and this is the purpose of the third moment. There needs to be a synthesis between what often appears to be two opposing points of view to bring together into some kind of unity, or wholeness, the insights, experiences, and historical facts shared and developed in the earlier pedagogical moments.

The term 'synthesis' implies that two conflicting positions lead to a third, resolving position. In classical philosophy, a dialectical method is used as a form of reasoning. An individual presents an argument, a second person presents a counter-argument, and tension is resolved through a process of critical negotiating, refuting, scrutinising, and synthesising opposing assertions. In mediaeval philosophy, especially in Aquinas's *Summa Theologiae* (1485), a dialectical method, or *a quaestio disputata*, took the following form:

1.   A question is raised.

2.   A provisory response is offered.

3.   The principle arguments in favour of (2) are offered.

4.   An argument against (2) is offered.

5.   (1) is addressed in light of (2), (3), and (4)

6.   Replies to each of the initial objections.

What is often referred to as 'Hegelian dialectics' incorporates a dynamic relationship between a thesis and an antithesis and a resulting synthesis or resolution between the two earlier states.[31] In a Chomskyan approach to pedagogy, a dialectical process will be treated in a similar way. Even so, while I agree with Hegel that reality is a process of continual change, I disagree that this change is influenced by and constantly moving toward some kind of Absolute, deity-like Spirit. As my understanding of dialectics will show, social change occurs through the interaction of people and their immediate environment, and not through the force or will of an entity beyond reality

---

[31] Interestingly, Hegel never used these terms. According to Walter Kaufmann, in his *Hegel: A Reinterpretation* (1966), Fichte was responsible for introducing the three-step process.

itself. Even so, I embrace a Hegelian understanding of dialectics as a conflict between a thesis and an antithesis that leads inevitably to a synthesis of ideas, and that a synthesis of ideas becomes, in turn, a new thesis, and the process continues in a dynamic fashion. Indeed, for Lonergan, a dialectical process of this sort aims at "a comprehensive viewpoint, and [proceeds] towards that goal by acknowledging differences, seeking their grounds real and apparent, and eliminating superfluous oppositions."[32] It involves a process of critiquing formerly acquired values and judgements, either to abandon them or to redefine them in light of new data.

The expression 'unity-in-diversity' is often associated with a dialectical process, and suggests that the whole can be realised through the rich individuality and complex interrelationships of the parts. The expression is developed in the works of Peter Kropotkin, who argues that fluctuations in population depend upon the complexity of the ecosystem.[33] If the environment is simplified and the variety of animal and plant species is reduced, then fluctuations in the population tend to get out of control and reach pest proportions. If, on the other hand, the diverse nature of an ecological system is preserved, then a degree of diversity or wholeness is enhanced and protected. For Murray Bookchin, the ecological principle of unity-in-diversity leads to greater participation for all members of the community. He states,

> The more differentiated the life-form and the environment in which it exists, the more acute is its overall sensorium, the greater its flexibility, and the more active its *participation* in its own evolution ... The greater the differentiation, the wider its degree of participation in elaborating the world of life.[34]

From a societal viewpoint, unity-in-diversity suggests that if one reduces, say, the variety and richness of expression, then one interferes with society's wholeness and destroys the forces that establish overall harmony and stability. Wholeness is achieved by challenging structures and actions that threaten the diversity and richness of society. The term 'wholeness' does not mean a Hegelian endpoint or totality in which no further development or growth is possible or meaningful. It represents an expression of the "varying

---

[32] Lonergan, *Method*, p.130.

[33] For example, see Peter Kropotkin, *Mutual Aid: A Factor of Evolution* (Montreal: Black Rose Books, 1989); Murray Bookchin, *The Ecology of Freedom: The Emergence and Dissolution of Hierarchy* (Montreal: Black Rose Books, 1991)

[34] Murray Bookchin, *The Modern Crisis* (Montreal: Black Rose Books, 1987), p.26.

degrees of the actualization of potentialities."[35] It is the unity that gives order to the parts - it is what has emerged so far from the process.

Fundamentally, the dialectical process is initiated through a frequently conflicting relationship between thematic dialogue and tradition. The only way a sense of unity, wholeness, or community can be achieved is if personal experiences, concerns, and joys of the present are brought into a dialectical relationship with tradition. It is only when the present and the past are brought together as parts of an ever-growing, developing whole that students can feel confident enough to imagine future possibilities.

The role of the teacher during this moment is to motivate students to acknowledge and attempt to resolve the tension between the two opposing points of view. This is best accomplished through a process of critical thought. The expression 'critical thinking skills' is a cheap and easy catchphrase used commonly in educational discourse to mean virtually anything that involves some sort of reflection. Besides the general slogan, critical thinking involves a degree of analysis and evaluation that extends beyond normal discourse, and in itself is an important feature of education. Naturally, everyone agrees that critical thinking is important in education - how could anyone argue otherwise? Critical thought goes far beyond simple reflection, a mechanical state of self-awareness, rote memory, and the regurgitation of facts. It incorporates a process of questioning, understanding, evaluating, and judging various forms of knowledge, either passed down through tradition or discovered through experience. In this sense, all knowledge is ultimately fallible. The use of critical thought in the classroom is not merely an intellectual exercise; rather, it invites students to examine critically the underlying ideologies that define their particular reality, refute them if necessary, and generate specific conjectures regarding a different vision of reality. At the same time, students are fully aware that any positions they may propose will be subjected to the scrutiny of additional refutations and perhaps discarded for a better, tentative proposal. Inevitably, the process of critical thought embodies a political element. It encourages students to reinterpret how power is distributed in society and imagine better ways to live in the world. Freire reminds us that "a teacher must be fully cognizant of the political nature of his/her practice and assume responsibility for this rather than denying it."[36] For Freire, this process involves the "development of the awakening of critical awareness,"[37] and is promoted, as we have already seen,

---

[35] Ibid., p.60.
[36] Ira Shor (ed.), *Freire for the Classroom: A Sourcebook for Liberatory Teaching* (Portsmouth: Heinemann, 1987), p.211.
[37] Paulo Freire, *Education for Critical Consciousness* (New York: Continuum, 1973), p.19.

in his problem-posing approach to education. Teachers, in this case, are part of a community in the classroom and work with students in a critical, creative, and dialogical manner to search for more liberatory ways of being. It involves moving students from what Freire calls a state of dehumanisation, that is, "a distortion of the vocation of becoming more fully human," to a state of humanisation, or "the overcoming of alienation" and the "yearning ... for freedom and justice, ... to recover their lost humanity."[38]

4. Transformation

Through the first three moments, students analyse dialogically, critically, and creatively both the present and the past. These moments, as important as they are in effective pedagogy, are oriented primarily toward critically reflective and creative activities, individually and collectively, but lack a concrete commitment to personal and social change. It is relatively easy to engage students, at least the majority of them, in reflective and creative classroom activities, but to move them beyond reflection to action is often a tremendous challenge for the classroom teacher. Even so, a movement from reflection, as embedded in earlier moments, to a moment that incorporates transformation is important in an effective pedagogy; otherwise, students regard the entire process as an exercise in empty rhetoric. Freire warns against focusing solely on either words or actions. He states,

> When a word is deprived of its dimension of action, reflection automatically suffers as well; and the word is changed into idle chatter, into *verbalism*, into an alienated and alienating 'blah.' It becomes an empty word, one which cannot denounce the world, for denunciation is impossible without a commitment to transform, and there is no transformation without action.

> On the other hand, if action is emphasized exclusively, to the detriment of reflection, the word is converted into *activism*. The latter - action for action's sake - negates the true praxis and makes dialogue impossible. Either dichotomy, by creating unauthentic forms of existence, creates also (sic) inauthentic forms of thought, which reinforce the original dichotomy.[39]

---

[38] Freire, *Pedagogy of the Oppressed*, p.28.
[39] Ibid., pp. 75-76.

In a similar fashion, Whitehead warns against what he calls 'inert ideas,' the 'evil of barren knowledge,' or the "aimless accumulation of precise knowledge, inert and unutilised."[40] He states,

> The importance of knowledge lies in its use, in our active mastery of life - that is to say, it lies in wisdom ... That knowledge which adds greatness to character is knowledge so handled as to transform every phase of immediate experience.[41]

The pedagogical moment of transformation bridges the gap between the way reality is, as expressed through the first three moments, and the way reality *should be*. It represents the active element of praxis and leads to a transformed reality rooted firmly in the past and the present. Praxis, in this sense, means a dynamic relationship between theory and practice; it means putting words into action. For Marx, the purpose of praxis is to improve the social conditions of the working class. People are defined by what they do - their nature and character are determined by their actions. The idea that praxis determines consciousness is the basis of Marx's scientific materialism. He states that "[t]he production of ideas, of conception, of consciousness is directly interwoven with the material activity and material relationships of men (sic) ... consciousness does not determine life, but life determines consciousness.[42]

For Marx, the material of life determines, to a significant degree, the shape of human consciousness. Theory is the expression and articulation of consciousness based on the material conditions resulting from praxis. Indeed, Marx insists that praxis must never be a theory void of a critique of existing social conditions. Criticism is efficacious only if it enables people to bring to self-consciousness the reasons why they are suffering and what they can do to change the causes of such anguish. Marx's emphasis on critical reflection and human activity provides the basis of his revolutionary praxis, a praxis informed by a critical understanding of reality.

Transformation implies change, that is, a deviation from normative patterns of belief and behaviour. Through transformative action, students re-imagine and re-create communities and traditions and re-prioritise values and lifestyles. Transformation requires personal, interpersonal, and structural changes. Personal transformation calls for changes in the way students regard

---

[40] A.N. Whitehead, *The Aims of Education and Other Essays* (London: Williams & Norgate Ltd., 1941), p.58.

[41] Ibid., p.49.

[42] Dermot Lane, *Foundations for a Social Theology: Praxis, Process and Salvation* (New York: Paulist Press, 1983), p.41.

themselves in relation to the world. It means redefining personal attitudes, lifestyles, values, perceptions, and beliefs. Personal transformation seeks to achieve a metanoia, or conversion, of the whole person. It embodies what Lonergan refers to as a 'conversion'. He states,

> By conversion is understood a transformation of the subject and his (sic) world ... a resultant change of course and direction. It is as if one's eyes were opened and one's former world faded and fell away ... Conversion is existential, intensely personal, utterly intimate. But it is not so private as to be solitary. It can happen to many, and they can form a community to sustain one another in their self-transformation and to help one another in working out the implications and fulfilling the promise of their new life.[43]

Thus, transformation leads to an ontological change, a new way of being in the world. But, it can also lead to interpersonal change as students interact with each other in the classroom. It suggests moving beyond the self and developing a new sensibility that stresses tolerance, unity-in-diversity, interdependence, and cooperation. It means striving for goals and worldviews that reflect the well-being of the majority of the community. Structural transformation seeks change in institutions that control and promote specific hegemonic ideologies and ensure the continued dominance of the status quo. Institutions of this sort include governments, schools, financial institutions, transnational corporations, and the mass media. Structural transformation calls for these institutions of power and influence to be changed so that they represent the interests of the society as a whole rather than the interests of a small, privileged minority.

Transformation requires courage, determination, a well-articulated sense of truth and morality, and an overall willingness to move beyond the status quo. Personal and social change occur as the result of a high level of individual and communal dialogue and critical thought. Forms of transformative action do not arrive pre-sealed in a package. Instead, students have to be creative, both individually and collaboratively, in the ways they transform themselves and society for the better. Transformative action can take various forms. For example, it might include refusing to purchase products that are manufactured by workers whose basic human rights are violated or simply discussing important issues with family and friends. For some, it might involve engaging in civil disobedience to oppose the unjust intervention of one's government in the affairs of another nation. It might imply not paying a proportion of one's

---

[43] Lonergan, *Method*, p.130.

taxes that would be used by the government for war or nuclear testing. It might include writing letters to government leaders and demanding changes in policies and procedures. It might also include organising a demonstration, insisting on the resignation of a particular individual in public office, or the development of community-based, grass-roots projects. The forms of transformative action are endless.

The dynamic nature of the pedagogy discussed above suggests that, as students move through the fourth moment and create change in themselves, and also in society, they continue to discuss, critique, and re-evaluate new experiences and recently discovered parts of the historical record. This naturally leads to a re-evaluation of the fourth moment and a re-application of the earlier moments, and the process continues in a dynamic, ever-changing manner.

Practical Limitations

The outcome of the educational process is often unpredictable, especially when one is in a classroom with many adolescents. Teaching involves an intricate, delicate, and highly complex relationship with students who enter the classroom with different experiences, values, and expectations. Regardless of its overall efficacy, a pedagogy, as described above, includes its own set of practical limitations.

First, the effectiveness of a Chomskyan approach to pedagogy is determined, in part, by its praxis-orientation. It focuses on both theory and practice, and students are invited to commit themselves to concrete forms of personal and social change. Critical consciousness-raising activities are relatively simple to initiate in the classroom. Frustration abounds when students are resistant to the idea of moving from theory to practice and implementing their ideas in reality. They often avoid commitment to action, perhaps for fear of failure, because it requires time and effort on their part, or maybe because peer pressure dictates otherwise. For whatever reason, bridging the gap between theory and practice can sometimes be a challenge for a classroom teacher, and it's a factor to be aware of at the outset. Sometimes, students simply do not want to take the step to action, and that is fine, too. There will be other opportunities for them to seek transformative action, but, at times, it is best to focus primarily on the rich educational experience offered through the first three moments.

Second, regardless of the dynamics and efficacy of any particular pedagogy, there are times when students are determined to resist all authentic efforts put forth by the teacher to create an interesting and challenging learning environment. There are days, as students often say, when they "don't want to think", especially about challenging and sometimes emotionally-charged subject matter. Resistance is expressed in numerous ways: passivity, anger, boredom, absenteeism, incomplete homework, tardiness, and cheating. Such behaviour is not foreign to the learning process. On the contrary, it reflects the many ways students are capable of resisting the norm or acting against the grain, so to speak. They are not always willing to travel so far with the classroom teacher, and sometimes they show signs of resistance. This highlights a preliminary note offered earlier, that is, that it's essential that teachers get to know their students well, and be able to detect signs of resistance, and adjust the pedagogy accordingly.

Third, time is always a factor. Teachers have to deliver a set curriculum within a matter of a few months. The time involved in a form of pedagogy that involves students in a few days of research and classroom presentations, in addition to the use of guest speakers, field trips, and other time-consuming activities, is often difficult to manage in a heavily content-laden course. For example, courses in the social sciences tend to offer a rather flexible curriculum with plenty of time for students to explore tangential ideas, but the volume of content in other courses, such as mathematics and the natural sciences, tends to restrict the time available for creative learning. Even so, in courses heavily laden with content, it is quite possible to restructure the delivery of the content to include the four pedagogical moments. For instance, in mathematics courses, it is often the case that later chapters include concepts and theorems discovered in earlier chapters. These repetitive components can be easily removed without any harm to the overall curriculum, and this will provide the teacher with a brief window of opportunity to use the pedagogy in a more creative fashion.

Inevitably, students can make teaching either a rewarding adventure or an arduous task. Even so, I believe the teacher's general attitude to the teaching and learning process determines, to a significant degree, the overall success or failure in a classroom setting. Teachers are trained in the intricate details of classroom management skills, so the issues cited above can be easily resolved. In many cases, the students are not the problem; rather, it's the teacher who defines the parameters of debate and cultivates the richness of the learning environment. There is a grain of truth in the position adopted by critical pedagogues that socio-political forces impact the effectiveness of the schooling process, and these forces can often create a difficult teaching and learning environment, but fundamentally it is what the teacher does in the classroom that determines whether or not authentic learning will occur. To blame the failures of public education on structural forces alone often appears to be a way of deflecting the blame elsewhere. Effective teaching takes place in a myriad of socio-political and economic environments, and to focus solely on outside forces becomes, at least for the classroom teacher, a rather irrelevant and purely academic topic of discourse.

In light of what has been discussed, I am well positioned to apply the pedagogy developed above in a concrete classroom setting. Even so, one should keep in mind that a pedagogy of this kind must be tried and tested in front of a group of students. It is relatively simple to develop a pedagogy, but its application is quite another factor. The success or failure of a particular pedagogy is determined, to a significant degree, by the teacher, but also by the dynamics of the students themselves. The beauty of teaching, especially in a high school setting, is its highly unpredictable nature. It is what makes teaching so interesting on a daily basis. There is never a dull moment amidst a group of teenagers, and the general effectiveness of a particular pedagogy does not guarantee success on any given day.

Application of a Chomskyan Approach to Pedagogy

In this section, I show how the four moments of the pedagogy developed above can be used in a classroom setting. This particular example is taken from personal experiences as a high school educator. It shows how the moments work in a dynamic fashion and, when applied in the proper way at the right time, lead to creative forms of transformative action. Over the years, I have applied a Chomskyan approach to pedagogy in various learning environments. In the following example, I focus on a lesson that relates to the business sector because the resulting analysis and transformative action correspond effectively to Chomsky's political interests. Nevertheless, it is worth mentioning that this pedagogy has a wide degree of applicability. For example, it has been used in a Grade 9 mathematics course in a lesson on the Pythagorean Theorem. Students were introduced to the theorem and then used it to measure distances in various areas of the school - cafeteria, hallway, foyer, football field. They learned about the life of Pythagoras and the founding of a Pythagorean community that promoted a strict ascetic lifestyle. This encouraged particular students to reconsider their dietary practices and adopt a vegetarian lifestyle. It has been implemented effectively in a Grade 12 philosophy course in a unit on ethics. Students explored various expressions of utilitarianism, especially how Peter Singer applies utilitarianism to an array of ethical issues. Students expressed sincere interest in his views on animal rights and eventually became active members of the animal rights movement. The pedagogy was used in an interesting fashion in a unit on logic and the study of syllogisms. Students were exposed to simple Boolean translations but also learned about the fascinating and often traumatic life of George Boole. They found it inspiring that a mathematical genius found the time and energy to devote himself to the needs of the poor and disadvantaged in society and also teach regularly in an adult learning centre. These motivated students to move beyond self-serving interests and reach out to the less-fortunate by volunteering in a local soup kitchen. The pedagogy has also been used in a high school retreat setting focussed on the theme of teen self-image. It encouraged students to critically explore the role played by peer pressure and the mass media in the perpetuation of specific teen images and to move beyond these artificial images to a deeper understanding of what it means to be human.

It is important to preface the following section with a brief commentary regarding corporate involvement in publicly-funded schools. The example to follow includes references to the relationship between schools and the business community. I have chosen this particular example because it relates well with Chomsky's analysis of the corporate sector. As a result of prevailing budgetary constraints in publicly-funded education, school boards are reaching out to the business community for financial support. School boards have developed business-education partnership programmes that enhance the presence of the business sector in the school community and, in return, provide schools with much-needed financial incentives. Specific guidelines and procedures clearly demarcate the aims and scope of the programmes. For example, in *Let's Do It Right ... Together!!!*, a document published by a school board in southern Ontario, businesses provide schools with corporate volunteers, mentors, advisory committee members, curriculum development advisors, facilities, grants, student awards, and corporate trainers. According to a resource guide published by the Toronto Area Partnership Network, a group that represents nine school boards, the primary purpose of business-education partnerships is to "foster student, teacher, and employee awareness of the importance of sharing resources, and also to demonstrate that sharing resources can directly impact community life now and in the future."[44] David Orr highlights the extent to which the private sector is willing to travel in order to establish profitable relationships with schools.[45] For instance, executives from various corporate enterprises are working diligently with government officials to "rebuild the whole [education] system" to "reach the performance

---

[44] This quote and reference to the details to follow can be found in two of my works: "Do we know the whole story? The Business-Education Partnership and Corporate Social Responsibility," *The Reporter: The Magazine of The Ontario English Catholic Teachers' Association,* 21(3), February 1996, pp.23-26; "The Business-Education Partnership: We shouldn't ignore corporate social responsibility." Canadian Centre for Policy Alternatives, *Education Monitor: Reporting on Education and Public Policy Issues* 1(1), November 1996, pp.22-23.

[45] David Orr, *Earth in Mind: On Education, Environment, and the Human Prospect* (Washington, D.C.: Island Press), 1994.

of a Toyota or Honda."[46] Orr mentions an interesting business-education partnership between Whittle Communications Corporation (founded by Chris Whittle) and various public schools. The corporation offers schools free access to Channel One, but in return, schools expose students to daily corporate advertising. According to Orr, the corporation's advertising reaches approximately eight million students. In addition, Whittle Corporation "intends to create 1,000 for-profit public schools (The Edison Project)."[47] Orr states,

> To make a profit on anticipated annual revenues of $10 billion, Whittle intends to reduce the educational bureaucracy, use a lot of educational technology and fewer teachers, employ students to clean up, ask for volunteers, and rely on economies of scale.[48]

The majority of partnership programmes are developed and implemented between individual school boards and the business community. For instance, a leading Canadian aerospace firm developed an intricate partnership with a school board in southern Ontario. The firm has designed various communications satellites and an $825 million arms system that was used to assemble and maintain components during the construction and operation phases of a $39 billion U.S. space station. The aerospace firm has invested time and money in local school-based partnership programmes. Corporate representatives interact on a regular basis with teachers and students through assemblies, classroom visits, consultation services, funding initiatives, and even student tours of the company site to promote the societal value of aerospace research and engineering. Teachers, school administrators, and school board officials regard such affiliations as pedagogically efficacious tools to encourage students to pursue careers in the high-tech industry. Fair enough, but this is precisely when the monsters appear in the classroom. This particular aerospace firm is ranked consistently in Canada's top few military contractors and a leading recipient of U.S. Department of Defense prime contracts. In the late 1980s, for instance, it produced components for the F-16C/D fighter and trainer aircraft in Brunei, Chile, Gabon, Morocco, Mozambique, and Turkey, and F/A-18 Hornet fighter aircraft in Kuwait. During the following decade, the aerospace firm produced components for Apache helicopters, F/A-18 fighter jets, military transport aircraft, and tactical air navigation systems used in countries that consistently violate human rights, including Malaysia, Kuwait, Israel, Thailand, and Brazil.

---

[46] Ibid., p.36.
[47] Ibid.
[48] Ibid.

This aerospace firm is a key player in Canada's involvement in military exports. The demand worldwide for weapons of mass destruction has increased at least ten-fold in recent years. Of the 28 million people who have been killed in more than 200 wars since 1945, more than half of them were innocent civilians who fell victim to the research and development efforts of aerospace firms.

Schools are, in many ways, a microcosm of society. As I noted earlier, the more traditional or conservative strain found commonly in schools legitimates an approach to teaching and learning that embraces the values inherent in a corporate worldview. Teachers and school administrators often respond in an uncontentious manner to the dictates of people in positions of greater authority, and students tolerate the hierarchical and often oppressive nature of the schooling process. It is often assumed that the primary purpose of education is to reproduce forms of knowledge that support the status quo. Rather than encouraging students to challenge the way things have always been, teachers play a significant role in the perpetuation of unrestrained competition, acquiescence, and self-serving individualism. They argue it is their moral obligation as public servants to preserve and protect the current state of affairs. Inevitably, this prevailing attitude can be challenged through the implementation of the pedagogy developed above.

Part of the Grade 11 social science curriculum addresses the issue of the role played by businesses in the local community. Needless to say, the topic is vast in scope, but the intent of the unit is merely to expose students to a few basic concepts and facts about specific businesses and the way they contribute to social and economic development.

A suitable theme for this lesson is 'business integrity.' I acknowledge that a significant number of my students come from families who own and operate profitable small companies. Therefore, business is in their blood, so to speak, and they enter the classroom dialogue with utmost respect for the business community. In order to initiate preliminary discussion about the topic at hand, I organise students into small working groups of no more than five members. The students are asked to address the following questions:

- Why do you always purchase specific brands of clothing or other consumer goods?

- While at school, where do you purchase drinks and snacks?

- Is there a relationship between the products you purchase and the commercials you watch in the media?

- Do you believe local businesses operate with a degree of integrity?

- In your opinion, do small businesses and transnational corporations operate under the same rules regarding integrity and social responsibility?

Even though some students appreciate the opportunity to share their thoughts with others about their consumption habits, others react with less enthusiasm and respond:

- Who cares? All I know is that I like the products I purchase.

- Why should I change my habits? What I decide to purchase and consume isn't anyone else's business.

- I only live once, so I should enjoy it.

- When it comes to business, it's all about profit.

- Why should I care if businesses act responsibly?

Students are encouraged to reflect on the significance of the questions and comments. I ask students to identify a few issues that reappear during the classroom dialogue, and they highlight (1) the compulsive desires of consumers, (2) the effects of television programming on purchasing choices, (3) the power of the business sector in society, and (4) how businesses act in a socially responsible way. A student from each group presents a summary of the group's responses to the questions. Even though the majority of students, at least initially, are unable to identify any significant relationship between the raised issues, certain students are insightful enough to recognise that perhaps their choice to consume particular products is influenced by a complex array of variables, including family values, peer pressure, the mass media, and specific business interests.

One can already detect some of the key qualities associated with a Chomskyan approach to education. For instance, the classroom is designed in a non-hierarchical fashion. The teacher is not dictating from the front of the classroom; rather, he or she is circulating among the groups of students, offering them suggestions and encouragement, and assessing the overall dynamics of the exercise. Also, the entire process begins with the life experiences of the learners. Students are encouraged to share their personal experiences and insights. The groups are organised in circles that automatically remove from the learning environment any sense of competition and also promote a cooperative milieu. The initial activity inspires students to freely inquire into and respond critically to the assigned questions and the responses of their classmates. They have the freedom to express their ideas in a reasonable and respectful manner. A sense of self-worth is enhanced, especially when students contribute to the group discussion or present the group's findings to other members of the class.

Tradition, the second moment of the pedagogy, involves a process of re-awakening historical consciousness. Students learn to re-evaluate past events and differentiate historical fact from fiction. Simply stated, the second moment provides all the facts in their appropriate place on the table. As I mentioned earlier, tradition, as a pedagogical moment, implies much more than merely absorbing prefabricated knowledge and so-called historical truths. It often involves creative research, critical data analysis, interviews, group participation, classroom presentations, report writing, and even guest speakers.

In this lesson, I review the historical content provided in the course textbook and highlight the various ways the business sector has changed over the years. I emphasise how the economy has been transformed from one that promotes competition between local small businesses to one controlled by the interests of a handful of transnational corporations. Students identify how a corporate-sector economy has impacted their family businesses. They also reflect on their particular family upbringing and identify some factors that influence the way they tend to consume products. Family upbringing plays a key role in their choices as consumers. Students are encouraged to discuss with family members why they purchase certain household items and explore how they lived their childhood with parents and grandparents. What was life like without a television? What did they do for entertainment? Students realise that, even though times were different two generations ago, newspapers influenced the lives of their grandparents in ways similar to how modern forms of media, including televisions, computers, and iPhones, influence modern lives.

To explore in greater detail the link between technology and consumer habits, I share with students three cartoons[49] and ask them to discuss with their group members the meaning associated with each cartoon. The first cartoon illustrates how advertising in the mass media is used to distort wants and needs. It shows five advertising executives planning ways to sell a new product. Under the cartoon, it states, "Of course no one NEEDS it, Willoughby! That's where you people in advertising come in." The second cartoon shows how television programmes often appear to be brief interludes between corporate-sponsored advertisements. It depicts a lady watching television and

---

[49] See Eleanor MacLean, *Between the Lines: How to Detect Bias and Propaganda in the News and Everyday Life* (Montreal: Black Rose Books, 1981), pp.48, 50, 125.

states, "A TV program is what they give us for watching commercials." Students related well to these two cartoons, primarily because they have been exposed to enough television programming and advertising to identify the issues from personal experiences.

Students continue their research and find that, on average, North Americans watch television for almost 30 hours per week or 13 continuous years of an average life span. Since 27% of prime-time is devoted to advertisements, on average, viewers watch the equivalent of three solid years of commercials.[50] Students learn that the average teenager has watched 200,000 televised acts of violence and 300,000 commercials.[51]

The third cartoon shows the *Toronto Star* building, and underneath, it states, "Freedom of the press belongs to those who own one". Initially, the message behind the cartoon - that information services are controlled by and serve the interests of the owners of media outlets - is difficult for the class to comprehend, partly because they assume that news is presented in an objective, accurate, and comprehensive fashion.

We consider some facts that support the message in the third cartoon. For example, in 1989, of 117 daily newspapers in Canada, 89 were owned by three corporations, and at the time of this particular classroom experience, the majority of dailies were controlled by two empires - Thomson and Southam. The Thomson chain, at that time owned by Ken Thomson, was the largest newspaper chain in Canada, providing printed daily news for over 2 million readers.[52] Thomson's holdings include more than 140 newspapers in North America, along with business interests in England and South Africa.[53] In 1993, profits in the newspaper division reached $174 million (US). Interestingly enough, in 1993, while employees, some with 18 years of service, were laid off, and employees earning less than $30,000 annually received wage rollbacks, the president of Thomson Corporation and the newspaper division chief earned $1.2 million (US) and $1.1 million (CA) respectively.[54] The second largest newspaper chain in Canada at the time of the lesson was Southam. In addition to the ownership of 14 daily newspapers, Southam also controlled Coles, the largest book retailer in the country.[55] In the television cable

---

[50] John Kavanaugh, *Following Christ in a Consumer Society: The Spirituality of Cultural Resistance* (New York: Orbis Books, 1981), p.25.

[51] Martin Lee and Norman Soloman, *Unreliable Sources: A Guide to Detecting Bias in News Media* (New Jersey: Carol Publishing, 1992), p.3.

[52] Maclean, *Between the Lines*, p.118.

[53] Ibid., p.136.

[54] *The Toronto Star*, Friday, May 20, 1994.

[55] MacLean, *Between the Lines*, p.119.

industry, Ted Rogers, then owner of Rogers Cable, purchased Maclean-Hunter for $2.8 billion (CA) to become Canada's "cable TV czar" with interests in cable television, telecommunications, publishing, broadcasting, and printing.[56]

Through a historical analysis of these facts, students appreciate the message behind the third cartoon. It is only natural, they argue, that newspapers and magazines they and their family members read reflect the interests of the owners. Students agree that it would be highly unlikely, for example, that an article criticising the business interests of Rogers would be published in *The Toronto Sun*. Students discuss critically a passage by Michael Czerny and Jamie Swift, who state,

> The Thomson empire, with its control of both newspapers and major department stores, provides an example of the dangers of having corporate connections between advertising and the media. The Bay, Simpsons and Zellers are major newspaper advertisers, whose displays of the latest fashions and sale items adorn many a page. Can a newspaper with those business connections be expected to report comprehensively or critically on the retail trade industry?[57]

For students, the message is clear: those who own the press have the power to determine what is fit for print, in order to serve their particular business interests. Also, students realise there is a strong working relationship between mainstream media and the elite. As Wallace Clement suggests,

> Actually, the overlap (of the media elite) with the economic elite is extensive, almost one-half the members are exactly the same people. Moreover, those not overlapped resemble very closely the economic elite. The conclusion must be that together the economic and media elite are simply two sides of the same upper class; between them they hold two of the key sources of power - economic and ideological - in Canadian society and form the corporate elite.[58]

At this point in the discussion, I present to the class Herman and Chomsky's Propaganda Model, as discussed earlier, and relate it to their findings. The

---

[56] Before the buy-out, Macleans-Hunter owned one television station and twenty-one radio stations in Ontario, Alberta, and Eastern Canada; 61.8% of *The Toronto Sun* (which also controls *The Financial Post*); published 200 periodicals, including *Maclean's* and *Chatelaine*; and 15 printing units.

[57] Michael Czerny and Jamie Swift, *Getting Started on Social Analysis in Canada* (Toronto: Between the Lines, 1984), p.103.

[58] Eleanor MacLean, *Between the Lines*, pp.120-121.

model is not a part of the school curriculum, but it offers students an opportunity to move beyond pre-defined boundaries of knowledge and explore other relevant material. Students then present some interesting findings. They focus on extremely wealthy and powerful members of the media elite who have extensive business interests beyond the media. For instance, at the time of this lesson, students learn that the CBS network is part owner of various publishing agencies, Columbia records, and the New York Yankees. The ABC network is part of PBC-Paramount, linked to Gulf & Western, an empire with business interests in sugar and breakfast cereal company plantations in the Dominican Republic, Paramount Pictures, the New York Rangers, and extensive media holdings throughout Latin America. RCA is owned by General Electric, which in turn owns the NBC network. Westinghouse owns major television-broadcasting stations, a cable network, and a radio-station network. Both General Electric and Westinghouse are powerful transnational corporations involved heavily in weapons production and nuclear power. Students discover that during the Gulf War, General Electric "manufactured or supplied parts or maintenance for nearly every major weapon system employed by the U.S. ... including the Patriot and Tomahawk Cruise missiles, the Stealth bomber, the B-52 bomber, the AWACS plane, and the NAVSTAR spy satellite system."[59] General Electric has also been identified on more than one occasion as one of the world's ten worst (most destructive) corporations, whose investment in nuclear weapons research "has created environment health, and safety nightmares across the United States."[60]

A student brings to the attention of the class the case of *National Geographic*. The environmentally-oriented magazine features a cover story about whether humanity can "save this fragile Earth," while on the back cover is an advertisement for McDonald's - notorious for its environmentally destructive activities in the Amazon rainforest. Students also critically reflect on and discuss an advertisement in a major weekly magazine that features a Vietnam veteran playing basketball on artificial legs supplied by Dupont. The advertisement reads,

> When Bill Demby was in Vietnam, he used to dream of coming home and playing a little basketball with the guys. A dream that all but died when he lost both legs to a Viet Cong rocket. But then, a group of researchers discovered that a remarkable DuPont plastic could help

---

[59] Lee and Solomon, *Unreliable Sources*, p.xviii.
[60] Russell Mokhiber, "Corporate Crime & Violence in Review: The 10 Worst Corporations of 1991," *Multinational Monitor* (December, 1991), p.14.

make artificial limbs that were more resilient, more flexible, more like life itself. Thanks to these efforts, Bill Demby is back, And some say, he hasn't lost a step. At DuPont, we make the things that make a difference."[61]

Without a doubt, students learn that DuPont definitely makes a difference. The same company that built the legs for Bill Demby also played a highly profitable role as a military contractor during the Vietnam War. Between 1964 and 1972, DuPont earned several billion dollars in Pentagon contracts, producing napalm, anti-personnel bombs, and heavy equipment for the U.S. war effort.[62]

After students consider a vast array of historical facts, it becomes clear to them how and why transnational corporations, including the company that owns the vending machine in the school, influence lives on a daily basis. At this point, I redirect their attention to the original issue, that is, the integrity of the business community and its influence on students' consumer choices. With a significant amount of preliminary research completed, students no longer resort to simplistic explanations as to why they purchase certain consumer goods. They realised that it is a complicated issue.

I invite a guest speaker from a local agency to discuss with students the activities of transnational corporations.[63] Students learn that the soft drink company that owns the school's vending machine began its activities in Canada in 1934. In 1965, it merged with other soft drink and snack companies to become one of the largest transnational corporations in the snack food and soft drink sectors.

In 1991, the company entered a soft drink joint venture in Burma.[64] At the time of the classroom presentation, the current annual production capacity is more than 54 million 10 oz. bottles of soft drinks, with plans to upgrade production to 140 million bottles. A company representative claimed that the

---

[61] Lee and Solomon, *Unreliable Sources,* p.53.

[62] Ibid., p.53.

[63] I contacted the director of the *Taskforce on the Churches and Corporate Responsibility* in Toronto. The agency was founded in 1975 by a coalition of Christian churches and religious orders to address issues of corporate responsibility. It undertakes research and action relating to the social and environmental impact of corporations, both public and private, and related government policies.

[64] The military government renamed Burma "Myanmar" immediately after the brutal events of 1988. Human rights groups claim the new name was introduced by the illegitimate government in an attempt to wipe the slate clean.

joint venture "is providing positive benefits to the citizens of that country."[65] Each of the approximately 250 people employed is paid more than twice the government's minimum wage. The company is a major sponsor of sporting events in Burma, supplying uniforms, trophies, and other products.

Burma is described by Amnesty International as a "State of terror." Initially, it was ruled by the State and Order Restoration Council (SLORC), but in 1997, SLORC was abolished and reconstituted as the State Peace and Development Council (SPDC), and recognised as one of the most brutal and destructive military regimes in the world. In 1988, the SLORC injured and killed tens of thousands of pro-democracy protesters. More recently, the regime has closed universities, enforced mass slave labour, condoned drug dealing, and placed democratic leader and 1991 Nobel Peace Prize recipient Aung San Suu Kyi, under strict house arrest. Human rights abuses have been extensively documented by Amnesty International, Asia Watch, and other agencies concerned about human rights violations.

In response to such atrocities, the international community stopped the flow of trade and aid to Burma, and since then, the country has been rapidly approaching bankruptcy. The SLORC (SPDC) managed to stay in power, in part because of revenues generated by private foreign investment and trade. According to the former U.S. Ambassador to Burma, Burton Levin, any hard currency received from foreign corporations is poured "straight into the army while the rest of the country is collapsing."[66]

The focus of the presenter's message is that by conducting business in Burma, the soft drink company is supporting the country's military regime. In fact, its joint venture business partner in Burma is a private trading company owned and controlled by the military regime. Needless to say, the company denies any affiliation with Burma's military regime. In a letter to the Sisters of Charity of Saint Vincent de Paul, it stated that "[the soft drink company] neither invests in nor supports political or military systems or governments. We invest in business and people. In the case of Burma, let me assure you that [it] is not in business with the Burmese government."[67] Students are insightful enough to know that by claiming political neutrality, one is siding with the status quo or, in this case, with the military regime. Conducting business with a repressive regime is inherently political - it lends political legitimacy to a brutal regime.

---

[65] Quoted from a letter in a file of the *Taskforce on the Churches and Corporate Responsibility*, Toronto, Ontario.
[66] Ibid.
[67] Ibid.

As a result of their own research and the findings presented by the guest speaker, students understand the intricate relationship between the media, their personal desire to purchase particular commodities, and human rights violations in other parts of the world. They understand that, in many cases, integrity and social responsibility do not play a role in the corporate sector. Students express mixed emotions: anger, sadness, powerlessness, and a strong sense that they are being manipulated by people in positions of authority. This pedagogical moment involves free and critical inquiry into ideas that are beyond the boundaries of normal discourse. It encourages in-depth research, self-directed and collaborative learning, and an ability to analyse and synthesise historical and often ambiguous information. Also, through continuous classroom dialogue, students develop a greater sense of self-worth and tolerance for the opinions of others.

The third moment offers students an opportunity to bring together into some kind of order or unity the information, insights, feelings, emotions, and personal experiences shared and developed in the earlier pedagogical moments. Attempts to generate a unified position begin with a formal classroom debate. The class is divided into two groups - one group represents the interests of the soft drink company, while the other group expresses the concerns of human rights activists. Both groups are assigned a general question: Does the company act with integrity in Burma? The purpose of the debate is not to emphasise a polarity of arguments but to highlight pertinent information that could provide a foundation for a coherent, well-informed and synthesised position. In each group, a student records the discussion taking place while others volunteer to defend the group's position against representatives from the other group.

During the classroom debate, both sides raised significant points. Arguments in defence of the company's business interests and the way it acts with integrity include (1) conducting business in Burma provides employment for the Burmese population, (2) the company's business ventures benefit economically the people of Burma, (3) it is simply an issue of demand and supply - what the public demands, the soft drink company supplies, and (4) the company is not interested in manipulating the public mind, but simply uses the mass media to inform the public about the availability of their products. Arguments claiming that the company's ventures in Burma lack a sense of integrity include: (1) conducting business in Burma; the company supporting a repressive military regime; and (2) the company and other transnational corporations use the mass media and government for their personal interests.

As a result, students leave the debate with a feeling that they are morally responsible for the commodities they purchase. They acknowledge that small businesses often embrace integrity as an integral part of their practices, but corporations tend to operate without any sense of moral or social accountability. They argue that if they purchase commodities from specific corporations, they might be condoning human rights violations or the destruction of the environment in other parts of the world. In addition, they highlight the importance of being media literate. They should watch television, read newspapers, and use other forms of technology in a critical fashion, and be aware of political biases and forms of manipulation. They acknowledge that it's virtually impossible these days to function in society without the use of technology; nevertheless, it should be used with caution.

This moment of pedagogy invites students to use their reasoning skills and unfold their latent powers as critical thinkers. They are encouraged to synthesise and evaluate conflicting points of view, solve problems, challenge traditional propositions, and offer feasible solutions in a collaborative and highly creative learning environment.

Inevitably, many students are anxious to move beyond words to action, to transform the world into a better place. Initially, as a result of the earlier moments, some students decide to make personal lifestyle changes. They try sincerely to escape a consumerist mentality that encourages the judgement of people according to what they possess. Personal relationships deepen in the classroom as students learn to appreciate values such as honesty, friendship, and respect. Others decide to reduce the number of hours they watch television and other sources of technology.

One highly creative response came as the result of some students who researched the relationship between corporate practices and environmental contamination. They considered the business ventures of corporations in the Maquiladora region and found that lax environmental regulations in northern Mexico enable corporations to dispose of hazardous industrial waste haphazardly and without any accountability. This leads to toxic levels of contamination in local streams and rivers. In turn, inhabitants of these communities consume food that is cultivated in the contaminated districts, and they, in turn, are confronted with long-term and often terminal health issues. One student responded to this dire situation by writing a poem that embodies her sense of disconnection from the earth, and the way people use the earth for their self-satisfying needs. It is an example of a unique and highly creative response to a lesson, a response that is far beyond the expectations of any standard curriculum. It is worth quoting in full.

Weeping Willow

On a warm summer day she looked outside to the fields, to the joy they portrayed and the wounds they could heal. Like the pain of a heart that has been newly broken, or the foul taste of lies that has been freshly spoken. So out did she go through the meadows and blades, to the trees that bestowed the most marvellous shade. But amongst all the joy that she thought she had found, was a comfort destroyed when she lay on the ground. She stared at the tree in whose shade she had crept, now quite shocked was she for the willow, it wept.

Why are you weeping, you willow I hear? Is it sadness you're keeping from those who draw near? Your branches do dangle and droop with despair, with sadness entangled in a desperate prayer. Oh, willow do tell, what makes for your sorrows? What's past has but gone, all we have is tomorrow. It may bring the sun, but may also bring a storm, and when the day's done, yet another shall form. And so is the way that the world sets to be, like your branches, we'll sway for eternity.

She rose to her feet, now set out to find a tree that would greet her with a happier kind. Of shades she could steal, for the willow was pain, but then did she squeal when it called out her name.

Daughter of Eden, you ask why I weep. I ask why your sins are so heavy and deep? You speak of tomorrow as a definite vow, but not of the sorrow your kind has bestowed. You speak of the sun but then hide in our shade, and when storms are all done, have your limbs been frayed? Do not speak of time as a work without end, for humanity's crimes do the trees apprehend. You see rivers running like a melodious tune, I see them as bleeding from a large, gaping wound. You see rolling fields alit with a glow, I see burning pastures in pain you can't know. You see critters running, they play and they're freed, I see my companions in a desperate need. So human you are to ask why I weep, as if it's bizarre when you've fallen asleep. While we who protect you, we who provide, are used and abused, we're rotting, we've died! But still you demand, you push and you prod, then look to the heavens and give thanks to God. You're cruel and contemptuous, your heart's filled with greed, and a God who acclaims that is one I don't need. So go, look to brew in the shade of another, but a tree who accepts you cannot be my brother. You see all these willows, you hear all our cries, but grief you won't show on the day that we die. And dried up we'll be when the fields are all burned, only then humanity will see that a tree must be earned.

And then it was silent, the willow had aired, to the girl be it violent the future they shared. So she sat in the meadow, she inhaled the breeze, and amidst all the willows she wept with the trees.[68]

Some students are not content with simple lifestyle changes or poetic reflections on the state of the world. The soft drink vending machine is still in the school, and they want it removed. How can a school community that embraces the values of justice, fairness, and human dignity sell products from a company that condones violence and oppression? The school principal accepts an invitation to join our class to discuss the matter of the vending machine. After explaining the current situation in Burma and the soft drink company's role in it, students requested that the vending machine and its products be removed from school property. The principal listens to the students with undue respect but informs them that the request is beyond his jurisdiction and should be directed to the school trustees.

Before the next meeting of school trustees, a few students meet after school and prepare themselves accordingly. Also, they decided to inform the general school population about the company's activities in Burma and their request to have its products removed from the school. An information flyer is designed and distributed throughout the school. More than 400 students agreed to sign a petition to boycott cafeteria services until the company's products are removed from the school. A copy of the petition is sent to local school trustees, the director of cafeteria services, members of the school board, and the principal of the school.

Over a short period of time, the vending machine became a popular topic of discussion for students and teachers alike. School trustees make it clear that a contractual agreement between the school board and the company forbids the removal of the vending machine, but the director of cafeteria services agrees to supplement the company's products in the cafeteria with other brands.

A final form of transformative action includes a letter writing campaign by students to the company's director of public relations. They express their concern about the company's business activities in Burma and express their urgent request for it to suspend all business activities with the Burmese military regime. Predictably, students do not receive a response from the company, but regardless of the final outcome, they feel assured their efforts play a small yet significant part in the process of social change.

The lesson highlights the overall efficacy of a Chomskyan approach to pedagogy, an approach that promotes both freedom of thought and expression

---

[68] Permission was obtained from the student to include her poem in this manuscript.

and a high level of creative and critical thinking. It can also lead to concrete forms of action for personal or social change. In the lesson cited above, the majority of students achieved a personal conversion experience of sorts. They realised that, even though the corporate sector significantly influences the way they see the world, it is possible to resist corporate influences and live a life defined by the principles of truth and goodness. A few students went a step further and pursued social change. In either case, the learning experience encouraged a process of self-realisation and significant personal transformation.

The transformative moment of this pedagogy invites students to move from theory to concrete forms of personal and social action. It encourages them to analyse critically the socio-political and economic factors that impact their lives. This moment also moves them from a state of acquiescence to one of self-appropriated disagreement or dissent. They learn that things do not have to remain the same - that it is possible to create significant personal and social change.

As I stated earlier, an effective pedagogy is not a step-by-step mechanical process. It does not mean that when students have arrived at a certain pedagogical moment, learning comes to an end. The dynamic structure of the pedagogy presented above suggests that any kind of transformative action leads back naturally to further investigation based on additional personal experiences and further reconsiderations of tradition. In a sense, a pedagogy of this sort is never-ending and reflects in structure and dynamics the overall nature of the learning process.

It is worth reiterating the fact that the overall efficacy of a pedagogy is determined, to a significant degree, by the character and attitude of the classroom teacher. It is absolutely imperative that the teacher is constantly aware of the dynamics in the classroom and is able to redirect the energy and thought processes of students. Also, the teacher must want to be in the classroom, spend valuable time with students, and be willing to explore ideas with them in a way that promotes experiential learning, classroom dialogue, creative thought, and various expressions of transformative action. Clearly, effective teaching comes in many forms. What works for one teacher may not work for another teacher. Approaches to effective teaching must be tried and tested in front of a group of students. Inevitably, it comes down to the dynamic relationship between one teacher and a group of students. In many respects, the classroom is a world unto itself.

In the following chapter, I revisit a discussion I had with Chomsky on education and offer some additional commentary. The discussion acts as an overall synthesis of some of the key ideas discussed in the manuscript.

Chapter 7

A Conversation with Noam Chomsky

In this chapter, I revisit a conversation I had with Chomsky in his MIT office two decades ago[1]. The purpose of the meeting is to explore some key themes in Chomsky's work that relate to education, and use them as a foundation for a critical analysis of the influence of members of the corporate sector, or what Chomsky calls "moral monsters", on public education. In some ways, the conversation provides a brief synthesis of some of the key ideas presented and developed in earlier chapters, but it also offers a personal touch. Often, thoughts and ideas expressed in a book appear rather detached from real human beings, but the themes explored in this conversation come directly from him. The conversation also includes ideas that are not included in the manuscript. At certain points, I offer commentary (in square brackets) to clarify an issue or to relate it to what was discussed in an earlier chapter.

I can recall the two of us sitting in his office, filled to capacity with books, articles, journals, and some cherished photographs. Immediately outside his office is a wonderful poster of Bertrand Russell. During our conversation, Chomsky was completely and authentically attentive to my questions and concerns and responded to them with an unexpected degree of interest and respect. Sometimes, it is difficult for me to believe that a person of such magnificent accomplishments and "arguably one of the most important intellectuals alive,"[2] would be willing to spend more than an hour of his extremely valuable time discussing ideas with a high school teacher. But that merely reinforces the overall public image of Chomsky as a fundamentally decent human being.

---

[1] Philip G. Hill, "Public Education and Moral Monsters: A Conversation with Noam Chomsky." The Canadian Centre for Policy Alternatives, *Our Schools/Our Selves* 10(2) January 2001, pp.73-92. I would like to thank CCPA for permission to include this conversation in my manuscript. There is a mistake immediately following the end of the conversation. The editor of CCPA mentions that, at the time of the interview, I was a "former" high school teacher. In fact, I continued to teach in a high school for an additional twenty years, and retired in 2019.

[2] *The New York Times Book Review*, February 25, 1979.

Human Nature

The conversation begins with a reflection on Chomsky's understanding of human nature. He argues that a clear understanding of what it means to be human should be the foundation of social and political thought. The concept of human nature has been explored at length in earlier chapters, and in the conversation, we focus on the elements of freedom and creativity. Even so, it is worth highlighting at this point that, fundamentally, Chomsky alludes to the fact that human nature is far too complicated to fully comprehend. Nevertheless, I think that his findings in linguistics and his political discourse offer substance to the subject.

[PH] *Humboldt states, "to inquire and to create - these are the centers around which all human pursuits more or less directly revolve."[3] In addition to inquiry and creativity, you recognise freedom as an additional component of human nature. Nevertheless, inquiry, creativity, and the pursuit of freedom are often absent in secondary education. In fact, adolescents often resist invitations to be creative, and would rather sacrifice these components of human nature in order to be part of the herd. What evidence do you have to suggest that inquiry, creativity, and freedom are the essence of human nature?*

[The question incorporates three possible components of human nature - inquiry, creativity, and freedom. In this manuscript, I reduce the components to freedom and creativity, because it is clearly evident that inquiry is part and parcel of human creativity.]

[NC] There is very little evidence, and Humboldt had no evidence either. There is no doubt whatsoever that humans have a rich and complex biological nature. But, the nature of human nature is not well understood. It's well beyond the reach of science. Science has a problem determining the nature of an insect. Nevertheless, our conceptions of human nature are also based on Humboldt. He expressed a rather standard Enlightenment view, pretty much the same view you find in Adam Smith, Kant, and so on.

---

[3] Noam Chomsky, "Toward a Humanistic Conception of Education." Quoted in Walter Feinberg and Henry Rosemont (eds.), *Work, Technology, and Education* (Urbana, Ill.: University of Illinois Press, 1975).

[PH] *Do you agree that one could achieve an understanding of human nature by observing the development of children?*

[With this question I was alluding to Chomsky's findings in linguistics. As I explored earlier, the creative element of human nature is apparent in the way all children acquire a language at approximately the same age. If I had more time, I would have pursued this topic further with him.]

[NC] You can find things out, but it's very important, especially in an era when science has a lot of prestige (merited or not), to be very clear about what is understood and what isn't understood. The fact is that when you get beyond molecules, understanding declines very sharply. When you hear confident pronouncements about anything involving the human sphere, you should be extremely sceptical. Economics, for example, has advanced as far as any subject in the social sciences, but it basically understands nothing about how the economy works.

[PH] *You state that human rights are rooted in human nature. Can you explain what you mean by this statement?*

[NC] Any conception of human rights, whatever it is - reactionary, conservative, reformist, revolutionary - is based on a conception of human nature. If you are a moral creature at all, that is, if you believe you are within the moral domain, your conception is based on some ideas, formulated or not, about what is good for human beings, and that means it's based on some conception of human nature. It makes sense to try to formulate that conception, and to see if you can find evidence to support it.

[Chomsky's response reflects an underlying assumption I assume in the manuscript, that is, that any approach to education incorporates an understanding of human nature.]

[PH] *Do the interests of the corporate sector reflect a very specific understanding of human nature?*

[NC] No. Remember, the condition is that you fall within the moral realm. You don't fall within the moral realm if you are a corporation. Corporations have been designated as persons by radical judicial activism, but that doesn't make them persons. In fact, if we go back to classical liberalism, the Enlightenment, and the foundations of modern intellectual thought - people like Adam Smith, James Madison, and others - these thinkers would have been appalled by the idea that corporations were given personal rights.

A corporation is an institution which exists in a framework of institutions. It is not a person. Maybe the CEO of a corporation is a human being. But, as a corporate executive, the CEO has responsibilities which are institutionally determined, and his responsibility is to be a moral monster. That's the requirement.

[PH] *He has a responsibility to his shareholders.*

[NC] He has a duty, a legal responsibility, to maximise profit and market shares, and that means to be a moral monster. He is given a little leeway for public relations purposes, but not much.

Thought Control

As I noted earlier, Chomsky's political works often make reference to the role played by the mainstream mass media in manipulating and perpetuating manufactured worldviews that enhance the interests of the corporate elite. He argues that powerful voices in the mass media, funded and controlled by the corporate elite, design and propagate ideologies that undermine independent thought and prevent the masses from developing a critical understanding and analysis of institutional structures and their functions.

[PH] *You suggest that the U.S. is "the most free and open society"[4] but has "the most sophisticated, well-guarded and effective system of indoctrination and thought control."[5] How can you explain this apparent contradiction? How can a society be free, open, and well-indoctrinated?*

[NC] It's not a contradiction. The two sides function together. As the capacity to control by force declines, we have to turn to other means of control. The obvious one is propaganda and indoctrination.

[I feel Chomsky is not entirely convincing here. I realise that mind control is necessary in a society that does nor rely on force, but, in this case, is it actually a free and open society?]

---

[4] Otero (ed.), Noam Chomsky: *Language and Politics*, p.599.
[5] Ibid.

[PH] *The parameters of debate are often well-defined by the powerful few.*

[NC] Fortunately, for those of us who want to know, people involved in thought control are very outspoken about it. For example, in the academic social sciences, public intellectuals, the public relations industry, business leaders, government leaders, and so on, are very frank. They mostly talk to each other, but the material is published.

In the 1920s, in the days when the masses thought they could participate in affairs, it was necessary to regiment the public mind like an army regiments its bodies. Otherwise, the public would actually become involved in public affairs, and that would have been unacceptable.

[PH] *In public education, the parameters of debate are often set by people of authority. Students are granted a particular degree of creativity and freedom, but the parameters are well defined. If students use their creativity and freedom to challenge the status quo, then the power held by decision-makers will be threatened.*

[NC] That's interesting ...

[PH] *Do you believe the parameters of debate are intentionally predetermined and controlled by the elite?*

[NC] Yes. I'm just completing my seventieth full-time year in a school. I suppose I have some experience. It's pretty obvious, you can see very clearly. Take a place like MIT, where I am now. Here, they encourage creativity and freedom for a very simple reason - it's a science-based university. Sciences survive on the basis of subversive ideology. Students have to learn to become subversive, to challenge authority.

[PH] *It's a very different situation across the river at Harvard University.*

[NC] Yes, that's a very different situation. When you move outside the sciences, you meet the opposite - control. They want to make sure you don't ask the wrong questions.

[PH] *John Snobelen, Ontario's former Minister of Education, in a speech to senior bureaucrats, stated, "If we really want to fundamentally change the issue in training and ... education, we'll have to make sure we've communicated brilliantly the breakdown in the process we currently experience. That's not easy. We need to invent a crisis. That's not just an act of courage. There's some skill involved."[6] In my opinion, this is a clear example of how members of the business community perpetuate intentionally what you call "necessary illusions" in order to justify to the public the policies and practices of the corporate sector. They create the illusion that public education is in a state of crisis, and that draconian cuts to funding and forms of privatisation are justified. I find it enlightening that a Minister of Education can announce publicly that he intends to invent a crisis to fir his policy, with virtually no public outcry. What does this suggest to you about what Alex Carey calls "grassroots propaganda"?[7]*

[NC] This is probably propaganda aimed at the elite. I'm sure he was not expecting to be read by the public. I don't know the case, but I'm assuming he was talking to colleagues who are expected to understand that it's necessary to invent a crisis. It's very common. When you want to privatise a system, turn it over to unaccountable tyrannies. That's what "privatise" means, and that's what corporations are, that is, unaccountable tyrannies. If you want to take some system out of the public domain, where the public can have some minor role in determining what it is, and put it into the hands of private tyrannies which are unaccountable, first you have to create a crisis. And that is standard.

If you want to privatise railroads, make sure they don't work. Cut back funding, infrastructure, to make them work so badly that people get disgusted with them, and then you can privatise them. The same with everything else. If you want to privatise education, that is, turn it over to private tyrannies, then you can either make it not work by underfunding or plan that it doesn't work. For example, in the United States, the propaganda in the Reagan administration around the Nation of Risk fraud, which is what it was, tried to undermine the whole of the education system.

Corporations are very clear about it. For example, a few years ago, major investment firms, like Lehman Brothers, started sending around brochures to their investors, saying, "Well, we've taken over the health system, we've taken a look at the criminal justice system ... "

---

[6] Quoted in the Canadian Centre for Policy Alternatives, *Our Schools/Our Selves* (December, 1995), p.12.
[7] Carey, *Taking the Risk Out of Democracy*, pp.87-108.

[PH] *Now, it's time for education ...*

[NC] The next big thing to take over is education.

Fifth Freedom

Chomsky argues persuasively that U.S. foreign policy is designed and implemented to create and maintain an international political and economic order which grants corporations access to cheap labour, valuable natural resources, profitable investment climates, export markets, and easy transfer of capital. To establish this scenario, the four fundamental freedoms - freedom of speech, freedom of worship, freedom from want, and freedom from fear - are subjugated to the fifth and most important freedom - the freedom of the corporate sector to rob and exploit on a global scale.

[PH] *According to the U.N. Commission on Human Rights (UNCHR), 40% of Third World countries eligible for military commodities are what Amnesty International calls "unexceptional violators' ' of human rights. Half of the countries have received Canadian military commodities. Canadian companies, for example, have more than $5 billion invested in Indonesia.[8] While the Canadian government has called for international arms embargoes with other nations, Indonesia remains Canada's second largest trading partner. What does this suggest to you about the Canadian government's economic interests and concern for human rights?*

[NC] There is a famous Canadian diplomat, John Holmes, who defined what he called the "Canadian idea." He said the Canadian idea is to stand up for your principles, but to find a way around them. And it's everyone else's idea too.

Canada's role in Indonesia has been disgraceful for a couple of reasons. Indonesia is a rich source of resources, investment opportunities, and markets, and Canada is specifics-oriented. For example, Canada, like the United States, was exalted over the Rwanda-style slaughter that took place in 1965. That event opened up the country to the Fifth Freedom, the freedom to rob and exploit, and it has been like that ever since.

[Chomsky is referring to John Wendell Holmes, Canadian diplomat and recipient of the Order of Canada. In the 1950s, Holmes was caught in a Cold War security net involving

---

[8] For more details, see Sharon Scharfe, *Complicity: Human Rights and Canadian Foreign Policy* (Montreal: Black Rose Books, 1996); Ernie Regehr, "Military Sales." In Robert Matthews and Cranford Pratt (eds.), *Human Rights in Canadian Foreign Policy* (Kingston and Montreal: McGill-Queen's University Press, 1988). pp.209-220.

the Canadian government, RCMP, and the Soviet Union that eventually destroyed his career as a diplomat. The sad unfolding of the events can be found in Lynda Hurst, "John Wendell Holmes: A Hunted Hero." *The Toronto Star*, Sunday, October 11, 2009.]

[PH] *The same old story!*

[NC] Yes, it's a very familiar story, and these are institutional issues. It's like corporations necessarily being moral monsters. States are not moral agents - people maybe, but not States.

Responsibility of Intellectuals

The term *intellectuals* represent a vast and complex array of professionals, including scientists, academics, journalists, and teachers. The term usually implies that these professionals are entrusted with the preservation and propagation of specific ideas and worldviews. As I highlighted earlier in the manuscript, intellectuals tend to be the most indoctrinated members of society. They are subjected to and internalise large doses of propaganda which they, in turn, transmit to the masses. Even so, Chomsky claims forcefully that it's the moral responsibility of intellectuals "to speak the truth and expose the lies" of governments and the corporate elite. This stance leads directly into a difficult area of discourse. Intellectuals are normally supported financially by salaries and grants provided by governments and the corporate sector. Therefore, for one to expect intellectuals to act morally and bite the hands that feed them is rather problematic. Nevertheless, Chomsky's own life events prove that it is possible to live a life of moral responsibility, but it takes hard work and many risks.

[PH] *One of the striking similarities between you and Bertrand Russell is your unending desire to speak the truth and expose the lies. I sense an underlying assumption in your efforts: when people know the truth, they will act the right way. Why are you convinced that people will change their ways of conduct in light of the truth, rather than act solely on selfish premises?*

[NC] I'm not convinced. I'm not convinced at all. But, that's the only hope there is. There is certainly no hope of people acting decently under the weight of lies. So, either it's either truth, or nothing.

[PH] *Do you witness a lot of encouraging behaviour on the part of workers to keep you motivated to continue your political efforts?*

[NC] Sure. The world is a lot better than it was two centuries ago, and it's a lot better than it was 30 years ago. Things have changed, mostly for the better, not entirely. But, there is a kind of uphill cycle of agonisingly slow progress. And it comes, not from gifts, but from popular struggle. The feudal system didn't disappear because the aristocrats decided to be nice and to have parliamentary democracy. Likewise, slavery didn't disappear because slave owners wanted to be nice people to the slaves. And it continues to the present. Women's rights, to the extent that they have been achieved, were not given, they were won.

[PH] *You suggest that in order to challenge current trends to privatise publicly-funded institutions, one requires a rare combination of qualities - courage, passion, tenacity, and self-confidence. These qualities are often associated with risks - we may lose our jobs, be denied access to promotions or contracts, or be alienated by our peers. Can we expect teachers and other professionals to challenge current trends, if the stakes, at least in the short-run, are often costly?*

[NC] It is true, one should not underestimate the costs. But, by comparative standards, those costs are pretty mild. We do not live in societies where these efforts lead to torture chambers, or assassination by death squads. These are things people face in most parts of the world, and have faced during most of history. The kind of costs that we face, by comparative standards, are pretty marginal.

[I shared this comment with numerous teachers who are involved in social activism, and it incited tremendous discussion. Granted, teachers in this part of the world do not live under the threat of imprisonment, torture, and death for their involvement in social change; nevertheless, the sacrifices they make, both at work and at home, are not regarded by them as being "pretty marginal." I have been personally involved with the struggle of teachers in Mexico, and fully appreciate what Chomsky is alluding to, but I am not entirely sure that similar efforts by teachers in so-called democratic nations can be treated as pretty marginal efforts. Chomsky has tremendous respect for teachers, so I assume what he meant to say is perhaps different to the way it was expressed]

[PH] *We should keep these things in perspective?*

[NC] Yes, we should keep these things in perspective. We are so privileged.

[PH] *In Mexico, the situation confronted by teachers is very different. Lives are lost daily.*

[This was confirmed through my work with the Trinational Coalition in Defence of Public Education. The Coalition emerged in the 1990s, in response to concerns about the impact of NAFTA on publicly-funded education. It is organised and led by teachers, teachers' unions, and academics from Mexico, the United States, and Canada. It is through discussions with teachers from Mexico that I learned about the extremely challenging conditions in which they work. In addition, I have worked in a high school in Mexico, and have witnessed first-hand the terrible working conditions of teachers. Also, a sister-in-law of mine works as an elementary school teacher in the State of Veracruz, and the relationship between a corrupt police force, the local drug cartel, and an equally corrupt teachers' union makes for a challenging teaching and learning environment.]

[NC] That's true. Teachers are killed and tortured, and so on. Here, it's very different. It could happen if you are, say, poor, Black, and from an urban ghetto. But, relatively privileged White people ...

[PH] *You state that "the main task for intellectuals," and I assume you include teachers in the term 'intellectuals,' "aside from resistance to repression and violence, is to try to articulate goals, to try to assess, to try to understand, to try to persuade, to try to organize." These can be extremely time-consuming activities. Work expectations and life outside the workplace demand a tremendous amount of one's time and energy. At the end of the day, the last thing a teacher wants to do is conduct research, attend community-based meetings, and so forth. Such a life leads to what you call a "schizophrenic existence, which seems to me morally obligatory and not at all impossible, in practice."[9] It may be morally obligatory, but do you believe it is a realistic expectation?*

[NC] These are human responsibilities. But, responsibility corresponds with privilege. The more privilege you have, the more responsibility you have. For example, if you are a couple, working an 80-hour week to put food on the table for the children, your responsibility is less than if you had a degree of education, freedom, opportunity, resources, and so on. Privilege often means relative freedom from certain causes. Then, people must make their own decisions ...

---

[9] Noam Chomsky, "Philosopher and Public Philosophy." *Ethics* 79(1), October 1968, pp.1-9.

[PH] *Moral responsibilities often conflict with current trends in society.*

[NC] Yes. In New England, the place where the Industrial Revolution began in North America, in the textile firms there was a very lively and keen interest in working class literature. Back 150 years ago or more, in factory guilds, men and women from the farms, labouring people, Irish immigrants [were engaged in study groups] ... One of the themes that they stressed was their "contempt for the new spirit of the age, gain wealth, forgetting all but self." That was 150 years ago. There was an effort at the beginning of the Industrial Revolution to drive out of people's heads normal human feelings - solidarity, cooperativeness, and so on. [It was tantamount] to the monsters who wanted nothing but to gain wealth, forgetting all but self, because that's the way the system works. It's not easy to do this.

In fact, a large part of the function of the whole indoctrination system, including schools, the popular arts, and advertising, and so on, is to try to turn people into that kind of creature. In the advertising and public relations industries, it's a very conscious effort. It is understood that one of the best ways to control people is to turn them into mindless consumers. It is interesting that this has been understood for hundreds of years.

Libertarian Socialism

I have considered in detail Chomsky's understanding of libertarian socialism. It is firmly rooted in the radical humanist values of the Enlightenment, classical liberalism, and anarchism. In addition, Chomsky often refers to progressive thinkers, including Dewey, independent socialists such as Bertrand Russell, and leading elements of anti-Bolshevik Marxism.

[PH] *You claim that "classical libertarian thought is opposed to State intervention in social life as a consequence of deeper assumptions about human nature and the need for liberty, diversity and free association."[10] Would you agree that, contrary to classical anarchist thought, we, in fact, need State protection from the corporate sector?*

[NC] It's not contrary to classical anarchist thought. Classical anarchist thought would have been more opposed to slavery, feudalism, fascism, and so on, than it would have been to parliamentary government. There was a good reason. Classical liberal thought, and anarchism coming out of it, were opposed to any

---

[10] Noam Chomsky, "Introduction." In Daniel Guerin, *Anarchism: From Theory to Practice* (New York: Monthly Review Press, 1970), p.xii.

concentration of power, that is, unaccountable concentration of power. It is reasonable to make a distinction between the more unaccountable and less accountable. Corporations are the least accountable. So, against the corporate assault on freedom and independence, one can quickly turn to the one form of social organisation that offers public participation and that happens to be parliamentary government. That has nothing to do with being opposed to the State. In fact, it's a sensible support for the State.

[This is an interesting comment. I am not sure if Chomsky's position on the relationship between classical anarchist thought and State protection is entirely accurate. As we saw earlier, libertarian socialism acknowledges the important role played by the State, but I am not entirely convinced that classical anarchists would agree. For instance, I already considered the anarchist views of Francisco Ferrer and Leo Tolstoy, and they were absolutely against the State. Also, both Michael Bakunin and Peter Kropotkin, and even contemporary self-proclaimed anarchists like Murray Bookchin and George Woodcock distanced themselves from the State. Granted, classical anarchists were against any form of hierarchy, including slavery, feudalism, and fascism, but they also included the State in this category.]

[PH] *In the United States and Canada, in the public health and public education sectors, workers have the option not to join a union. In Canada, this applies directly to nurses and, to a certain degree, to administrators in public education who have been removed entirely from teachers' associations. This choice is impacting significantly the dynamics of organised labour. In light of such changes, do you believe that anarcho-syndicalism is the most effective route to pursue, in order for one to challenge trends to privatise publicly-funded institutions, or perhaps, a from of anarcho-communism in the tradition of Peter Kropotkin and Elisee Reclus?*

[NC] First of all, the right not to join a union was the traditional right. There was a long struggle to gain the right to be a member of a union. The norm was to destroy unions. Unions were hated by concentrated power. Unions were subjected to tremendous attack.

In popular culture, for example, for the past 150 years, a major theme has been to try to undermine and discredit unions. Two or three days ago, there was an interesting article in the leading international business daily, *The Financial Times* in London, about the establishment in England of training corporations on how to break up unions, borrowing American ideas and developments, and so on. It was pretty frank. Businesses don't like unions, and they have to work on ways of undermining and destroying them.

One of Thatcher's main goals was to destroy the union movement, and, in particular, the mine workers, because they were militant and organised. In fact, she destroyed the British mining industry, not so much because it was uncompetitive - it was competitive - but, the destruction of the industry was an extremely important goal because unions are a democratising force. They enable people to work together.

Actually, the attack on unions is, in a way, very much like the attack on social security, public education, and so on. All of these institutions are based on the idea that people should help one another, and that is unacceptable. The idea that people should help one another is extremely dangerous because then what?

What is the best way? Not by theoretical ideas - communitarian approaches, anarcho-syndicalism, and so on. We have real life struggles. We can have long-term goals, too. It makes sense to have them. And those long-term goals should be discussed and debated, but you have immediate struggles over a wide range of alternative long-term goals, like those you mentioned. There is a common agreement on the problems to be faced right now.

[It is worth noting that Chomsky did not address the reference I made to the anarcho-communist views of Kropotkin and Reclus. I anticipated that the question would motivate him to comment on the important role played by unions in social change, especially because he often refers to the works of anarcho-syndicalist Michael Bakunin, but it would have been interesting to hear his position on anarcho-communism. On occasion, Chomsky makes a brief reference to Kropotkin, but he clearly favours anarcho-syndicalism.]

[PH] *In my opinion, there is a link between community-based business-education partnership programmes and corporate-funded regional, national, and international institutions. In Canada, for example, there are between 15,000 and 20,000 business-education partnership programmes. The primary aim of the programmes, promotion material, guidelines, and methods of evaluation are very similar. In Ontario, school-based and Board-based programmes often seek advice from corporate-funded regional institutions, such as the Toronto Area Partnership and the Learning Partnership. These regional bodies rely heavily on national groups like the Conference Board of Canada, Business Council on National Issues, Canadian Chamber of Commerce, right-wing think tanks like the C.D. Howe Institute and the Fraser Institute, and intellectual forums such as the International Partnership Network and the OECD. When I discuss these links with my colleagues, I am often regarded as some sort of conspiracy theorist, or wacky and paranoid political animal. Do you believe such links are coincidental, or designed and implemented intentionally?*

[For information regarding the intricate relationship between publicly-funded education and the corporate sector, see my report: *Ontario Catholic Education and the Corporate Sector* (Institute for Catholic Education, 1997).]

[NC] It would be amazing if they weren't professing the same thing. They have the same general interests.

[PH] *Do you believe there is an intentional link?*

[NC] I assume so. I would be very surprised if it weren't an intentional link. People communicate it to them. It is a relatively small group of people with very common interests and a high degree of class consciousness. The business world is very Marxist, super Marxist. When you read business publications, it is like reading vulgar Marxism. They pretty much understand what they are struggling for.

[PH] *In 1996, a report by the Lehman Brothers stated that education could replace health care as the politically hot industry for private sector involvement.[11] What does this report suggest to you about the future of publicly-funded education?*

[NC] What it suggests is that people should have the same understanding the Lehman Brothers have. [The business community] wants to destroy democracy, social growth, social solidarity, mutual support for people, sympathy - the traditional ideals that normal, decent human beings struggle for.

[PH] *Michael Apple refers to what he calls "intensification," that is, the many ways the "work privileges of educational workers are eroded" by people of greater authority.[12] Through a process of intensification, teachers are unable to 'stand back' from the schooling process, in order to reflect on and challenge forms of injustice and oppression in the workplace. They are too busy with busy work - compulsory over-evaluation of students, endless and often unnecessary supervision duties, meetings, and so on. The time required to dialogue critically with others is not available. Do you believe attempts in recent years to intensify the workplace are, in fact, intentional acts on the part of powerful decision-makers to marginalise and pacify workers?*

[NC] It could be an intentional act. I don't know the details, but what you describe is part of a much broader tendency which more or less falls under a particular concept of efficiency. There is a highly developed concept of efficiency which has been designed so that efficiency is determined essentially by profit margins. One of the consequences is that costs are transferred to individuals. These costs are not measured. And that's all over

---

[11] Lehman Brothers, *Investment Opportunity in the Education Industry,* 1996.
[12] Michael Apple, *Teachers and Texts: A Political Economy of Class and Gender Relations in Education* (New York: Routledge, 1988), p.41.

the economy. So, take, say, doctors. In privatised health systems, you can get higher efficiency by some measures, but only by not counting the costs transferred to the individuals. Doctors spend 40% of their time filling out forms. That's not counted. If the patient waits an hour in an office or emergency room, that is not counted. And this happens all over the place.

[PH] *In education, it might be a question of inefficiency. When we are overworked, we become highly inefficient.*

[NC] Yes. Efficiency is an ideological construct. It is not an objective notion. There are measures of efficiency by which it is efficient to increase costs. Take, say, something as simple as the measuring of the gross domestic product. There are easy ways to increase the gross domestic product. For example, don't repair the street. When you drive, your car gets destroyed, and you have to go to a mechanic and buy new parts, and that all increases the gross domestic product. In fact, increasing pollution is a good way to increase the gross domestic product. It makes people sick, they have to go to doctors, to medical establishments, and so on.

[PH] *In 'Primer of Liberation Education,' Joel Spring suggests that, based on principles of libertarian education, decision-making regarding education spending should be determined by the individual, not by school boards.[13] Do you agree that a proposal of this nature coincides with attempts in recent years by corporate-funded organisations to introduce charter schools into the domain of publicly-funded education?*

[NC] Students should have a role, but there's nothing wrong with a democratically elected community board. There are a lot of ways to arrange public education. Charter schools and voucher schools, we need to look at them case by case. There are negative features to the general concept, and it does undermine public education. You are undermining the conception that I should care if the kid down the street has an education.

---

[13] Joel Spring, *A Primer of Libertarian Education* (Montreal: Black Rose Books, 1975).

[PH] *You state that "schools function in many ways as instruments of indoctrination ... Students are rewarded for obedience and passivity."[14] "Schools are the first training ground for the troops that will enforce the muted, unending terror of the status quo."[15] Nevertheless, you also claim that "it is possible in practice for schools to foster the creative impulses that are rather natural from childhood on and to encourage a constant willingness to challenge established doctrine and authority."[16] How can we, as educators, reconcile these two apparently conflicting aims of education?*

[NC] They can't operate at the same time. They are two opposing conceptions of education. Which conception wins out depends on the successes of popular struggle. It is perfectly clear why there should be an effort to turn the schools into institutions of indoctrination and regimentation, and if people don't want that, they will have to struggle for it. But these can't co-exist, side-by-side.

[This was a rather unanticipated response to my question. I think it is quite possible to foster a creative impulse in schools and other institutions that act as instruments of indoctrination. In fact, it is the motivating factor behind the personal teaching experiences explored in this manuscript. The personal experiences expressed in the manuscript show clearly that it is possible for teachers and students to expand the parameters of debate within an institutional setting. Granted, at times, there are prices to be paid - reprimands, alienation, job loss, and so on - but, regardless of the price, it is possible to seek a greater sense of freedom and creativity than what is permitted by institutional powers.]

[PH] *Milton Friedman states, "few trends could so thoroughly undermine the very foundation of our free society as the acceptance by corporate officials of a social responsibility other than to make as much money for their shareholders as possible."[17] In recent years, concerned educators have proposed that school boards implement codes of conduct to ensure that corporations which violate human rights or exploit the environment do not participate in business-education partnership programmes. Do you believe codes of conduct could be an effective tool to protect schools from privatising efforts of big business?*

[NC] First of all, Milton Friedman is basically correct, but he didn't go far enough. It has nothing to do with freedom, it has to do with tyranny. But if you replace the word 'freedom' by 'tyranny,' he is basically correct.

---

[14] Otero (ed.), *Noam Chomsky: Language and Politics*, p.393.
[15] Noam Chomsky, "Some thoughts on intellectuals and the schools." Ibid.
[16] Ibid, p.393.
[17] Quoted in Heather-Jane Robertson, *No More Teachers, No More Books: The Commercialisation of Canada's Schools* (Toronto: McClelland & Stewart, 1998), p.284.

It would undermine the conception of private tyranny for corporate executives to try to meet conditions of social responsibility. But, that doesn't go far enough. They have a legal responsibility not to be concerned with issues of responsibility. Now, why do they do it at all? For public relations. For the same reasons why dictatorships can be benevolent. Under certain conditions, a dictatorship will act in a benevolent fashion. Take, say, Nazi Germany - an extreme case. Nazi Germany did conduct a kind of social revolution in which people made many gains in their individual lives. And that was part of the reason they were so popular. And it was done very consciously.

[PH] *A wise educator once said the aim of education is "the education of individuals who are well integrated, free and independent in their thinking, concerned about improving and enhancing the world, and eager to participate in making life more meaningful and worthwhile for all."*[18] *Do you know who stated these words of wisdom?*

[NC] It sounds like John Dewey.

[PH] *It was your father.*

[NC] Really! Well, he was a Deweyite. That's straight from Dewey.

[PH] *Do you have anything to add to your father's view on education?*

[NC] I could add something, but it would be more or less the same thing.

---

[18] Quoted in Barsky, *Noam Chomsky*, p.11.

Conclusion

[A]s a corporate executive, the CEO has responsibilities which are institutionally determined, and his responsibility is to be a moral monster.

(Noam Chomsky in discussion with author)

It is assumed in this manuscript that any approach to teaching and learning is based upon an understanding of human nature. That is, it is assumed that what one tries to do as a teacher in the classroom reflects, perhaps in an inarticulate fashion, what it means to be human. If, on the one hand, one practises a form of pedagogy that encourages rote memory, acquiescence, obedience, strict classroom management, punishment and reward, boredom, and other qualities of a traditional approach, then one assumes that human beings are by nature passive, malleable, uncritical empty vessels, and future cogs in a vast machinery of production and consumption. If, on the other hand, one practises a pedagogy that promotes creative and critical thought, collaborative learning, dialogue, and freedom of thought and expression, then one assumes that human beings, by their very nature, seek fundamental creative and liberatory principles.

A significant part of this manuscript is devoted to an exploration of human nature. What does it mean to be human? Are humans merely modified apes, or is there something truly unique about the human species? Through a fairly detailed exposition of key ideas in Chomsky's linguistics and political discourse, I hope it has become evident that the essence of human nature includes freedom and creativity. Also, I have shown that it is possible to develop and apply a Chomskyan approach to pedagogy based on his findings as a linguist, left-libertarian political thinker, and educator.

On any given day, the overall effectiveness of a pedagogy is influenced by a myriad of variables, including, in my case, the hopes, aspirations, anxieties, and often unpredictable behaviour of teenagers. Pedagogies, like new shoes, have to be tried and tested. They have to be applied, modified, and developed to meet the needs and expectations of a particular group of students. What works for one group of students may not work for another group. There is no simple formula for success in the classroom, but the qualities promoted by a Chomskyan approach are key parts of the equation. If one begins with an understanding of human nature that promotes freedom and creativity, then, it would appear, one is on the right path. There will be many obstacles along the way, but the path is pointed in the right direction.

Young children are terrified of monsters. They run and hide and wait until the monsters are gone. These monsters are not real - they are simply the product of a child's highly creative imagination. In schools, the monsters, or what Chomsky calls the "moral monsters", are real. As indicated in the epigraph above, Chomsky refers specifically to CEOs of large corporations as moral monsters, but one can easily modify the expression to mean any and all aspects of education that contradict the overall aim of a Chomskyan approach to pedagogy. Commonly, monsters of this sort are not easily recognisable, but their presence is felt everywhere - in curriculum development, teaching methodologies, teacher-training programmes, student evaluation procedures, business-education partnership programmes, and even, as I noted, on school posters and vending machines. They promote a particularly oppressive and dehumanising understanding of human nature. In many respects, these monsters are like a gentle undercurrent that slowly pulls one away from the shore, and only after it is too late does one realise that the current existed at all. The damage has been done.

Educational policy and procedures are defined and implemented by school boards that are funded and controlled by ministries of education. These ministries, in turn, embrace the interests and concerns of their major financial contributors, including members of the corporate sector, large financial institutions, and other significant political and economic forces in society. This is where the political element in education becomes blatantly obvious. Even though governments' rhetoric emphasises the attributes of publicly-funded education and the importance of the individual learner; nevertheless, in reality, the picture is often quite different. It is true that local school boards and ministries of education rhetorically nod in agreement about the urgency of improving schools, but the underlying interests that promote these messages are often driven by the business community. Publicly-funded schools may be funded by the public, but they tend to serve the needs of the corporate elite. Historically, isn't that the primary function of public education, to serve the interests of the private sector?

A Chomskyan approach to education offers teachers a legitimate alternative to a predominantly conservative approach to schooling. It empowers teachers and students with the tools necessary to remove monsters from the classroom. It creates truly authentic, experientially-based teaching and learning experiences, challenges acquiescence, encourages creative and critical thought, promotes the free expression of ideas, enhances reasoning skills, creates a participatory and communal classroom environment, and treats students with reverence. This approach also invites students to seek ways to transform current socio-political and economic forces to coincide with human nature. Teachers embrace wholeheartedly both a love of learning and the richness of tradition. They want to spend valuable time with students, exploring their exciting ideas, and coming to know them as authentic human beings. Teachers encourage students to move beyond words and seek an ontological change - a change of being itself. In most cases, this involves a process of intellectual or moral conversion, that is, a form of self-appropriation that uses truth and goodness as overarching guiding principles.

Thirty years ago, a local school board official evaluated my teaching as the final part of the provincial teacher licensing process. I was a relatively young and inexperienced teacher at the time and cherished the opportunity to explore interesting ideas with high school students. I do not recall most of my brief interaction with the evaluator, but I do remember one piece of valuable advice he offered me. He told me to always hold onto my idealistic vision of education, that is, do not conform to the norm, and do not be afraid to swim against the current.

I kept the advice close to my heart throughout my years as an educator, and it acted like a rudder, constantly pointing me in the right direction amidst tremendous obstacles. The greatest challenge that confronts teachers today is the ability to develop and maintain a sense of hope in the classroom and share it in an enthusiastic manner with their students. If one loses hope, then conditions in education will continue to worsen. With hope, there is always a glimmering light on the horizon, and I feel a Chomskyan approach to pedagogy offers teachers this sense of hope. I will grant Chomsky the last words in the manuscript. He states,

> If you assume that there is no hope, you guarantee that there will be no hope. If you assume that there is an instinct for freedom, that there are opportunities to change things, then there is a possibility that you can contribute to making a better world.[1]

---

[1] Quoted in goodreads.com

Bibliography

Alston, Charlotte. *Tolstoy and His Disciples: The History of a Radical International Movement.* London: I.B. Tauris, 2014.

Apple, Michael. *Ideology and Curriculum.* New York: Routledge, 1979.

_____. *Teachers and Texts: A Political Economy of Class and Gender Relations in Education.* New York: Routledge, 1988.

Aquinas, Thomas. *Summa Theologiae* (5 Volumes). Notre Dame, IN.: Ave Maria Press, 1948.

Archambault, Reginald D. (ed.). *John Dewey on Education.* Chicago: University of Chicago Press, 1974.

Archer, William. *The Life, Trial, and Death of Francisco Ferrer.* Honolulu, Hawaii: University Press of the Pacific, 2001.

Aronowitz, Stanley and Giroux, Henry. *Education Under Siege: The Conservative, Liberal, and Radical Debate Over Schooling.* South Hadley, Mass.: Bergin and Garvey, 1985.

_____ and _____. *Postmodern Education: Politics, Culture, and Social Criticism.* Minneapolis: University of Minnesota Press, 1991.

Avrich, Paul. *The Modern School Movement: Anarchism and Education in the United States.* Princeton, New Jersey: Princeton University Press, 1980.

Barsky, Robert F. *Noam Chomsky: A Life of Dissent.* Toronto: ECW Press, 1997.

_____. *The Chomsky Effect: A Radical Works Beyond the Ivory Tower.* Cambridge, Mass.: MIT Press, 2007.

Baum, Gregory. *Religion and Alienation: A Theological Reading of Sociology.* New York: Paulist Press, 1975.

_____. *Theology and Society.* New York: Paulist Press, 1987.

Bazelon, David. *Power in America: The Politics of the New Class.* New York: The New American Library, Inc., 1963.

Bell, Daniel. "Labour in the Post-Industrial Society." *Dissent* (Winter, 1972).

Berwick, Robert C. and Chomsky, Noam. *Why Only Us: Language and Evolution.* Cambridge, Massachusetts: The MIT Press, 2016.

Bickerton, Derek. *Language and Species.* Chicago: University of Chicago Press, 1990.

_____. *Adam's Tongue: How Humans Made Language, How Language Made Humans.* New York: Hill and Wang, 2009.

_____. *More Than Nature Needs: Language, Mind, and Evolution.* Cambridge, Massachusetts: Harvard University Press, 2014.

Bickman, Martin (ed.). *Uncommon Learning: Thoreau on Education.* Boston: Houghton Mifflin Company, 1999.

Blaisdell, Bob (ed.). *Tolstoy as Teacher: Leo Tolstoy's Writings on Education.* New York: Teachers & Writers Collaborative, 2000.

Bloomfield, Leonard. *Language.* London: George Allen & Unwin, 1933.

Boas, Franz. *Handbook of American Indian Languages.* Washington: Washington Printing Office, 1911 & 1922.

Bookchin, Murray, *The Modern Crisis.* Montreal: Black Rose Books, 1987.

_____. *The Philosophy of Social Ecology: Essays on Dialectical Naturalism.* Montreal: Black Rose Books, 1990.

_____. *The Ecology of Freedom: The Emergence and Dissolution of Hierarchy.* Montreal: Black Rose Books, 1991.

Bowles, Samuel and Gintis, Herbert. *Democracy & Capitalism: Property, Community, and the Contradictions of Modern Social Thought.* New York: Basic Books, 1986.

_____. *Schooling in Capitalist America: Educational Reform and the Contradictions of Economic Life.* New York: Basic Books, 1987.

Bray, Mark and Hayworth, Robert (eds.). *Anarchist Education and the Modern School: A Francisco Ferrer Reader.* Oakland: PM Press, 2019.

Carey, Alex. *Taking the Risk Out of Democracy.* Sydney: University of New South Wales Press, 1995.

Chomsky, Noam. *Syntactic Structures.* The Hague: Mouton & Co., 1957.

_____. *Cartesian Linguistics.* New York: Harper & Row, 1966.

_____. "Philosopher and Public Philosophy." *Ethics* 79(1), October 1968.

_____. *The Logical Structure of Linguistic Theory.* Chicago: The University of Chicago Press, 1975.

_____. *Morphophonemics of Modern Hebrew.* New York, 1979. Originally a 1951 University of Pennsylvania MA thesis, revised version of a 1949 University of Pennsylvania BA thesis.

_____. *The Washington Connection and Third World Fascism.* Montreal: Black Rose Books, 1979.

_____. and Herman, Edward. *After the Cataclysm: Postwar Indochina & the Reconstruction of Imperial Ideology.* Montreal: Black Rose Books, 1979.

_____. *Rules and Representations.* New York: Columbia University Press, 1980.

_____. *Towards a New Cold War: Essays on the Current Crisis and How We Got There.* New York: Pantheon Books, 1982.

_____. *The Logical Structure of Linguistic Theory.* Chicago: University of Chicago Press, 1985.

_____. *On Power and Ideology.* Montreal: Black Rose Books, 1987.

_____. *Turning the Tide: The U.S. and Latin America.* Montreal: Black Rose Books, 1987.

_____. *Deterring Democracy.* New York: Hill and Wang, 1991.

_____. *Necessary Illusions: Thought Control in Democratic Societies.* Concord: Anansi, 1991.

_____. *Year 501: The Conquest Continues.* Montreal: Black Rose Books, 1993.

_____. *The Prosperous Few and the Restless Many.* Berkeley, California: Odonian Press, 1993.

_____. *What Uncle Sam Really Wants.* Berkeley, California: Odonian Press, 1993.

_____. *Secrets, Lies and Democracy.* Tucson, Arizona: Odonian Press, 1994.

_____. *World Orders Old and New.* New York: Columbia University Press, 1994.

_____. *Class Warfare*. Monroe, Maine: Common Courage Press, 1996.

_____. *Language and Problems of Knowledge*. Cambridge, Mass.: The MIT Press (eighth printing), 1996.

_____. *Powers & Prospects: Reflections on Human Nature and the Social Order*. Boston: South End Press, 1996.

_____. *The Common Good*. Tucson, Arizona: Odonian Press, 1998.

_____. *The Architecture of Language*. New Delhi: Oxford University Press, 2006.

_____ and Michel Foucault, *The Chomsky-Foucault Debate on Human Nature*. New York: The New York Press, 2006.

_____. *The Science of Language: Interviews with James McGilvray*. Cambridge: Cambridge University Press, 2012.

_____. *The Minimalist Program* (twentieth anniversary edition). Cambridge, Massachusetts: The MIT Press, 2015.

Chomsky, William. *Hebrew: The Eternal Language*. Melrose Park, PA: Jewish Publication Society of America, 1957.

Cook, V. J. and Newson, Mark. *Chomsky's Universal Grammar*. Malden, Massachusetts: Blackwell Publishing, 2007.

Cramer, Jeffrey S. (ed.), *The Quotable Thoreau*. Princeton: Princeton University Press, 2011.

Crowe, Frederick E. *Old Things and New: A Strategy for Education*. Atlanta, Georgia: Scholars Press, 1985.

Czerny, Michael and Swift, Jamie. *Getting Started on Social Analysis in Canada*. Toronto: Between the Lines, 1984.

Darwin, Charles. *On the Origin of Species by Means of Natural Selection*. London: John Murray, 1859.

_____. *The Descent of Man and Selections in Relation to Sex*. London: John Murray, 1871.

_____. *The Expressions of the Emotions in Man and Animals*. London: John Murray, 1872.

_____. *The Formation of Vegetable Mould Through the Action of Worms*. London: John Murray, 1881.

Dennett, Daniel C. *Darwin's Dangerous Idea: Evolution and the Meaning of Life*. New York: Touchstone, 1995.

Dewey, John. *Experience & Education*. New York: Collier Books, 1963. Originally published in 1938.

_____. *Democracy and Education*. New York: The Free Press, 1966. Originally published in 1916.

Dickens, Charles. *Hard Times*. New York: W. W. Norton, 1966. Originally published in England in 1854 by Bradbury & Evans.

Edgerton, William. *Memoirs of Peasant Tolstoyans in Soviet Russia*. Bloomington: Indiana University Press, 1993.

Feinberg, Walter and Rosemont, Henry (eds.). *Work, Technology, and Education*. Urbana, Illinois: University of Illinois Press, 1975.

Freire, Paulo. *Education for Critical Consciousness*. New York: Continuum, 1971.

_____. *Education for Critical Consciousness*. New York: Continuum, 1971.

_____. *Pedagogy of the Oppressed.* New York: Continuum, 1987.

Friederici, Angela D. *Language in the Brain: The Origins of a Uniquely Human Capacity.* Cambridge, Massachusetts: The MIT Press, 2017.

Galbraith, John Kenneth. *The Culture of Contentment.* Boston: Houghton Mifflin Company, 1992.

Goodman, Paul. *Compulsory Miseducation and the Community of Scholars.* New York: Vintage Books, 1966.

Guerin, Daniel. *Anarchism: From Theory to Practice.* New York: Monthly Review Press, 1970.

Hargrove, Barbara. *The Emerging New Class: Implications for Church and Society.* New York: The Pilgrim Press, 1986.

Hauser, Marc D. *The Evolution of Communication.* Cambridge, Massachusetts: The MIT Press, 1997.

_____. Chomsky, Noam and Fitch, W. Tecumseh. 2002. The language faculty: What is it, who has it, and how did it evolve? *Science* 298:1569-79. Also included in Larson et al., *The Evolution of Human Language.*

Herman, Edward S. *The Real Terror Network: Terrorism in Fact and Propaganda.* Boston: South End Press, 1982.

_____. and Chomsky, Noam. *Manufacturing Consent: The Political Economy of the Mass Media.* New York: Pantheon Books, 1988.

Highest, Gilbert. *The Art of Teaching.* New York: Vintage Books, 1977.

Hill, Philip G. "Do we know the whole story? The Business-Education Partnership and Corporate Social Responsibility". *The Reporter: The Magazine of the Ontario English Catholic Teachers' Association,* 21(3), February 1996.

_____. "The Business-Education Partnership: We shouldn't ignore corporate social responsibility." Canadian Centre for Policy Alternatives, *Education Monitor: Reporting on Education and Public Policy Issues* 1(1), November 1996.

_____. *Ontario Catholic Education and the Corporate Sector: A Report Submitted to the Institute for Catholic Education.* Toronto: Institute for Catholic Education, 1997.

_____. "Public Education and Moral Monsters: A Conversation with Noam Chomsky." The Canadian Centre for Policy Alternatives, *Our Schools/Our Selves* 1(1), 2001.

Hull, David. "On Human Nature," *Proceedings of the Biennial Meeting of the Philosophy of Science Association,* 1986 (2).

Humboldt, Wilhelm von. *The Limits of State Action.* Cambridge: Cambridge University Press, 1969. Originally published in 1852.

Illich, Ivan. *Deschooling Society.* New York: Harper & Row, 1971.

Kaufmann, Walter. *Hegel: A Reinterpretation.* Notre Dame: University of Notre Dame Press, 1988.

Kavanaugh, John. *Following Christ in a Consumer Society: The Spirituality of Cultural Resistance.* New York: Orbis Books, 1981.

Kirylo, James. *A Critical Pedagogy of Resistance: 34 Pedagogues We Need to Know.* Boston: Brill Publishers, 2013.

Kropotkin, Peter. *Mutual Aid: A Factor of Evolution.* Montreal: Black Rose Books, 1989. Originally published in 1902.

_____. *Fields, Factories and Workshops.* Montreal: Black Rose Books, 1994. Originally published in 1898.

Lane, Dermot. *Foundations for a Social Theory: Praxis, Process and Salvation.* New York: Paulist Press, 1983.

Larson, Richard, Deprez, Viviane, and Yamakido, Hiroko (eds.). *Evolution of Human Language: Biolinguistic Perspectives.* Cambridge: Cambridge University Press, 2011.

Lee, Martin and Soloman, Norman. *Unreliable Sources: A Guide to Detecting Bias in News Media.* New Jersey: Carol Publishing, 1992.

Lenneberg, Eric. *Biological Foundations of Language.* New York: John Wiley & Sons, Inc., 1967.

Lieberman, Philip. *The Biology and Evolution of Language.* Cambridge, Massachusetts: Harvard University Press, 1984.

_____. *Human Language and Our Reptilian Brain: The Subcortical Bases of Speech, Syntax, and Thought.* Cambridge, Massachusetts: Harvard University Press, 2000.

_____. *Toward an Evolutionary Biology of Language.* Cambridge, Massachusetts: The Belknap Press of Harvard University Press, 2006.

Lonergan, Bernard. *Method in Theology.* New York: Seabury Press, 1979.

Lucas, Victor. *Tolstoy in London.* London: Evans Brothers Limited, 1979.

Lyons, John. *Chomsky.* London: Fontana Press, 1991.

Macedo, Donaldo. *Literacies of Power: What Americans are not Allowed to Know.* Boulder: Westview Press, 1994.

_____ (ed.). *Chomsky on MisEducation.* New York: Rowman & Littlefield Publishers, Inc., 2000.

MacLean, Eleanor. *Between the Lines: How to Detect Bias and Propaganda in the News and Everyday Life.* Montreal: Black Rose Books, 1981.

Magee, Bryan. *Philosophy and the Real World: An Introduction to Karl Popper.* La Salle: Illinois: 1982.

Mailer, Norman. *The Armies of the Night: History as a Novel, The Novel as History.* New York: The New American Library, Inc., 1968.

Matthews, Robert and Pratt, Cranford (eds.). *Human Rights in Canadian Foreign Policy.* Kingston and Montreal: McGill-Queen's University Press, 1988.

Mayhew, Katherine Camp and Edwards, Ann Camp. *The Dewey School: The Laboratory School of the University of Chicago 1896-1903.* New York: D. Appleton-Century Company, 1936.

McGilvray, James. *Chomsky: Language, Mind, and Politics.* Cambridge: Polity Press, 1999.

_____. *The Cambridge Companion to Chomsky.* Cambridge: Cambridge University Press, 2005.

McLaren, Peter and Leonard, Peter (eds.). *Paulo Freire: A Critical Encounter.* New York: Routledge, 1993.

_____. *Pedagogia, Identidad y Poder: Los Educadores Frente al Multiculturalismo.* Santa Fe: Homo Sapiens Ediciones, 2003.

Mokhiber, Russell. "Corporate Crime & Violence in Review: The 10 Worst Corporations of 1991." *Multinational Monitor.* December 1991.

Murphy, Daniel. *Tolstoy and Education.* Dublin: Irish Academy Press, 1992.

O'Hare, Padraic (ed.). *Tradition and Transformation in Religious Education.* Birmingham, Alabama: Religious Education Press, 1979.

Orelus, Pierre W. *On Language, Democracy, and Social Justice: Noam Chomsky's Critical Intervention.* New York: Peter Lang Publishing, Inc., 2014.

Orr, David. *Earth in Mind: On Education, Environment, and the Human Prospect.* Washington, D.C.: Island Press, 1994.

Osler, William. *The Student Life and Other Essays.* London: Constable's Miscellany, 1928.

Otero, C.P. (ed.). *Noam Chomsky: Radical Priorities.* Montreal: Black Rose Books, 1981.

_____ (ed.). *Noam Chomsky: Language and Politics.* Montreal: Black Rose Books, 1988.

_____ (ed.). *Chomsky on Democracy and Education.* New York: RoutledgeFalmer, 2003.

Otto, Rudolf. *The Idea of the Holy: An Inquiry into the Non-Rational Factor in the Idea of the Divine and Its Relation to the Rational.* London: Oxford University Press, 1950.

Pateman, Barry (ed.). *Chomsky on Anarchism.* Oakland: AK Press, 2005.

Peck, James (ed.). *The Chomsky Reader.* New York: Pantheon Books, 1987.

Pelikan, Jaroslav. *The Vindication of Tradition.* New Haven, CT.: Yale University Press, 1984.

Perkins, Ray (ed.). *Yours Faithfully, Bertrand Russell: A Lifelong Fight for Peace, Justice, and Truth in Letters to the Editor.* Peru, Illinois: Open Court Publishing, 2002.

Popper, Karl. *Unended Quest: An Intellectual Autobiography.* New York: Fontana/Collins, 1982.

_____. *The Open Society and its Enemies.* London: Routledge, 2011.

Pruyn, Marc, and Huerta-Charles, Luis (eds.). *Teaching Peter McLaren: Paths of Dissent.* New York: Peter Lang Publishing, 2005.

Rachels, James. *Created from Animals: The Moral Implications of Darwinism.* Oxford: Oxford University Press, 1990.

Rai, Milan. *Chomsky's Politics.* New York: Verso, 1995.

Redfearn, David. *Tolstoy: Principles for a New World Order.* London: Shepherd-Walwyn Publishers, 1992.

Robertson, Heather-Jane. *No More Teachers, No More Books: The Commercialisation of Canada's Schools.* Toronto: McClelland & Stewart, 1998.

Rogers, Carl. *On Becoming a Person.* Boston: Houghton Mifflin Company, 1961.

Rousseau, Jean-Jacque. *A Discourse on Inequality.* London: Penguin Books, 1984. Originally published in 1755.

Ruse, Michael. *Taking Darwin Seriously: A Naturalist Approach to Philosophy.* New York: Prometheus Books, 1998.

Russell, Bertrand. *On Education, Especially in Early Childhood.* London: Unwin Paperbacks, 1976.

_____. *Education and the Social Order*. London: Unwin Paperbacks, 1977.

_____. *Autobiography*. London: Unwin, 1978.

_____. *Principles of Social Reconstruction*. London: Routledge, 1997.

_____. *Mortals and Others: American Essays 1931-1935*. New York: Routledge, 2009.

_____. *Unpopular Essays*. New York: Routledge, 2009.

Sayre, Robert F. (ed.), *Henry David Thoreau: A Week on the Concord and Merrimack Rivers, Walden; or, Life in the Woods, The Maine Woods, Cape Cod*. New York: The Library of America, 1985.

Scharfe, Sharon. *Complicity: Human Rights and Canadian Foreign Policy*. Montreal: Black Rose Books, 1996.

Schweitzer, Albert. *The Philosophy of Civilization*. New York: Prometheus Books, 1987.

Searle, John. "Chomsky's revolution in linguistics". *The New York Review of Books*, June 29, 1972.

Shor, Ira *Critical Teaching and Everyday Life*. Boston: South End Press, 1980.

_____ (ed.). *Freire for the Classroom: A Sourcebook for Liberatory Teaching*. Portsmouth: Heinemann, 1987.

_____. *Empowering Education: Critical Teaching for Social Change*. Chicago: University of Chicago Press, 1992.

Shotton, John. *No Master High or Low: Libertarian Education and Schooling 1890-1990*. Bristol: Libertarian Education, 1993.

Skinner, B. F. *Verbal Behavior*. New Jersey: Prentice-Hall, 1957.

Smith, Neil. *Chomsky: Ideas and Ideals*. Cambridge: Cambridge University Press, 1999.

Spring, Joel. *A Primer of Libertarian Education*. Montreal: Black Rose Books, 1975.

Suissa, Judith. *Anarchism and Education: A Philosophical Perspective*. Oakland: PM Press, 2010.

Sullivan, Edmund. *Critical Psychology and Pedagogy: Interpretation of the Personal World*. Toronto: OISE Press, 1990.

Tait, Katharine. *My Father Bertrand Russell*. New York: Narcourt, Brace, Jovanovich, 1975.

Thoreau, Henry David. *Walden, or Life in the Woods*. Boston: Ticknor and Fields, 1854.

Tolstoy, Leo. *War and Peace*. New York: W. W. Norton, 1966. First published in book form in 1869.

_____. *Anna Karenina*. New York: W. W. Norton, 1970. First published in book form in 1878.

Walls, Laura Dassow. *Henry David Thoreau: A Life*. Chicago: University of Chicago Press, 2017.

Whitehead, Alfred North. *The Aims of Education and Other Essays*. New York: The Free Press, 1929.

Wilson, Edward O. *Sociobiology: The New Synthesis* (twenty-fifth anniversary edition). Cambridge, Massachusetts: The Belknap Press of Harvard University Press, 2000.

_____. *From So Simple a Beginning: The Four Great Books of Charles Darwin.* New York: W. W. Norton & Company, 2006.

Witherell, Elizabeth Hall (ed.), *Henry David Thoreau: Collected Essays and Poems.* New York: The Library of America, 2001.

Woodruff, Paul. *Reverence: Renewing a Forgotten Virtue.* Oxford: Oxford University Press, 2001.

Index